MAD GAME

The NBA Education of Kobe Bryant

ROLAND LAZENBY

MASTERS PRESS

NTC/Contemporary Publishing Group

Library of Congress Cataloging-in-Publication Data

Lazenby, Roland.
    Mad game : the NBA education of Kobe Bryant / Roland Lazenby.
       p.   cm.
    ISBN 1-57028-225-0
    1. Bryant, Kobe, 1978–   2. Basketball players—United States—
Biography.   I. Title.
    GV884.B794   L393   2000
    796.323′092—dc21
    [B]   99-045112

Photograph credits: Page 1: copyright © NBA Photos/Bill Baptist; Page 23: copyright © NBA Photos/Garrett Ellwood; Pages 41, 79, 137, 235: copyright © NBA Photos/Andrew D. Bernstein; Page 181: copyright © NBA Photos/Barry Gossage; Page 295: copyright © NBA Photos/Glenn James

Interior design by Nick Panos

Published by Masters Press
A division of NTC/Contemporary Publishing Group, Inc.
4255 West Touhy Avenue, Lincolnwood (Chicago), Illinois 60712-1975 U.S.A.
Copyright © 2000 by Roland Lazenby
Printed in the United States of America
International Standard Book Number: 1-57028-225-0

99 00 01 02 03 04 LB 19 18 17 16 15 14 13 12 11 10 9 8 7 6 5 4 3 2 1

Dedicated to Dean and Maxine Foster,
for conveying to me their love of life and knowledge.

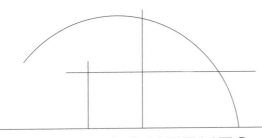

CONTENTS

ACKNOWLEDGMENTS   VII

INTRODUCTION   XI

1 THE DREAM'S EMBRACE   1

2 THE SHADOW GAME   23

3 ASCENSION   41

4 LAKERSVILLE   79

5 THE MIKE ALIKE   137

6 LOST WEEKENDS   181

7 LEGENDS OF THE FALL   235

8 LOVE TRIANGLE   295

INDEX   315

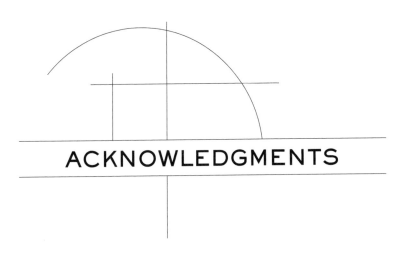

ACKNOWLEDGMENTS

It's difficult to list all the people who've helped, particularly for someone like me, who has had the benefit of so much help from so many people. The interviews always prove to be the fascinating part of my work, and I am indebted to people who take time from their busy lives to discuss their perspectives on events.

For this project, Kobe Bryant showed himself to be decent, honorable, and remarkably mature. He was understandably guarded in some of his comments. He will obviously have his own book to write someday, when he feels more comfortable fully discussing his feelings. In the short term, however, he was gracious in answering my questions, just as he was gracious in enduring the pressures that fell on him in 1999.

In fact, I come away from this project with a refreshing view of the Lakers organization and its players. Somehow, they've gotten the rap of being young and spoiled, but I found no great evidence of that in my time around them. If they were guilty of anything, it was perhaps trying too hard, wanting to win too badly, and letting that get in the way of their understanding one another—but that hardly makes them any different than the rest of us.

In my interviewing, I received extraordinary cooperation from a range of people in the Lakers organization, including Derek Fisher, Rick Fox, Shaquille O'Neal, Jerry West, Larry Drew, and other unidentified sources. In addition, Tex Winter, now an assistant coach with the team, took the time to offer his trademark candid view of events, as did Steve Kerr and Jeremy Treatman, a writer and protégé of Kobe Bryant. Beyond that, Michael Jordan, Kurt Rambis, Del Harris, Nick Van Exel, Eddie Jones, Andrew Bernstein, Pat Williams, Travis Knight, Tyron Lue, Peyton Manning, James Franklin, Derek Harper, Gary Vitti, Charles Barkley, Scottie Pippen, and Magic Johnson all gave graciously of their time.

Likewise, I owe much to a variety of journalists, many of whom are friends and associates. At the head of that list are Lakers broadcaster Larry Burnett (and wife Barb) and veteran hoops writer Mitch Chortkoff, who has covered the Lakers for the better part of four decades and who always takes time to explain the organization to me.

This book would not have been possible without the outstanding writing and reporting of a variety of people, including Tim Kawakami, Mark Heisler, J. A. Adande, Bill Plaschke, Scott Howard-Cooper, and Lonnie White of the *Los Angeles Times*; Howard Beck, Karen Crause, and Kevin Modesti of the *Los Angeles Daily News*; and Mark Emmons, Steve Bisheff, Mark Whicker, and Rany Youngman of the *Orange County Register*.

The many crucial works on Kobe Bryant include those by Ian Thomsen at *Sports Illustrated*; Chris Mundy at *Rolling Stone*; Samuel Davis and Donald Hunt at the *Philadelphia Tribune*; Shaun Powell and Greg Logan at *Newsday*; John Smallwood at the *Philadelphia Daily News*; Mike Wise of the *New York Times*; Allison Samuels and Mark Starr at *Newsweek*; Steve Wilstein at the *Rocky Mountain News*; David DuPree, Greg Boeck, David Leon Moore, and Peter Brewington at *USA*

Today; Steve Dilbeck at Gannett News Service; Craig Barboza at USA *Weekend*; Kevin E. Boone at the *St. Louis Post Dispatch*; Ken Dawidoff at the *Bergen Record*; and Ken Vance at *The Columbian*.

Also Jorge Ribeirio of *Hoop* (Japan), Brad Turner of the *Riverside Press Enterprise*, Brian Golden of the *Antelope Valley Press*, Steve Dilbeck of the *San Bernadino Sun*, Frank Girardot of the *San Gabriel Valley Tribune*, Brian Patterson of the *Daily Breeze*, Ricardo Jiminez of *La Opinion*, and Jim McCurdie of the *Long Beach Press Telegram*.

Also the work of Lacy Banks, John Jackson, and Rick Telander at the *Chicago Sun-Times*; Terry Armour, Sam Smith, and Skip Bayless at the *Chicago Tribune*; Johnny Ludden and Glenn Rodgers at the *San Antonio Express-News*; Jonathan Feigan and Michael Murphy at the *Houston Chronicle*.

Also of tremendous value was Joe Layden's juvenile biography, *Kobe!*, and Robert Caro's biography of Lyndon Johnson, *The Path to Power*.

At NTC/Contemporary, I have a long list of people to thank, including publisher John Nolan, who believed in the project, editor Ken Samelson, whose understanding and encouragement were invaluable, senior project editor Julia Anderson, text editor Chris Benton (a master fixer), and subsidiary rights manager Susan Jensen, all who made *Mad Game* a most pleasant publishing experience.

Then there's my editor at the *Chicago Sun-Times*, Bill Adee, who is always willing to listen and offer encouraging words, plus Tom Bast, who supported the project in the first place, Paul Chung (for his excellent advice and support), Lindy Davis, publisher of *Lindy's Sports Annuals*, and the fine folks at Pro Sports Xchange.

Thanks also to the media relations directors at the NBA and its various teams, truly the most professional group in all of sports: John Black, Tom Savage, and Erikk Aldridge at the

Lakers; Tim Hallam and Lori Weisskopf at the Bulls; Harold Kaufman at the Hornets; Tim Frank at the Rockets; Tom James at the Spurs; Joe Safety at the Clippers; Joel Glass at the Magic; and Matt Williams and Maureen Lewis at the Wizards—all were most helpful.

Best of all was the support of my family—Karen, Jenna, Henry, and Morgan, who make me such a lucky guy.

INTRODUCTION

*"Every night, as soon as I hear the
introduction, I feel like a little kid. I
don't think I'll ever lose that."*

—KOBE BRYANT

The first time I met Kobe Bryant he greeted me with a soul
shake. Never mind that I was a middle-aged reporter with
a tape recorder. He offered up a little skin, then the hooked
fingers and the tug. Very old school. Very smooth. Yet also
reeking with youthful enthusiasm.

And why not?

He had all the reason in the world to be happy. It was
November 1996, and he had just finished playing the game in
which he had scored his first NBA field goal. Yes, his Lakers
had lost, but even that couldn't get in the way of this momen-
tous occasion. He was 18 years old, at the time the youngest
player ever to appear in an NBA game. Just months after taking his last high school exam in Ardmore, Pennsylvania, and
escorting diva-in-waiting Brandy to his senior prom, he had
become a member of the glittery Los Angeles Lakers. Playing
pro basketball had been his dream since he was a toddler
watching his own father, Joe "Jelly Bean" Bryant, compete in
the NBA.

Now Kobe was standing in the visitors' locker room at the
Charlotte Coliseum, inhabiting the special moment with his
new teammates, who all eyed the press warily. Unlike the rest

of them, Bryant actually greeted reporters as they filed in to do postgame interviews.

"How ya doin'?" he asked, flashing a 100-watt smile to go with the soul shake.

His progress at the opening of that first season had been impeded by injuries that kept him out of action. Then, even when he did return to duty, he found Laker coach Del Harris using him sparingly. For the first time since grade school, he had spent long stretches on the bench.

"I'm just taking it as a learning experience, sitting back and getting to watch the guys," he said. "You see so much sitting on the bench. . . . Even though you're sweating and saying, 'Man, I want to be out there,' you just have to be patient and just learn."

His first action hadn't come until the fourth game of the season, against the New York Knickerbockers in Madison Square Garden, when he recorded his first pro score with a free throw.

The next game in Charlotte brought his first basket, a three-pointer, which he scored despite the booing of the local crowd. Just months earlier, he had been Charlotte's top draft pick, but his agent, Arn Tellem, had forced a trade away from the team because Bryant wanted to play for the Lakers. To get him in a trade, Lakers executive Jerry West had given up veteran center Vlade Divac, a prize for the Hornets. But some Charlotte fans had interpreted Bryant's efforts to go to Los Angeles as arrogance, so they showered him with boos when he entered the game in the second period.

He responded nervously, missing four of his first five shots, yet perhaps the most impressive thing to veteran observers was how quickly and easily Bryant got those shots. Despite the misses, he scored five quick points against the Hornets. He finally notched his first NBA basket with a deep jumper. "It felt good," he said. "When I first took that three-point shot, I believed it was gonna go down. First it felt good, then it felt a little short. I kinda leaned back, eyein' it. When it went down, I was like 'Shewww! My first three-pointer.'"

He also rang up three equally quick turnovers, including a play where he stepped out of bounds in his eagerness to get to the basket and dunk.

Asked about the play, Bryant said, "When I caught the ball in the corner, at first I said, 'I'm gonna shoot it. All right! I'm gonna stroke it.' But then I saw this big ol' lane under the hoop and I started lickin' my chops. I said, 'Oh, man, I'm gonna finish this.' But I was overexcited. My back step was a little too long. That was just being overanxious getting to the hoop. I'm like 'Man, if I can just get to that block, I can get this dunk! I'm there! I'm home. I'm free.' So that was a little overanxious right there."

Perhaps the most telling factor in Kobe Bryant's first few weeks in pro basketball was the nickname affixed to him by Shaquille O'Neal, his seven-foot-one, 330-pound teammate. O'Neal had watched Bryant dunk in his early practices and had seen him basking in the media glow as reporters gravitated to him in the Lakers' locker room. So the big center had decided to call him "Showboat."

Bryant sensed that it was not entirely a term of affection.

It was one of his first indications that, while he was eager to embrace pro basketball, pro basketball's players and coaches were not entirely enthusiastic about embracing him. After all, the NBA was a game of hard-faced older veterans, men armed with tough lessons they had learned along the way.

Kobe Bryant, on the other hand, was expectant and brimming with talent and intelligence and ambition and good looks. Yes, he had spent his short life studying the game. "Growing up, all I did was watch basketball and play basketball," he explained. "It was just natural for me." But his youthful experiences were hardly thought to be authentic by NBA standards. The league presented its own special curriculum, and the only way for Kobe Bryant to learn it was to live it.

"He's gonna be a good pro," Lakers assistant coach Larry Drew said of Bryant at the time. "But he has a lot to learn about the NBA game. He loves to play. He wants to be out there regardless. But he understands that this is a learning process and a slow process."

Kobe himself, though, didn't see it that way. His short journey over the ensuing seasons would bring its share of harsh, bitter moments. But his positive nature wouldn't allow circumstances and criticism to turn him away from what he saw as his destiny. "I won't let them break me," he said again and again. "I'm in this for the long haul. I want to learn."

What follows then is an attempt to document the unique education of a determined young athlete, one seemingly unafraid, and sometimes unaware, of the consequences.

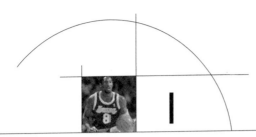

THE DREAM'S EMBRACE

"This kid is really, really driven."
—LARRY DREW

When Kobe Bryant works the ball, he reminds me of something, but I can't figure out exactly what. Maybe a large bird, like some kind of young condor ready to take flight. He flexes his body and his focus to the right, the ball moving rhythmically from fingertip to fingertip between his legs, his arms flaring to the sides like wings, while his neck stiffens and his eyes grow still. He seems to be looking nowhere and everywhere at the same time. Then he shifts to the left and assumes the same strange birdlike pose. Maybe it's the way he arches his neck. I almost expect him to cluck.

Here, during his private practice time in the Great Western Forum, in the early days of his third NBA season, as Kobe Bryant spends yet more time polishing his signature move off the dribble, this motion from side to side seems a little freaky. Who knows how many hours he's spent working alone, perfecting this shifting approach? It's the product of a young lifetime. Right. Left. Right. Left. Over and over again.

If you're defending him in a game, there's nothing comical, nothing birdlike, about this posture. In the context of a game, this move is absolutely threatening, reptilian, like a cobra mesmerizing its target before the strike. It's the setup for his crossover dribble. His neck arches oddly as he prepares to flex his fake. The eyes freeze because he's locking in the peripheral vision, surveying the floor without giving up his intention. "I can still see the court," he says. "Even if I have my head down sometimes, I can see it."

This is the exact moment when the defender reaches maximum anxiety. Which way will Kobe go?

"It's the rhythm," Kobe explains. "The defender can't do anything about it. He'll either back up or close the gap even more. As for the eyes, it depends on who's guarding you. Some defenders like to look right here at your belt buckle. Other defenders like to look in your eyes. To see if they can follow the basketball."

So Kobe goes birdlike on them. Flex right. Flex left. Explode. His rear end sags like a dragster grabbing traction, and he's off to the hole. This, of course, is what NBA opponents fear most from Kobe Bryant. In the jargon of the business, he's "long" at six-foot-seven, which means he has the reach and leaping ability and quickness and athleticism to knife his way through a defense and get to the basket for a dunk. If he doesn't dunk, he often draws a foul, and because he shoots hundreds of free throws a day, he's an 84 percent foul shooter. Either way, his penetration adds up to trouble for opponents.

Unless, of course, it adds up to trouble for Kobe himself. He's still learning when to slip into the attack mode and when not to. The learning process itself has been frustrating for his Los Angeles Lakers teammates and coaches. "You can see when he goes into brain lock," observes one longtime Lakers staff member. "He'll dribble about 15 times between his legs, and then he'll try to beat three defenders going to the basket. When he does that, a couple of things usually happen. He either gets in trouble and takes a bad shot, or he makes a bad pass."

Kobe works the ball again. His head bobs ever so slightly on his long neck. If this were a video, I'd maybe use "Surfin' Bird" as a soundtrack.

But it's not a video. It's practice. Kobe Bryant's personal practice. His teammates have long gone, and he's still here in the grand old Forum, where the championship banners and the retired numbers of former great Los Angeles Lakers are hanging about the court, urging him on to glory.

Not that 20-year-old Kobe Bryant needs any urging. He is absolutely and completely obsessed with basketball, so locked in the embrace of his ambition that you wonder if maybe you should be worried about him.

"This kid is really, really driven. I haven't seen it in a player in a long time, not to that extent," Lakers assistant coach Larry Drew confides.

"It's unparalleled," Del Harris, Kobe's coach during his first two NBA seasons, says of his work ethic. "He doesn't waste a minute. Before practice, after practice, during the summer, whenever. Kobe doesn't waste any motion."

"I drive myself," Bryant explains, saying that work is far more important than play. "I like to go out and have fun and have a good time. But I just don't feel right. While I'm out having a good time, I could be playing basketball or something, could be lifting weights. I could be working on something."

"You remind me of what I've read about Lyndon Johnson trying to get elected to Congress in 1937," I tell him.

"Oh yeah?" he says. "How so?"

"Well," I explain, "Johnson wanted to be elected so badly that he almost ruined himself physically and mentally trying to reach his objective. He walked all over his rural Texas district, knocking on doors, shaking hands, doing whatever it took to succeed. He did get elected, but he couldn't really celebrate because by Election Day he was in the hospital suffering from exhaustion."

It's not that Kobe Bryant is headed toward any type of exhaustion. He's too superbly conditioned—physically and emotionally—for that to happen. But there is this balls-out quality to the way he approaches life in the NBA that generates immense pressure, pressure that would quickly consume less talented young players (and there are many of those).

Some of his urgency certainly has to do with his team's circumstances as the 1999 season opens. The schedule was shortened to 50 games due to wrangling over the labor agreement between the league's owners and players. In Los Angeles, all that means is a compression of the circumstances.

The Lakers, after all, are Hollywood's team, and owner Jerry Buss and executive Jerry West and the team's fans hold tremendous expectations for a championship. The young Lakers have shown impressive growth during the regular season in each of Bryant's first two campaigns, although a playoff defeat by the Utah Jazz dampened the team's outlook in 1997.

Then came a 61–21 record in 1997–98, and hopes surged in Los Angeles after the Lakers swept the pugnacious Seattle Super Sonics in the second round of the playoffs, which led to yet more premature talk of a championship. But then the Lakers again lost to the veteran Utah Jazz led by Karl Malone and John Stockton in the Western Conference finals in a humiliating sweep. "I don't have a clue how to beat these guys," Lakers point guard Nick Van Exel admitted to reporters, a confession that factored into Van Exel's being traded away to Denver after the season.

The disappointment from eight months ago still hangs over this team, and talk persists that guard Eddie Jones and center Elden Campbell are being discussed in trade talks with the Charlotte Hornets. It seems that Buss, a studious poker player, is determined to shuffle and reshuffle until he deals up a winning hand.

It's no wonder that these young Lakers seemingly drip with

pressure, except that they spend much of their time denying to reporters that they feel any at all. The truth is, just about all of the figures associated with the team, especially Shaquille O'Neal and Bryant, have much at risk in terms of reputation, future, and standing in the game. It's a good thing they're all well paid. Bryant himself has just signed a new $71 million contract. O'Neal's way of deflecting the circumstances is to remind reporters repeatedly that NBA pressure is nothing, that real pressure is faced daily by the homeless scrounging for a meal. It's a valid point. Still, these young Lakers are very much a product of their rare, hypercompetitive environment. "There's a lot I want to accomplish in my life," Kobe admits. To gain and hold on to status, they must advance, which in part means giving Buss, West, and Lakers fans the championship they so badly crave. If anything, the pressure has increased with the dawning of 1999, because the shortened season means that every game is much more important in deciding a team's chances for the playoffs.

The mitigation to these circumstances, at least in Kobe's mind, is his absolute hunger to play. The long months off nearly drove him to distraction, except that he used his off-season time wisely, studying hours upon hours of videotape of his opponents so that he would know the best way to defend them once the season started. He also trained ferociously, spending day after day in the weight room, adding pounds of muscle to his young body.

The results of this effort were obvious when the Lakers season finally opened on February 5, 1999, at the Forum against the Houston Rockets. The Rockets had recently traded for longtime Chicago Bull Scottie Pippen, the game's most masterful small forward, and it was Bryant's challenge to defend him. Kobe had spent much time in the off-season conducting a study of Pippen's defensive technique, and he viewed this first game as a test of what he had learned. In the first period alone

Bryant blocked 2 of Pippen's shots, and for the game the young Laker hounded Pippen into missing 14 of his 18 shots. Pippen finished with just 10 points, while Bryant scored 25. Just as important, Bryant used the newly added muscle to grab a career-high 10 rebounds, all immensely valuable in driving Los Angeles to a 99–91 win over a key Western Conference opponent.

The euphoria over the Friday night victory coursed through the Forum crowd and the Lakers roster only to crash hard just hours later. On Sunday afternoon the Utah Jazz came to the Forum, and although the Lakers played well and had the lead for most of three quarters, Stockton and Malone executed their crafty pick-and-roll offense at the end of the game and won yet again.

Afterward, the disappointment and frustration, even a sense of confusion, fouled the air in the Lakers locker room. The team's confidence, so high just hours earlier, now sagged toward panic. Already there had been renewed talk in the media of the firing of coach Del Harris, the trading of Eddie Jones, and the signing of wacky free-agent forward Dennis Rodman. Many observers feared that adding the eccentric Rodman to the roster would only deepen the young team's confusion.

Making matters worse, there were signs that West and Buss were clashing behind the scenes over the direction and future of the team. Clearly the famed Laker franchise was in disarray, with management and players alike seemingly strangling on the pressure they had imposed on themselves.

In the chaos after the Utah loss, Kobe stood in the locker room amid a group of interviewers and smiled. Yes, the Jazz were wily, he said. Yes, it hurt to lose to them yet again. But the Lakers would learn from the circumstances, he promised.

"We'll figure it out," he said. "We'll be all right."

The Confidence Game

His means of making himself and the team better quite often begin here, with his extra private practice time.

As we talk, Kobe again executes his flex move, his eyes strangely fixed. Then I realize what he reminds me of. One of those raptors in *Jurassic Park*. He shifts again in this predator's pose. Very freaky. But that's the way it is with genius, I think. Very unsettling. Because genius is much more than talent. It's talent that has an uncompromising level of commitment. Genius is talent that's willing to take risks.

And that's Kobe Bryant. He's living on the edge of his testosterone-laced dreams. Totally obsessed. Totally committed. Totally talented. Putting every part of himself into making himself the greatest, into being dominant, what he and other young players call "the man."

For years Bryant has reviewed edited videotape of pro basketball's greatest players, breaking down their every move, their finest moments. "I've watched tape of everybody," he says. "I've watched Hakeem, I've watched Magic, I've watched Malone. I've watched everybody. I've watched Pistol Pete. Earl the Pearl. Nate Archibald. I've watched all of them."

"What's the most amazing thing you've seen in all that tape?" I ask.

"The most amazing thing I've seen?" he says.

"Yeah," I say. "Of all those great players and great moments on tape, of all those great moves, is there one that really stands out, that blows you away?"

"Not really," he says. "Because I think I can do it all. When I was growing up, nothing really impressed me that much because I thought I could do it. You know what I mean?"

How big does this confidence get? "You think you could beat Michael Jordan in one-on-one, don't you?" I ask.

He gives me a look that says "Puh-leeze."

"I'd love to play him," he says and smiles.

This uberconfidence comes from the bedrock that is his family and his upbringing. The son of journeyman NBA player Joe Bryant, Kobe was reared in an atmosphere of expectation and steeped in the belief of his impending ascension to the throne of basketball. This confidence is his greatest strength. It is the armor that has protected him against a business that is very capable of using him up quickly and throwing him away. Yet the same confidence is also the dynamo at the heart of his greatest difficulty. It inspires envy in teammates and opponents alike and helps to cast him in some eyes as an arrogant young know-it-all.

"I think his confidence in himself may at times be misperceived," says Lakers teammate Rick Fox. "It may be seen as arrogance, to the point that he knows everything and is always having to be right. He strives for perfection."

Bryant's combination of confidence and perfectionism has a strong double edge, Fox observes. "It makes the lessons painful. And it can be intimidating to others, especially if those others don't see themselves as being as perfect as they would like to be."

In other words, older teammates have been taken aback by such confidence in one so young, Fox says. "In a team sport, it can be a turnoff. You strive to be the best you can be, but it's OK in a team sport to admit that you're not perfect and that you have to rely on teammates. It's OK to admit that you need to be encouraged and they need to be encouraged and lifted up. It's a brotherhood thing."

It's not that Bryant's an egotist, although some critics argue that he is. He's pleasant, unflappable in his diplomacy and good manners, and makes frequent use of his easy smile. But it's not difficult to push aside that demeanor and find a sharp, hard edge to his approach. He has a huge need to fill, and he knows what he wants. In high school he discovered the elation of athletic dominance. He had a series of games in which he scored 50 points on the way to taking his team to a state championship. It was a masterful control of his environment, and it proved addictive. There would be the five players from the other team, all scrambling to stop him, all absolutely defenseless in the face of his faking, snaking sorties to the basket and his abrupt pull-up jumpers. In the ensuing months many observers would come to compare him to Michael Jordan. And there were many obvious physical reasons to liken him to Jordan, but the greatest reason was a sharklike hunger they share for dominating.

Phil Jackson, Jordan's coach in Chicago, once explained it to me like this: "Some nights Michael could take on a whole team. They'd say, 'That son of a gun, he beat us all to the basket.' As a coach, you can run that videotape back over and over. You say, 'Look at this guy go around that guy and that guy. He beat four guys going to the basket that time.' That's destructive. That's something that Michael's been known for, and I know it grates at the heart of the other team. It's an amazing feat this guy has been able to accomplish. But I think his power is very addictive."

Indeed, Kobe Bryant has tasted that power, that addiction. "I feel like I'm conquering somebody," Kobe says of those moments. Which explains why he longs to unleash it each time he steps on the court, the only problem being that basketball is a five-man game and such displays aren't often considered appropriate in the hierarchy of the talented Lakers. Jordan himself took a half dozen seasons learning when to give in to his cravings and when not to. Then again, Jordan didn't have to learn to share the offensive spotlight with a massive and effective weapon like O'Neal. Bryant has heard repeatedly in his Lakers tenure that the team's primary offensive option is O'Neal. For the most part, Kobe Bryant has no major trouble with this reality. But he does find the running of all of the Lakers offense through the huge center to be more than a little stifling.

As a result Bryant has become fascinated with the archaic triangle offense used by Jordan and the Chicago Bulls, because that offense, among other things, called for a motion among the players in which the center frequently vacated the low post and faced up to the basket. By doing that, the Bulls then allowed Jordan to post up near the basket, using his size, strength, and creative ability to score over other teams' guards.

Bryant has these similar post-up skills but seldom has the opportunity to display them because the low post in Lakerland is Shaq's domain. "He's a very good low-post ballplayer, because he has good footwork," Lakers assistant coach Larry Drew says of Bryant. "He's good on both blocks, and he really, really uses both hands well. His left hand is solid. He has so much confidence in taking that little left-hand jump shot that it's just unbelievable."

But the opportunites for Bryant to approach the game like Jordan did have been few. "It becomes tough to do," Drew admitted, "because when you have Shaq he's gonna command a lot of attention down there. And there's just not enough room to post two guys up down there. With Shaq in the game, that's Shaq's territory down there.

"With Shaq there, one thing Kobe is learning is to pick and choose his spots when he can, so he can possibly get down there a little bit. He just has to learn how to pick and choose the spots. It will get to a point when Kobe goes into the low post that teams will come and double-team him. That's gonna work to our advantage. He has the potential to work down low, he has a good midrange game, and he has a good perimeter game. He's very versatile. You try to take advantage of all the things he can do."

Bryant first became familiar with the triangle offense as a reserve running it in practice against the Lakers starters in 1996. He immediately saw the possibilities the triangle, or triple post, would provide him for relating to his teammates while still achieving his personal goals. At the same time that recognition deepened his trouble because he knew the Lakers had no plans to change.

In 1998, with his frustration running high, he admitted that his difficulty in facing several defenders could be blamed in part on the Lakers' lack of offensive organization. "When I see three guys coming at me, I start looking out of the corner of my eye to see who I can hit with a pass," he told me. "Sometimes guys will be out of position, so I'll take a shot, you know?

"If you look at a team like Chicago, where they have a very guard-oriented team, when Michael and Scottie draw double teams, everybody knows where to go," he added. "Everybody has a certain spot, whether it's ducking into a corner, ready for the open shot, everybody knows where to go. It's a system. We have that here with Shaq, but now I think it's time to add it from the guard standpoint. If I'm drawing double teams, then we have to know where to be, where to go. It's just random right now. We're running around with our heads cut off. We don't have any spacing because everything's all clogged up."

The losses to Utah added to this frustration because the Jazz used sophisticated split cuts in their offense to create shots and open up the floor. Bryant has approached Del Harris about adding similar motion and looks to the Lakers, but Harris showed no interest in that.

His maturity has been taxed heavily by the situation, and most game nights he still obviously struggles with the issue. His answer, in the short term, has been to accept the circumstances the best he can. For the long term, he keeps studying. He recently asked me for the phone number for Tex Winter, the Bulls coach who concocted the triangle offense. As the season winds toward its conclusion, Kobe will phone Winter for a far-reaching discussion of basketball philosophy. As a favor, I also add a phone number for Jordan because it's obvious that Bryant craves Jordan's guidance on this issue.

"What would you ask Michael?" I ask.

He thinks a long while and replies, "I would ask him how to incorporate math into the game."

It's another way of addressing the age-old hoops dilemma of the individual versus the group. It's the question that makes basketball such a wonderful game, such a challenge. And Kobe Bryant's earnest, probing approach to the issue speaks much about his unique character.

The issue has been clouded by all of the media attention directed at Bryant, much of it stemming from the comparisons with Jordan.

These comparisons have been made by coaches, other players, scouts, and the media since Bryant entered the NBA in 1996. Some within the Lakers organization think Bryant has taken these comparisons to heart, to his own detriment. "He even runs like Michael Jordan," says one obviously frustrated Lakers staff member. "It's not good for him. The great basketball players try to take complicated things and find simple ways to do them. Kobe with all his switching of the ball from hand to hand and faking takes simple plays and tries to make them complicated."

Yet even this criticism connects him to Jordan. For more than a dozen years, Tex Winter made the same complaint about Jordan. "He's more of a high-wire act, you know," Winter observed in 1998 as Jordan was on his way to leading Chicago to its sixth league championship. "He's into degree of difficulty instead of just working, just trying to be real fundamentally sound."

As the most prominent of a generation of young players seeking to emulate Jordan's dominance and magnetism, Kobe's brief NBA career has brought a constant sifting through this and other of the game's mysteries. With his frustrations has come the first light of understanding that those questions proved complex for Jordan and are even more so for those who seek to be like him.

Although Kobe obviously views Jordan as a role model and craves information about him and the game, he, too, has become wary of the comparisons. A young reporter interviewing him after a performance early in the 1999 season asked him, "Were you trying to do some things that Michael would do out there? Is that a constant thought in your mind?"

"Yeah," Bryant replied sarcastically, "that ran through my mind exactly when I was making the moves: 'This is how Michael would do it.'"

He smiled and added, "No. Please."

The young reporter persisted, however: "Do you ever try to emulate Jordan's moves, though?"

"No," Kobe repeated and laughed sarcastically. "That's a good question, though."

As the reporter thanked him and walked away, Kobe turned to other reporters nearby and said, "Damn, when I go like this"—then he let out a huge gasp—"people say, 'Golly, he breathes just like Mike!'"

Standing Alone

Kobe interrupts his practice dribble here in the Forum and asks me what I think of Allen Iverson, another of the generation of young stars following Jordan.

I tell him that the Philadelphia 76ers star has never been anything but a gentleman when I've dealt with him. "Al's cool," Kobe agrees as he resumes his dribble. "We talk."

Then I tell him that Tex Winter has told me he thinks Iverson is the best player in the league.

Kobe is visibly disturbed by this news. He stops his dribble and issues a vow that, given time, people will clearly see that he, Kobe Bryant, will be the best. He wants to absolutely dominate the NBA in three years, he tells me.

His phrase for this is "bustin' out." The cusp of the lockout-shortened 1999 NBA season was not the time to bust out, he tells me. But his time will come in three years.

"I just want to take over," he says. "I want to be the man."

That, it seems, is the raw essence of Kobe's world. Where the self-imposed expectations and pressures are huge, and the confidence is even bigger. What else would you expect from the crown prince of professional basketball? He's 20 years old and already experiencing his third NBA season. At age 9 he broke down his first video scouting tape. By 11 he was taking on his father's Italian League teammates in one-on-one and holding his own. By the eighth grade he was cutting his teeth on those high-test summer pickup games in Philadelphia against college-level talent. At 18 years and 4 months, he became the youngest player ever to start in an NBA game.

Four months into his first NBA season, he won the slam dunk competition at the 1997 All-Star weekend. Twelve months later the league's fans elected him a starter on the 1998 Western Conference All-Star team, which opened the door for the league and its broadcast partners to feature Kobe Bryant and Jordan on their promotional billboards, newspaper advertisements, and televised commercials leading up to the game.

It was a rapid elevation of status for a 19-year-old, someone who wasn't even a starter on his own NBA team. And it elicited a hugely negative reaction, one from which Bryant is still staggering a year later.

"I thought it was inappropriate," Harris said of the buildup given his young player. "The NBA is in on it. Kobe is just gonna have to learn to deal with those things because he's a worldwide personality already. He's known literally worldwide. He's doing commercials for major products. He has billboard-size photos of him in Europe, for example, for Adidas. I've seen them."

Harris said he was surprised over the summer of 1997 to encounter the huge ads in Barcelona, near the site where the Olympic Games were conducted in 1992. "I already knew when he signed a $5 million deal with Adidas that they were going to use him. And Adidas is bigger in Europe than it is in the U.S. But 30-foot posters and billboards were a bit of a surprise. I saw them just outside the Olympic facilities in Barcelona.

"You come right down the steps just below the fountain, and on one side they got one of Kobe's feet. And the other foot is on the other side. With Kobe wearing Adidas shoes 30 feet high."

For the white-haired, scholarly Harris, it was way over the top. "He's a good guy," Harris said in 1998. "And he's bright. But everybody's trying to rush him into being something that no 19-year-old can ever be, including Michael himself. Michael was Michael Jordan from North Carolina at age 19, and he didn't become Michael until he was about 27. And he didn't become MJ until he was 30. It didn't happen like that. Michael Jordan wasn't a media creation. He wasn't anything that everybody was hoping for at age 19. The guy got cut from his high school team at 15. He made it through immense talent but hard work over a period of time. And that's the way Kobe will have to make it."

During that interview I reminded Harris that Bulls coach Phil Jackson had put much time and effort into protecting Jordan from the pressures that shoved him in the wrong directions. "Are there ways that you can protect Kobe?"

"It's out of my control," he replied.

The fact that Bryant was shoved into the spotlight ahead of dozens of older, more accomplished players created substantial problems for both the player and the team. Bryant explained to me that in the wake of the wash of media attention, his teammates thought he had become conceited.

Aware that there might be a problem, he said he had tried to maintain an even keel. Before the attention, he had been playful and brash, talking the same trash to his teammates that they talked to him. But in the aftermath of the 1998 All-Star game, they interpreted his playfulness as newly discovered ego.

"It seemed like they wanted to show me," he says.

Suddenly, his teammates seemed determined to teach him harsh lessons. As a result Kobe Bryant was alienated from his teammates, a factor that would become increasingly obvious as the 1999 season unfolded.

"I do my own thing," he explains when asked about off-court relationships.

The situation did generate a substantial wave of envy among other players, both teammates and opponents, admits teammate Rick Fox. "Whenever you're climbing the ladder at a rapid pace, the people at the top are wary. They have the grasp of power and the limelight, and they've climbed that ladder to get it. They don't want to give that up too easily. And they'll do whatever they can to knock you down. Even if you are a teammate. Kobe experienced that at the All-Star game. He said he was just being himself, but you know what? He's quickly becoming one of the main marketing tools of the NBA, which means that someone else isn't."

As Bryant himself says now of the promotional buildup, "I could have done without all that. That's something that the NBA wanted to do, that they felt like they needed to do. It was a growing process for me. It made me mature a lot faster, being under the microscope like that. I would have been happy to let my game speak for itself."

But, he added, "the league is always looking for something splashy, something spectacular. It's always a formula that they look for. They look for energy, they look for excitement."

One apparent resource in healing this alienation could be the addition of 37-year-old guard Derek Harper, who was brought to the team by management in hopes of supplying much-needed veteran leadership.

Asked about Bryant, Harper says, "We sit on the plane together. We eat together. We talk a lot. He'll be great because of his work ethic. He's the first guy here and the last guy to leave every day. Very hungry."

It's obvious that the media buildup and expectations have had a dramatic effect on Bryant's development, Harper says. "Everybody has already pushed him to be the man, especially now that Michael has retired. Everybody is saying this is the guy who is going to carry the torch. And that's a lot of pressure for a young kid."

Even so, Harper says he hasn't cautioned Bryant to take it easy on himself. "Because he won't," Harper says, pointing out that Kobe is merely pursuing his destiny. "He really really has this thing that he wants to be the best. There's no use in him taking it easy. He may as well go for it just the way that he's doing."

There seems, however, to be no shortage of people who think Kobe Bryant should go slower. To some he has become something of a symbol for a generation of young players who have received immense playing and product endorsement contracts without really having accomplished much as players to earn those rewards. So his confidence serves to engender the debate about him. Whose fault is it anyway? Is it Kobe's for having such a hugely presumptive nature? Is it the greed of the marketing minds of the National Basketball Association for promoting and hyping him before he has earned it?

There is, of course, another answer, one that his critics don't want to consider. That answer is that Kobe Bryant does deserve this rapid rise to stardom, that he has paid a huge personal price for it, that he has paid that price willingly.

Winter, the wise old assistant coach of the Bulls who has spent considerable time studying Bryant on videotape, wonders if the young star truly realizes the costs of his approach. "He's exceptional in his desire," Winter says. "That's one of the reasons he's so fine a player at such a young age. But on the other hand, I think there's gonna come a time when he realizes there's more to life than basketball. Right now, it's mighty important to him. There'll come a time, when he's older, that he'll level off on the desire. He's gonna regret not having had the opportunity for the college experience."

He could have gone to the best of universities. With a flair for writing, solid high school grades, and a score of 1080 on the Scholastic Aptitude Test, Kobe offered a tantalizing package to college recruiters as he closed out his career at Lower Merion High in 1995 and 1996. His whirling dunks and effervescent style had thrilled crowds for four seasons in the Philadelphia suburbs. But as the months peeled away and he neared the decision, it became increasingly clear that his intentions were focused on becoming a professional.

Kobe says that University of North Carolina coach Dean Smith was the first college coach to read the situation clearly and backed off from recruiting him. Smith's ardent rival in the storied Atlantic Coast Conference, Duke University coach

Mike Krzyzewski, read the same intentions. But Krzyzewski made it clear that he couldn't live with himself if he didn't make the maximum effort to persuade Kobe to go to college at Duke and spend some time discovering himself and his game.

So the Duke coach did his persuasive best to turn Kobe away from an early NBA choice. (Out of appreciation for that effort, Kobe says he remains a Duke fan, although he says he spends little time watching the college game.) Ultimately, he turned away from Krzyzewski and embraced the NBA.

Likewise, the NBA embraced him. The league, though, just wasn't sure what to do with him. Was Bryant a point guard, commonly called a "one" in the NBA? Was he an off guard, better known as a "two"? Or a "three," NBA jargon for a small forward?

Having played only against high school competition, where he frequently played in the post, Kobe himself wasn't sure. "One, two, or three, I don't worry about it," he said at the time. "I just go out and play."

The NBA, a business that seemingly lives only for today, is far from an ideal environment for a young player's journey of self-discovery. There's room for hardly any practice or teaching time in a schedule that includes 82 regular-season games and as many as another two dozen or more playoff and exhibition games.

Basically, pro basketball offers a whirl of fast-paced travel with virtually no supervision away from the game. Each professional player is a corporation unto himself, meaning that, as longtime coach Chuck Daly once explained, each team is a collection of small corporations, each vying for playing time, media attention, and lucrative product endorsement contracts. Such a cold environment can be fraught with problems for an uninitiated 18-year-old.

To guard against that, Kobe's parents, Joe and Pam Bryant, abandoned their Pennsylvania home to move to Los Angeles to help him negotiate the challenges. Ultimately, though, the off-court family support could carry him only so far. He would have to thrive on the court to survive. In short, that has meant finding a way to blend his hunger, his talents, and his drive with those of his older, more experienced Lakers teammates. His smile and his confidence mask just how difficult the adjustment has been, just how difficult it remains. But all of those factors will become increasingly evident as the 1999 season unfolds, as his conflicts with teammates bubble, as one hard NBA lesson after another gets sketched out on Kobe Bryant's slate.

Each of his two seasons has been fraught with hard lessons. And now the spring of 1999 has brought more of the same, while the patience of his teammates, his coaches, and Lakers fans wears thin.

"He's a 20-year-old kid in an environment that no other 20-year-old kids find themselves in," says Rick Fox. "He has the pressures not so much of being an NBA player, but the pressures of his status as an up-and-coming superstar, of being handed supposedly the accolades that it took other superstars years to earn. He's getting those things already. A lot of people would probably envy his ability and envy his position. But personally I don't. At age 20 I just wanted to be in college. I just wanted to play and get an education and have fun. But the NBA is the real world; this is a working environment for him. This is all he's ever known as a kid. He's had dreams and aspirations and goals of what his life would be like. He obviously wanted to be a professional basketball player, and he wants to be a great player. I don't think he thinks of anything else. I don't think he wants anything else."

Unless, perhaps, it would be a sudden Lakers conversion to the triangle offense. Otherwise, Kobe Bryant seems quite happy hanging his chin out in front of the sport he loves. "He handles himself quite, quite well for all that pressure laid upon him," says Lakers assistant coach Larry Drew. "If you ask him, he welcomes pressure. He won't acknowledge that it's something that can affect his game. He's the kind of person who welcomes any challenge whatsoever. And if the challenge is to carry the torch for the league, he'll welcome that with open arms. That's really putting a lot of pressure on yourself. That really is. When I was a player, I always tried to just be the best player that I could be. When you're thinking of being the best player ever to play the game, that pressure is tremendous, especially when a guy like Michael Jordan has accomplished what he has accomplished."

Yet Drew admits that Bryant's confidence and talent have made him a believer, despite the obvious frustrations of the Lakers coaching staff. "The thing I like about it is that he's never satisfied," the assistant coach says. "If you become satisfied with yourself, you tend to reach a comfort level. But he's never satisfied. That's why I think, when his career is over, he has a chance to be mentioned in the same breath as a Michael Jordan. Because he is driven."

If there is relief from the circumstances, Kobe Bryant doesn't want it.

"What do you do besides basketball?" I ask him. "What do you do to get away from everything?"

"I do a lot of things," he replies. "Personally, I just like to hang out with my family. I really do. But, the thing about it, in the summertime when I'm just relaxing and hanging out with my cousins, they all play basketball."

He laughs at this.

"So it all revolves around basketball," he says. "We'll wind up going to the movies and eating popcorn. But one of us starts mouthing off and talking trash or whatever, so then we gotta leave the movie and go play one-on-one or something."

"But is there anything that erases your tapes, that gets you away from the pressure?" I ask.

"Basketball does that for me. I don't need to get away from this," he says, nodding to the court around him. "When I play this, I'm getting away from everything else. You know what I mean?"

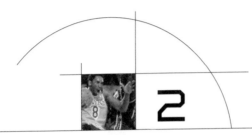

2

THE SHADOW GAME

> *"Everybody goes through life looking for the magic code. I found it at an early age."*
> —KOBE BRYANT

The contest is over, the postgame media interviews completed. Kobe Bryant gives one last straightening tug to his tie and steps out of the visitors' locker room. The venue is an old building, with a long narrow hallway crowded with well-wishers, friends, and other supplicants. It's mostly insiders—media representatives, players' relatives, and others of that ilk—so there's no chirping for autographs. Still, Kobe can feel the love, the tingle his celebrity sends through the faces along the walls, so he looks straight ahead and steps quickly. Twenty feet down the hall someone touches his arm. A familiar face. With the familiar face is an attractive, well-dressed young woman. They're introduced. Kobe smiles, rolls out a brief bit of his charm, and seems intent on making his exit to the team bus. Sensing opportunity slipping away, the young woman casts aside all pretension. She has to close this deal in a hurry.

"What's your hotel?" she asks.

It's a question Bryant hears more times than he can count, one that he has grown accustomed to evading as easily as he squeezes past an opponent's clutching down-screen.

"The chicks are all over him because he's Kobe Bryant," says an old friend from Pennsylvania. "He doesn't let them get close."

In the past, he has used high school friends to screen his contact with women. In Los Angeles, it is his older sisters, Shaya and Sharia, who help him avoid the groupies and meat puppets.

"They screen calls whether I like it or not," Bryant explained to *Rolling Stone* magazine in 1998. "You have your fun. I'm human. But I don't like selling myself short or spreading myself thin. I have too many things I want to accomplish."

"He doesn't even date," says Lakers vice president Jerry West. "He focuses everything he has on basketball."

"I'm ashamed to say," Bryant says, "but I'm buried in my profession."

He's also acutely aware of the precedents.

It was in 1979 that a 19-year-old Magic Johnson had come to the Lakers from Michigan State and discovered that Los Angeles was the world's casting couch, a place populated with beautiful young women eager to be seen with an NBA star. Johnson followed the lead of veteran Lakers guard Norm Nixon, so adroit as a ladies' man that his Lakers teammates called him "Sav" or "Wa" for "savoir faire." The hotel lobbies where the team stayed crawled with women eager to meet Nixon. The young Johnson observed the phenomenon and declared that he wanted to be like Norm.

Before long, he had exceeded Nixon's wildest dreams. Johnson would later figure that he was having sex with 300 to 500 women per year. How strange did it get? At the height of his satyrism, Johnson would have one or two women waiting for him in the Lakers team sauna immediately after games. There he'd cavort, then throw on a robe and return to the locker room in time to do his postgame media interviews.

These liaisons came with a cost as Johnson racked up one venereal cold after another over the years, leading one team official to joke about Johnson in training camp in 1990, "If that f——er doesn't have it, you can't get it."

The legion of women in and around the Forum Club grew so thick during the Showtime era that Laker trainer Gary Vitti began dispensing condoms to the players. Johnson, however, declined to use them. He said he didn't need protection. After all, he was the Magic man.

Citizen Kobe?

By most accounts, Kobe Bryant emerged in the mid-1990s from a basketball fairy tale, a cocoon of nurturing, to become a full-blown phenomenon. The son of an NBA player. Raised in Europe. Schooled on the hard courts of Philadelphia. Groomed for glory and superstardom.

The doubters, however (and there are a few), have dogged the family since Bryant first made known his thoughts about jumping to the NBA right out of high school. Where some observers see an exceptional upbringing, the doubters look to his childhood for the seeds of unhappiness that an unrealistic agenda will bring him, as if Bryant is destined to become the modern NBA's Citizen Kane, trapped by a dysfunctional karma in a Xanadu of loneliness and regret.

For this group of doubters, Bryant's Rosebud might well be the tiny Lakers jacket that his parents dressed him in as a baby. What's significant about the jacket, which remains stored in the family house back in Philadelphia, is that at the time Kobe's father was just finishing a four-year stint playing for the Philadelphia 76ers and on his way to a tenure with the San Diego Clippers.

The doubters would suggest that the tiny Lakers jacket embodied the elder Bryant's frustrations with pro basketball. As Joe "Jelly Bean" Bryant has explained, it was the Lakers in 1979 who were welcoming young Magic Johnson, a basketball aberration at six-foot-nine. It was significant that not only could Johnson pass and handle the ball brilliantly, but his coach at Michigan State, Jud Heathcote, had allowed him to play point guard. In the entire history of college basketball, no coach had ever designated a six-foot-nine player as a point guard, but as Heathcote explained many times, Johnson was so brilliant, "he had to have the ball."

Heathcote's reward for pursuing this unconventional approach was that Johnson used his open-court brilliance to lead his Spartans to the 1979 NCAA title. Johnson then left college after that championship season and moved to the Lakers, who despite early difficulties would also decide to turn the ball over to Johnson as a six-foot-nine point guard. That decision resulted in the Lakers' winning the 1980 NBA championship with the rookie Johnson being named the Most Valuable Player of the championship series.

For his part, Joe Bryant was left only to wish that he could be Magic Johnson. Jelly Bean, after all, was nearly 6-foot-10, thin at 200 pounds, with his own special flair for passing and handling the ball. But that playing style was thought to be inappropriate for a big man when Joe Bryant entered LaSalle University in 1972. He had just led John Bartram High to the Philadelphia Public School Championship that spring. It was at Bartram where Joe Bryant acquired the nickname Jelly Bean, supposedly based on the fact that young fans would bring him candy when the Bartram team played. He was an exceptional high school player and could have gone to Notre Dame or Maryland or another top program. Instead he chose to stay close to home and play for coach Paul Westhead at LaSalle.

"Joe Bryant played at LaSalle for me for three years," recalled Westhead, who would later coach the Lakers and clash with Magic Johnson. "Joe was a man ahead of his time. People look at Kobe and say, 'Hey, where did he come from?' Well, you know Joe was as quick and as fast and as flashy and about four or five inches taller. Joe had a lot of pizzazz and the potential for greatness and at times would exhibit it."

In two varsity seasons at LaSalle, Joe Bryant averaged 20.7 points and better than 11 rebounds. His junior year, in 1974–75, he led the Explorers to a 22–7 record and Westhead's first NCAA tournament invitation. Joe Bryant scored 25 points with 14 rebounds before fouling out in LaSalle's overtime loss to Syracuse in the first round. The Orangemen would play their way into the Final Four, but that produced no real moral victory for LaSalle. The NCAA loss would be Bryant's last college game.

He had met Pam Cox, a Slippery Rock student whose brother John "Chubby" Cox was a guard for Villanova. Joe Bryant and Pam Cox had known each other since childhood when their grandparents lived in the same Philadelphia neighborhood. They met again one night when LaSalle played Villanova, and from there the courtship blossomed. He was big and amiable and had a lot of class. She was pretty and smart and sweet. And they both came from strong families.

"Really good families," emphasized Pat Williams, who was general manager of the Philadelphia 76ers at the time. "Pam Cox was a stunningly beautiful woman. A gorgeous, gorgeous woman. And Joe was a trophy, very personable, very pleasant, just a happy-go-lucky kid. He was a local legend, a playground legend. He was big and very flamboyant, a ball handler, a '90s type of player. He was his son 20 years before Kobe arrived."

By the end of the 1975 college season, Joe Bryant was married with a child on the way, so he filed for financial "hardship status" to enter the NBA draft. Seeing his size and skills, the Golden State Warriors, who had just won the NBA title, selected him with the 14th overall pick of the first round. If only he and the Warriors had come to terms, Joe Bryant would later tell people, he might have been able to play in the league's Western Conference, where his skills would have fit in with an open-court game.

As it was, Joe Bryant's agent and the Warriors did reach a

verbal agreement, but under the NBA rules of the day each team had to tender its offers to rookies by September 1, or the rookies became free agents. "I don't know exactly why, but the Warriors delayed in tendering the offer," Pat Williams recalled. "Maybe a secretary was late typing up the agreement."

As the deadline neared, Joe Bryant's agent, Richie Phillips, phoned Williams and alerted him to the circumstances. Several days past September 1, Phillips phoned Williams again to say that Bryant was available because he still hadn't received the offer. "Joe was free to sign with anybody he wanted," Williams recalled. "I felt bad for the Warriors, but you gotta do what you gotta do."

In the summer of 1975, the Philadelphia 76ers were a team eager to spend money for talent. In 1973 they had finished with 9 wins and 73 losses, the worst record in NBA history. To make matters worse, their 1974 first-round pick, Marvin Barnes, chose the ABA rather than play for the struggling franchise in Philly.

To change that image, the Sixers began throwing down big money to bring in players. Soon reporters would begin calling them "The Best Team Money Could Buy." Joe Bryant came along at just the right time to collect the largesse. Philly promptly signed him to a five-year deal worth better than $900,000, a fat plum in that era. The paychecks, however, came with a cost. The 76ers were his hometown team, but it was Eastern Conference basketball. "They put me under the basket," Bryant would later lament, which meant that his ball-handling skills would go unused.

It also meant that if he wanted playing time he would have to trade elbows with veteran forward Steve Mix. That proved to be a tall order for a thin rookie forward who really wanted to be a guard. It was Mix who got the major minutes, although Bryant averaged a respectable seven points a game.

More important, in retrospect, was that the timing would offer Joe Bryant a unique perspective on the perils and rewards of a teenager's jumping right from high school to the NBA. The Sixers were desperate for help at center when they learned of a 6-foot-10, 250-pound high schooler in Florida who was said to have the mature body of a man. They investigated and discovered that, sure enough, Darryl Dawkins displayed astounding physical maturity. Afraid that other NBA teams would find out about him, the Sixers put Dawkins's high school coach on a six-year retainer as a scout with the idea that he would "baby-sit" Dawkins and keep him out of any postseason high school tournaments. To make sure no one accused them of taking advantage of the situation, they gave Dawkins, the fifth pick of the first round in 1975, a $1.5 million contract for five years.

When Joe Bryant arrived at training camp in the fall of 1975, he found a bubbling chemistry. The 18-year-old Dawkins, self-dubbed "Chocolate Thunder," would become known for his verbal creations, such as his imaginary planet, Lovetron. With the 24th overall pick in the same draft, Philly had brought in an unbridled young guard, Lloyd Free, from little Guilford College in North Carolina. Also gifted with a verbal creativity, Free dubbed himself the "Prince of Mid Air" and later changed his legal name to World B. Free.

With the American Basketball Association crumbling, the club added center Caldwell Jones and chain-smoking All-Star forward George McGinnis, the possessor of an ugly but often effective game. A year later the club would add ABA star Julius Erving with a $6 million deal.

With their spending spree, the Sixers had amassed one of the all-time collections of basketball personalities, with Free, Dawkins, Erving, Doug Collins, Mix, Henry Bibby, Mike Dunleavy, Fred Carter, Harvey Catchings, Terry Furlow, and McGinnis all seeking to assert themselves. For good measure, the club threw in Gene Shue, an old pro guard with a liking for offensive basketball, as the coach.

"We ended up with this incredible high-wire act," Pat Williams said of the roster he assembled, "kind of a traveling circus with Gene Shue playing ringmaster. Gene had the toughest job in the world trying to keep that act in line. They all wanted to play, they all wanted to shoot, they all wanted to score."

Coming off the bench with "Chocolate Thunder" and "World B. Free" meant that "Jelly Bean" wouldn't get many shots, much less the opportunity to handle the ball. Reporters began describing him as a "defensive specialist," and by his second year his scoring average had dipped to 4.4 a game.

Williams recalls that both Dawkins and Bryant were immensely frustrated with their playing time that first season, a situation that would only worsen over the next few years as the Sixers kept spending and adding more talent to the equation. Williams, though, recalled that Jelly Bean's father, Joseph Bryant, Sr., a distinguished gentleman who walked with a cane, was at every game, supporting his son and taking in the strange scene.

From the enigmatic McGinnis to the ebullient Dawkins to the quick trigger on Free's jumper, the Sixers offered Shue the chemistry test of all time. "We have the best of one world— the playground," the coach told reporters. In that Sixers mix of players, Joe Bryant's personality glowed like a warm rock. It didn't take him long to become one of Gene Shue's favorites, although that didn't necessarily translate into playing time.

Kobe's father played four seasons in Philadelphia, the highlight of which was the 1976–77 campaign when the Sixers powered their way into the NBA Finals against Bill Walton and the Portland Trial Blazers. With Bryant playing about 10 minutes a game, the Sixers had won the Atlantic Division with a

50–32 record. Against Portland, they held home-court advantage and promptly claimed the first two games in the series. But then Walton cut his long hair and Dawkins imploded in a tiff with Portland's Maurice Lucas. In the aftermath Dawkins smashed up a bathroom in the locker room and publicly accused his teammates of not coming to his aid during the brouhaha. The momentum changed, the Blazers came alive and swept the next four games to take the title, a stunning reversal that rocked the Sixers franchise.

"It's a bad scene," Erving admitted afterward.

Indeed, Gene Shue wanted McGinnis traded, but it was Shue himself who was ousted the following season in favor of Billy Cunningham, who had been a fan favorite as a Sixers player.

It was about 15 months after that championship fiasco, on August 23, 1978, that the third and last of Joe and Pam Bryant's children was born. They named him Kobe after a Japanese steakhouse in King of Prussia, Pennsylvania. While his family life was blossoming wondrously, Joe Bryant's professional career encountered increasing turbulence. Seeking to reduce the zaniness factor in the club in 1978, Cunningham came to Pat Williams and asked the GM to trade Free. The Sixers could find no takers—"We tried everywhere to trade Lloyd Free," Williams said—until Shue, who had landed in San Diego as coach of the Clippers, finally agreed to take him in a trade.

In exchange, the Clippers gave the Sixers their first-round draft pick for 1984, which would become Charles Barkley.

That off-season of 1978, the Sixers brought in forward Bobby Jones, which only served to shove Bryant farther down in the playing rotation. "Jelly Bean was doomed," Pat Williams recalled.

A year later, early in the 1979 off-season, Cunningham again visited the GM and this time asked him to trade Bryant. "Billy told me, 'He just doesn't fit. He's 25 years old. We gotta do something with him,'" Williams recalled. "Jelly Bean never could play with consistency. Never could shoot with consistency. He never really had a position. Very talented. A character. Very loose and flamboyant. But when he got out on the floor, you never knew what he was going to do."

The problem was, the Sixers couldn't find anyone interested in a trade. "There were no takers," Williams recalled. "We can't get a nibble. Then, at the last minute just before the season starts, Gene Shue says he'll take him. Gene was an offensive coach. He needed talent."

In October 1979, the Sixers traded Joe Bryant to the San Diego Clippers for their 1986 first-round draft pick. Once again, Williams had laid the groundwork for Philadelphia's future. The pick that Joe Bryant was traded for would become center Brad Daugherty, the only problem being that Philly management promptly traded him to Cleveland in 1986 for Roy Hinson and $800,000.

"The sportswriters in Philly still rail about what a boner that one was," lamented Williams, now an Orlando Magic executive.

It was in San Diego where Jelly Bean would finally become a double-digit scorer, averaging better than 11 points per game and better than 2,000 minutes of playing time a season in three years with the Clippers.

It was also young Kobe's first southern California connection. The family's collective memory now conjures up images of a three-year-old Kobe, dressed in a little Clippers uniform, performing dunks on a small plastic goal and telling his mother that he would someday play in the NBA, just like Daddy, what Kobe would later describe as his discovery of the code.

The Clippers' fortunes, however, were beginning a pronounced sag. In 1981, an L.A. lawyer by the name of Donald

Sterling took control of the team, beginning a long run as the NBA's most meddlesome owner. Gene Shue was promptly replaced by Paul Silas, setting in motion a downward spiral of regularly changing coaches and players. By Joe Bryant's third season in San Diego, the Clippers' record had dipped to a dreadful 17 wins and 65 losses. He would "break out" with phenomenal games, scoring a high of 32 in one season and 34 in another. But struggling teams are usually terrible places to try to establish consistency, and that has always seemed the case with the Clippers.

As fate would have it, Joe Bryant was packaged with a second-round pick and traded for another second-round pick to the Houston Rockets for 1982–83. There, unbeknown to both father and son, his career would intersect with Kobe's. Joe's last NBA coach would become Kobe's first two decades later. Del Harris was in charge of the Rockets. He had managed to coach the club into the 1981 league championship series against the Boston Celtics in a stunning run of playoff upsets, but afterward center Moses Malone had departed for Philadelphia. By the time Joe Bryant got to the Rockets, they were truly and intentionally awful, trying to dump games through the spring of 1983 in a race to see who could get the number-one pick in the draft to take University of Virginia center Ralph Sampson. It would seem almost impossible to be worse than the Clippers team Joe Bryant had just left, but the Rockets were. They lost 68 games that season on their way to snagging Sampson.

Like any sane competitor, Joe Bryant would try to repress much of that misery, but he did come away from the experience with the lasting impression that Del Harris liked to talk an awful lot. A pleasant and gentlemanly man with a deep sense of faith, Harris was given to droning on and on during the frequent pauses in Rocket practices.

Despite the unpleasant circumstances, there was no great friction between Bryant and Harris. Asked about Kobe's father in 1998, Harris recalled, "He played for me with the Houston Rockets. He had good ball-handling skills, but he was not near the athlete that Kobe is. He was bigger overall, about six-foot-nine. I don't know how he got the name Jelly Bean, but it fit. He was a good guy, had a great personality. He was a smart guy, but he was a little bit into the flair part of the game himself."

In other words, it was said about Jelly Bean that he sometimes seemed to enjoy making simple plays unnecessarily complicated, a sin that his son would later be accused of. Once asked if he saw similarities between Joe and Kobe, Del Harris replied, "They're nothing alike. The only similarity is that both have great ball-handling skills. His dad's passing skills were as good as anybody playing at that time, except Magic. Joe was a good guy, a pleasant guy to be around, but more of a fun-loving guy. Kobe is focused, businesslike. Joe's affable nature was the outstanding thing about his character, whereas focus and determination are Kobe's. I suspect Joe helped him with that. It's not necessarily like father, like son. Sometimes a father will teach his son to do the things he felt like he could've done better and maybe didn't."

The postmortem on Jelly Bean's NBA tenure would confirm that he was a good guy. But in the final analysis he was too good, too sweet, too carefree.

"He was a goofball," one longtime Lakers official recalled sourly. "He threw away his NBA career."

After the Rockets closed out their miserable 1983 season, they released Joe Bryant. As can be imagined, those late days in Houston didn't pass without some bitterness. The more success enjoyed by Magic Johnson, the greater Joe Bryant's sense of what might have been. "He comes into the league with all that fancy stuff," Bryant told reporters as his days in Houston were drawing to a close, "and they call it Magic. I've been doing it all these years, and they call it 'schoolyard.'"

Over There

With three young children to feed, Bryant tried for a time working in Houston. Rockets owner Charlie Thomas liked his affable manner and was supposedly eager to put him to work in his network of businesses. But Joe Bryant missed the game dreadfully and soon found himself back in Philadelphia, connecting with his roots.

It was Philly hoops legend Sonny Hill who got him hooked up to play in Europe in 1984, thus setting the stage for Kobe's unique and wondrous childhood. Within weeks the family had packed up and moved to Rieti, Italy, where Kobe would begin school just days after his sixth birthday. Sharia was eight, Shaya seven. They didn't know the language, but they spent afternoons teaching each other through word games. Within months they had found a comfort level in a world vastly different from the one they had left behind.

It was just the first of many bonding experiences for the Bryant clan. As strangers in a strange land, the children and their parents learned what it meant to depend on one another. With each passing year in Europe, the bonds grew tighter, the family members closer, giving them a strength, a unity that would last long after they had returned to the States. Asked in 1999 about friendship, Kobe Bryant said he didn't have many friends, that his family members were his friends. "I have a large family," he explained.

As might be expected, the cultural change also brought a shift in Joe Bryant's basketball life. Although soccer was a much bigger spectator sport in southern Europe, Italians still displayed a passion for their local basketball teams. American hoops imports usually found the money to their liking and a schedule that actually allowed for a family life, as opposed to the NBA grind of three or four games per week and constant travel. In Italy, the focus was on practices, usually held twice a day, which is unthinkable in American professional basketball. Games, on the other hand, usually amounted to no more than one per week, most often on Sundays.

Where Joe Bryant had felt constrained by the NBA, he quickly took to the competition in Italy and found stardom at the pace of 30 points per game. If he felt like trotting out his flair, no problem. The fans merely sang songs in praise of his skills. "You know the player who's better than Magic or Jabbar?" went one set of lyrics that Kobe committed to memory in Italian. "It's Joseph, Joseph Bryant!"

His biggest fan was the little boy who followed him to practice most days. "He just played with so much charisma," Kobe recalled of his father's play in Europe. "He taught me to enjoy the game."

Enjoy is perhaps one description. *Totally and absolutely consumed* was mostly Kobe's approach to basketball even at that young age. In retrospect, his time in Italy became the most comprehensive basketball school one could imagine. "I started playing basketball over there," he said, "which was great, because I learned fundamentals first. I think most kids who grow up here in America learn all the fancy dribbling. In Italy, they teach you true fundamentals and leave out all the nonsense."

For starters, he studied more videotape than the heartiest of NBA drones serving as assistant coaches. His grandparents in Philadelphia kept the connections with American culture alive by sending a steady flow of videotapes of sporting events, mostly basketball games, and TV programs, with a heavy helping of "The Cosby Show." By far the most important were the basketball games, which came at the rate of about 40 per season. Joseph and Kobe would pore over them together, taking note of all the key subtleties, the footwork and positioning, the drop steps and jab steps, the various offensive and defensive styles.

"My grandparents would tape a lot of basketball games and send me the footage over in Italy," Kobe explained. "I used to watch everybody from Magic to Bird to Michael to Dominique Wilkins. I used to watch their little pet moves and add them to my game."

He used the freeze frames and slowed tracking to review sequence after sequence, with his father often pointing out key elements. When Joe was away, Kobe pursued his studies alone, virtually memorizing entire sequences, especially those that revealed player tendencies. By age nine he had put together his first scouting tape, a look at Atlanta Hawks guard John Battle. Michael Jordan, too, had begun his mesmerizing assault on the NBA's hierarchy in those days. But without question the star of the Bryant household and Kobe's young life was Magic Johnson. The Lakers were in the midst of their Showtime heyday, their run of championships highlighted by Johnson's dazzling ball handling and exceptional leadership, which in turn made them a network darling. Young Kobe's room and his heart were shrines to Johnson with a poster on the wall and Johnson's number 32 as his jersey number. However, his main focus on the Lakers great came at the video monitor, where Kobe would play and replay Johnson's highlights.

The only problematic aspect of Kobe Bryant's Italian basketball "school" came when he attempted to put what he saw into practice. Soccer was the dominant recreational sport there, meaning that Bryant would have to pick and politic his time on the playground for basketball. When he did play with

Italian children, he often found himself playing soccer goalie. Eventually his parents would put up a hoop at home, but even then his approach to the game was solitary of necessity. Joe would play one-on-one with him when available, but with so many hours a day in Italy dedicated to professional practice it wasn't humanly possible for his father to play enough to slake Kobe's great thirst.

So Kobe played alone, in imaginary games against himself. "Shadow basketball," he called it. "I play against my shadow." That, of course, involved intense visualization of the NBA opponents he had stored in his imagination from the video screen. His pursuits were strikingly similar to those of Jerry West four decades earlier as a skinny kid in the West Virginia hills, those hours and hours alone at an outdoor hoop.

It was not entirely solitary for Kobe. Weekday afternoons after school he would go with the old man to his team practices, where he would continue this pursuit at a sideline hoop while Joe's team ran the floor. Before long Kobe had developed the art of luring one of Joe's teammates into a game of one-on-one. And on Sundays, when his father's team played, Kobe would make the most of halftime, using the empty court to conduct his shadow games and shooting and dribbling routines, often to the applause and wonderment of the crowd.

Through all of it Joe was his companion and guide. The personality traits that had perhaps made the father less than he could have been as an NBA player were just the things that made him a world-class parent. The gentle, judicious nature made him a teacher that Kobe could love and trust and helped to create a powerful bond between the two. "My father never really came to me and said, 'OK, son, you have to do this and that,'" Kobe explained. "I came to him and asked him when I needed help."

He clearly had his own hoop dreams, and they were stoked far beyond any influence provided by his father.

And by no means was this Italian schooling just basketball. In all, Joseph Bryant spent another eight pro seasons in Europe, playing and coaching in Italy, Spain, and France. Young Kobe traveled extensively, viewing a range of wonders from the Alps to the Vatican to the ruins of Rome to the romantic wonders of the Venetian canals. The knell for this wondrous experience came with a late-night phone call in the fall of 1991. Kobe's grandparents called with the stunning news that Magic Johnson had announced that he had contracted the HIV virus and was retiring from basketball. The next morning, Pam and Joe broke the news to Kobe without going into the details of exactly what was forcing the Lakers star from the game. It didn't matter. The 13-year-old was crushed. He cried, he struggled to eat, a mourning that lasted more than a week.

At the time, Joe's career had come down to a fragile little team in France, while his kids attended a Swiss school just across the border. After 16 seasons playing pro ball, he halted his pursuit of his own particular brand of hoops magic just weeks after Johnson's announcement. The Bryants packed up and moved back to the Philadelphia suburbs, where the children would find a substantial challenge reacquainting themselves with American culture. Kobe, an eighth grader, in particular, would find difficulty confronting the urban African-American experience. The eight years abroad had left him with a unique identity. His schoolmates in the Philadelphia suburbs would marvel at the new brother in class with the strange accent. Asked in 1999 what effect his time in Europe had had on him, Kobe simply replied, "I jump high. Everything else is groomed Italian style."

In that sense Jelly Bean's basketball journey had taken him just as far as he needed to go. Very quickly it was becoming Kobe's turn, and the pace would quicken to a blur.

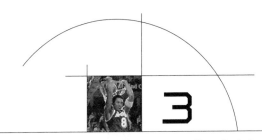

3

ASCENSION

> *"Whenever I step on the court, I think of that—that my father went through this and now I'm going through it."* —KOBE BRYANT

T he counselor had seen kids like this before. They were all like this. They all believed they were headed for the NBA, for huge glory and even huger paychecks. This was the Sonny Hill Community Involvement League, where the best young talent in greater Philadelphia went at each other on sultry summer evenings. The swagger factor ran deep with these young players. That's the way it is with hoopsters. It's a game of confidence, and playing it well can bring huge surges of power, confidence so great that it can blind whoever possesses it.

And so it was the mission of the Sonny Hill League to build that confidence in young players while at the same time forcing them to see the light. If it sounds like a delicate balance, it is. But over the decades Sonny Hill had refined his league into a Philly specialty, the basketball equivalent of a cheesesteak. A former five-foot-nine guard in the old semipro Eastern League, Hill was by nature an organizer. Professionally he had started life building membership in a local labor union. Later he would evolve into a radio talk show host, a fund-raiser, even a player representative. First and foremost, though, he was a lover of the game, and he would use his many skills to shape his summer leagues as an expression of that love. Some observers would insinuate that Hill's approach had a few too many hard edges, but Hill and his defenders would point out that they were shaping all the negatives and the energy of the streets into something positive. That was what made the experience real.

First Hill founded the Baker League, a four-team summer circuit organized in 1960 for pro players. In those early years, Hill staged the games on outdoor courts at a recreation center in north Philadelphia. Admittedly, his motivations were selfish. He wanted to keep his own career going, and many of the Philly-area pros were frustrated trying to find court time in the off-season. To remedy that, Hill put together his league with the help of Charles Baker, a local politician. Later the scene shifted to the basement of the Bright Hope Baptist Church before finally finding a home in air-conditioned McGonigle Hall at Temple University.

With his community roots, Hill was quickly able to attract a range of NBA stars in the early days, from Guy Rodgers to Wilt Chamberlain to Bill Bradley to Earl Monroe to Julius Erving to many, many others, all eager to use the off-season competition to add to their games. The Baker League became a place where they could trot out their individual flair for thousands of fans, many of whom never got to see an NBA game. Local legend Earl the Pearl made a habit of arriving late to games, sending a buzz through the crowd as he made his way courtside. "He'd duck his head into Rev. Bill Gray's Bright Hope Baptist Church gym, and fans would spread the word. 'Magic is here. Magic is here. MAGIC is HERE!'" recalled writer Donald Hunt, a longtime observer of Philadelphia basketball.

From Chamberlain's rim-clanging dunks to Monroe's ball-handling wizardry, the Baker League offered up the rarest of nightly displays. Through his efforts, Hill had connected the commercial upper echelon of the game back with its playground roots, the street labs where hoopsters cooked their skills. It was the setting where style and substance evolved at a pace that constantly defined and redefined basketball. Such an environment posed a variety of obvious threats to established pros, but Hill's league found a way to minimize those threats.

Bill Bradley quickly discovered how valuable that connection could be. He has credited Hill with helping to restore his confidence over the summer of 1968 after a terrible NBA rookie season. A Rhodes Scholar, Bradley had studied in England for two years after graduating from Princeton in 1965, during which his skills eroded. In the wake of his rookie failure, Bradley spent that fated summer of 1968 working days as a community volunteer in Harlem (when's the last time an NBA player did something like that?), then taking a train down in the evening for the Baker League games.

"We played in the basement of that church. I was still trying to play guard, and Sonny was very positive," Bradley once recalled for *Sports Illustrated*. "He told me I could do it. That was an important summer for me in terms of restoring my confidence, getting back some of the skills I had lost, getting the chance to go against great players like Earl Monroe and Wali Jones, and, above all, making a good friend [in Hill]."

It was about the time that Hill added amateur competition to his formula by founding the Sonny Hill Community Involvement League, a 47-team network that over the years has provided a mix of hoops, academic tutoring, and career counseling for better than 10,000 young players.

It was the Baker League that brought Hill the high profile, but the amateur league would prove to be the grounds for his greatest influence. The operation of the pro league grew more difficult as the 1990s unfolded, with the escalation of player salaries and teams' worries about injuries. The Sonny Hill League, meanwhile, evolved into what many see as the ultimate amateur basketball proving ground. That was why Joe Bryant made sure that when the family returned to the States each June he would take Kobe, starting at the unprecedented age of 10, down to the Hill League to begin his hardcourt education. After years in Europe, Joe Bryant, himself a protégé of Sonny Hill and a graduate of the Philly playgrounds, knew that the Sonny Hill League would provide Kobe the perfect introduction to the urban hoops experience. It was there that he would have to learn to survive. The competition often overwhelmed him in those early years, but it didn't destroy him. To the contrary, he toughened with each experience and found confidence in his father's persistently positive approach.

"This is where I can work hard and make the best of that hard work," Kobe said at the time of his early experience in the Hill League.

"I believe Kobe is out here most summers, not because I started a trend or anything, but he really wanted to play this game at a young age," Joe Bryant told the *Philadelphia Tribune* in 1994. "We see it as educational."

In those early days Kobe was viewed as something of an oddity, a preteen venturing a little further than maybe he should. After all, by the time he arrived there, the Sonny Hill League had produced a vast number of college and even professional players. In time, though, Joe Bryant's boy would come to be considered Sonny Hill's most famous product.

"Kobe actually grew up in this league," coach Tee Shields explained to reporters in 1995.

Part of that upbringing included the first confrontation with his future. Kobe was still quite young that day when the counselor for the Sonny Hill League was scanning the player applications for problems. Beside the category that asked for future career plans, Kobe had listed "NBA."

The answer represented just the kind of unrealistic attitude the league wanted to guard against.

For the Sonny Hill League, basketball is the carrot used to lure youths away from the treacherous pitfalls of Philadelphia's hard streets. The game is certainly prized, but the emphasis is that basketball is a means to an end, not the end itself. Players in the league are taught to plan for their futures but not to figure on the NBA as being that future.

So the counselor admonished Kobe. Only one in a million make it to the NBA, the counselor said, so you have to plan on a future other than basketball.

"I'm going to be that one in a million," Kobe replied. After all, he explained, Magic Johnson had done it. Michael Jordan had done it. "Why not me?"

It was just the level of confidence and expectation that his father had encouraged in him. Others would later label this air of assumption in Bryant pure arrogance. Many would find it hard to stomach. Others were simply awed by seeing someone so young with such a sense of purpose, not to mention an elevated skill level.

In fairness to Kobe, his answer to the counselor was entirely logical because he wasn't your routine young player. If nothing else, his bloodlines dramatically increased the odds of his finding a career path in professional basketball. Not only had his father enjoyed a 16-year career in the pro game, but his mother's brother, John "Chubby" Cox, had played at Villanova, then transferred to the University of San Francisco where he became a fine college guard. Chubby Cox even did a short stint in the NBA. Beyond the sheer genetics of Kobe's karma, there was the environmental influence that had seized him even before he could walk. Once the Bryants moved back to Philadelphia, the family tradition took an even firmer hold on his life. John Cox joined Joe Bryant on the faculty at Kobe's personal institute of advanced training.

"My dad and uncle Chubby spent a lot of time with me," Bryant explained. "They worked on my shooting, rebounding, and defense. In addition, they encouraged me to play hard all the time."

Their efforts meant that he bordered on a technical, fundamental purity, even as an eighth grader. Because of its European gestation, his game lacked the street ball elements, the crossover dribble and the array of twitches and ankle-breaking fakes. But that didn't matter. He would acquire those facets over the years of going against the best amateur talent in the country at the various summer camps and leagues. In the process he would make himself into a considerable offensive weapon, somebody capable of getting a shot as often as he wanted.

"You know, I grew up in Philadelphia," he explained. "You go down to the playground, you play. If you can't get your own shot, you can't play. So that started at an early age."

Among those to get an early view of Kobe in the Hill League was Eddie Jones, a six-foot-six forward at Temple who quickly realized he was witnessing something special. "Even back then, when he was 13, he could play," Jones recalled. "Even back then he could bust people."

Kobe was so good that Jones began dropping by the Bryant house to make sure Kobe had a ride to pickup games that included local college talent. The more he watched him, the more Eddie Jones thought that Kobe might just be the best young player he had ever seen. Jones wasn't alone in that perspective.

Kobe had spent only a few days in organized public school basketball upon his return from Europe in early 1992 before he came to the attention of Gregg Downer, the young coach for Lower Merion High School in suburban Philadelphia. It was during the first months of 1992 that Downer began hearing about the new eighth grader at nearby Bala Cynwyd Junior High. Supposedly the newcomer was six-foot-two and just killing opponents in the junior high competition. So Downer invited him over to the varsity practice at Lower Merion.

The first obvious sign that day at the Lower Merion gym was when the prospect walked in with his six-foot-nine father. Somebody mentioned that the old man had been an NBA player, but Joe Bryant didn't come on strong that day, preferring instead to stay in the background to allow Kobe the moment. It was just a few minutes into the scrimmage when Downer realized he was watching someone with pro-level skills, a mere kid who was cutting up his varsity with ease. Downer had played a little college ball himself and still played competitive recreation league games. So something prompted him that day to take on the eighth grader himself in a little one-on-one. Huge mistake. The coach suffered the same fate as his players and the same fate as Joe Bryant's European teammates—embarrassment at the hands of a 13-year-old.

Downer would come to discover over the ensuing months that Kobe had a startling work ethic. He pushed himself through a grueling self-improvement schedule that included road work, weights, and seemingly nonstop basketball. It was obvious to anyone who watched him even in his early teens that not only was he on a highway to the big time, but Kobe Bryant was intent on getting into the passing lane. Where was he headed? To a destination that only he could see.

King of the Aces

Jeremy Treatman was a young correspondent for the high school sports staff of the *Philadelphia Inquirer*'s "Neighbors" section when he first got a look at Kobe as a 14-year-old freshman at Lower Merion during the 1992–93 season. Treatman was immediately awed by his skill, and although the correspondent would write only a few paragraphs about Kobe, he would look back at that first story a few years later and smile at his advice to his readers. "Remember this name," Treatman wrote.

That introduction would prove to be the beginning of a friendship between the writer and Joe Bryant, and eventually with Kobe as well. Like others, Treatman was immediately impressed by the young player's drive and his sense of purpose. "He was 14 years old and about six-foot-two," Treatman recalled. "He wasn't dunking or anything then. He was really thin. In fact, he broke his kneecap because somebody just bumped knees with him. That's how thin he was."

The injury meant that Kobe missed the last few games of his freshman season. The Aces went on to a 4–20 finish, the product of a long, draining season in which Kobe averaged about 18 points a game and led Lower Merion in rebounding.

Another thing that impressed Treatman that first year was that even then the young player was burning with thoughts about Lower Merion winning a state championship in basketball. A suburban school with a population that was about 90 percent Caucasian, Lower Merion hadn't won a state hoops title since 1943. The idea of Lower Merion rising up in the Philly high school basketball hierarchy was almost comical at the time, Treatman said. "No one else on the team in those early days was even thinking of a state championship. But that's what Kobe wanted, and eventually he made it happen, almost single-handedly."

Treatman remembered being impressed that Bryant would even stay at a place like Lower Merion when he easily could have gone to one of the Philly powerhouses. But Kobe clearly liked the idea of taking his suburban school to the title. He also liked the surprise he created in opponents that first season.

"The first couple times we played inner-city schools, there'd be a buzz about me," Kobe once explained. "Half of 'em would say, 'Oh, he's soft, from the suburbs.' "

Despite his frustration with his team's heavy losses that first season, Bryant still produced some absolutely spellbinding displays of athleticism, a development that raised eyebrows in Philadelphia high school basketball circles.

From that point on there were frequent rumors each season that he was transferring to this school or that one, but Treatman came to see that the gossip had no basis in fact. "The most impressive thing to me about his high school days was the fact that he wanted to stay at Lower Merion," Treatman said. "There were all these rumors about him transferring to one of the city powers, but he didn't want to do that. He was determined to make Lower Merion a winner before other people even thought about it."

Part of this allegiance seemed to stem from the high regard Kobe held for Gregg Downer's coaching, Treatman recalled. "Downer's pretty sharp. He knew what he had in Kobe. He took a lot of pressure off Kobe. He was the kind of coach who would come in the locker room after a tough loss and put all the blame on himself. He was in control, and Kobe had a lot of confidence in him and would listen to him. Gregg Downer had a big influence on Kobe's life."

His taking the blame for the losses that first season was a means of shielding Kobe from the intense pressures the player put on himself. Downer also hadn't hesitated to let Joe Bryant work with the team that first season as an assistant coach, another factor in Kobe's appreciation for the head coach.

One of Treatman's delights was watching Joe Bryant's passion as a coach, both at Lower Merion and at nearby Akiba

Hebrew Academy, a private school where he coached the girls' team. Unfortunately, Joe had to relinquish both of those jobs after the '93 season because he was hired as an assistant coach at LaSalle.

The people who knew Joe Bryant as the flamboyant young player for the Sixers were surprised at how he had matured. He was still a happy-go-lucky guy, but his whole focus seemed aimed at being the best father possible. The elder Bryant's sunny personality was a hit with Treatman. The more time he spent around them, the more the writer came to admire the strong bonds between father and son.

"It was exactly what all father-son relationships should be," Treatman recalled.

Most impressive was Joe Bryant's measured approach. His son's personal drive was clearly pushing the basketball experience along, but the father always seemed to follow close enough without ever really intruding. There was strength when Kobe needed it. There was freedom when he didn't.

"I just love my father for being there for me," Kobe said at the time.

Soon Joe Bryant and Treatman were fast friends, so much so that when Joe Bryant began coaching Kobe on a team in the Narberth League, another Philly summer league, Treatman helped him draft the players.

"He's still one of the nicest people I've ever met," Treatman recalled in a 1999 interview. "It was special the way he made those girls at Akiba Hebrew feel as their coach. I'll never forget it. He went way beyond the call of duty. He'd even run with them during drills. It was funny to watch this six-foot-nine guy who had played in the NBA running and teaching these girls who had never dribbled a ball how to play basketball. And he taught them. They loved him. They literally cried when he left for LaSalle."

Kobe, meanwhile, allowed his knee to heal that spring, then went right back to work. In the wake of the dismal season, he stepped up the intensity of his workouts and videotape study. He was moving toward six-foot-four, which made him even more of a factor in the Hill and Narberth Leagues and in basketball camps during the off-season. At the time, Kobe wasn't even the best ninth- or tenth-grade player in the region. That distinction belonged to Tim Thomas, a willowy six-foot-nine forward from New Jersey who would wind up at Villanova for a year before moving on to the NBA. But Kobe would soon catch and eclipse Thomas in the eyes of the numerous scouts and basketball recruiting experts.

"The difference was Kobe's work ethic and determination," Treatman said. "High school players really don't work on their crafts, their skills, anymore. They play a lot, but they don't do the work to develop certain facets of their games. You'd never see a young Kareem Abdul-Jabbar today with that sky hook. So many young players today think that because they have talent and athletic ability that's enough. But Kobe was absolutely unique in his willingness to do that work. That's where his parents came in."

Although Pam Bryant stayed in the background, she too had a remarkable bond with her children. Kobe drew much of his singular determination from her strength. "She's been as much of an influence on him as Joe has been," Treatman said. "I don't think that he goes a day without talking to her, even today."

For observers, the combination of individual skills work and the constant competition in Philly's leagues and camps translated into meteoric progress for Kobe. Added to his fundamentals was an increasing number of playground moves, crossover dribbles, and whatnot. His increased size and strength also stepped up the intensity of the one-on-one contests he waged with his father. With each day it became clearer that Kobe was nearing the time when he could actually beat Joe. Perhaps because of this increasing threat, Joe stepped up the physical nature of his play. Kobe's competitiveness was becoming almost uncontainable, which left him complaining that Joe was resorting to the physical play as a means of "cheating" to win. Sometimes it was good-natured. Sometimes it wasn't. They'd go at each other so hard that Pam Bryant would angrily break up the games, especially if Joe managed to fatten Kobe's lip with an elbow.

Regardless, he could sense his increasing power, and his confidence soared with the extra work and his rapid growth. Just as important was the sense of pride he took in his basketball mind. No one studied the game as much as he did.

"I was like a computer," he would recall. "I retrieved information to benefit my game."

It certainly sounded arrogant, but it was the truth.

That mental benefit was substantial in Kobe's rise to basketball prominence. So was the offensive approach that Downer used for Lower Merion's Aces for 1993–94.

"Wherever I went, I'd be thinking of different ways to utilize Kobe's athleticism, to get him the ball," Gregg Downer recalled. "He was incredible."

The coach weighed the benefits of a motion offense versus a scheme that would put the ball in Kobe's hands most of the time. "Why run a motion offense when you can have the ball in Kobe's hands?" Treatman asked. "Kobe brought the ball up a lot of times his 10th-grade year."

He would cross midcourt and deliver the ball to the wing, then go set up inside for the Aces' "seal play," where Kobe would seal off his defender, receive the post pass, and score with either hand.

The proceedings engrossed Treatman, who realized he was witnessing the unfolding of something special. "He was automatic from the inside, automatic from the outside, plus he had this beautiful pull-up, midrange shot. At the time, there were maybe five NBA players who could finish inside, finish outside, and had a nice midrange game."

The only problem, Treatman said, "was that there was a jealous senior point guard at the time. Kobe would score seven in a row, and this guy would come down and jack up a jumper rather than get the ball to Kobe."

It's a common conflict in basketball for an uncommon few. Some players are so skilled, so advanced, that their games come into conflict with traditional notions of team play. The better they play, the more their teammates struggle to find a role. It became a common theme in Michael Jordan's tenure with the Chicago Bulls. On a smaller scale it was the same for Kobe Bryant and the Merion Aces.

In Kobe Bryant's final season of high school play, a range of professional teams would begin reviewing videotape of his performances. Among those would be the Lakers. Mitch Kupchak, the L.A. general manager, would later reveal that the Lakers' scouting staff looked at those tapes and remarked that Kobe Bryant appeared to be the most selfish player they'd ever seen.

Informed of that evaluation during an interview, Treatman, who would serve as an assistant coach at Lower Merion during Kobe's senior year, was obviously wounded. "We thought he was such an unselfish player. That's what upsets me so much about this selfish crap. His high school teammates probably understand Kobe better than his Lakers teammates do."

"We still made an effort to play team ball," Downer said. "Kobe had an obligation to exercise good shot selection, just like every other kid on the team. There were times that he was taking what I considered to be bad shots, and he came out of the game."

"To hear people calling him selfish is kind of stunning," Treatman said. "As good as Kobe was, we won a state championship based on his ability to pass the ball and share it with his role-playing teammates. Kobe, with his basketball pedigree, understood that better than anybody."

Selfish or not, Kobe Bryant was clearly a scoring machine. By the end of his sophomore season he would come within 80 points of the 1,000 career scoring mark. He averaged 22 points and 10 rebounds for the 1993–94 season. Better yet, the Lower Merion Aces suddenly challenged for the Central League title and finished with a 16–6 record.

During the season, Treatman had attempted to get his preps editor at the *Inquirer* to allow him to do a story on Joe and Kobe Bryant. In an editorial meeting the writer pitched the angles. A bright young player. Son of an NBA player. A youngster who spoke Italian. "Kobe and Joe Bryant just don't do it for me," the editor replied. "Get off it."

Publicity or not, Kobe marched on, with more off-season work, more fine showings in the Sonny Hill League and in the high-test summer camps. Working days that literally stretched from 9:00 A.M. to 9:00 P.M. and beyond, Kobe played in six different leagues and attended two summer camps. He even made an appearance at the highly regarded Adidas ABCD All-America camp at Fairleigh Dickinson University as one of only four rising juniors invited. In another year the camp would become the platform for his rise to prominence, but in the summer of 1994 he was just a good young player hoping to mature.

"I enjoy playing against great competition," Bryant told reporters at the time. "That's how you get better. I knew that playing for Lower Merion I would be facing the best players from the suburban area. I knew that the Sonny Hill League would give me a chance to face the top players from the city. The ABCD All-America camp put me up against the best players in the country."

For the 1994–95 season, Downer sought a similar upgrade for the Lower Merion schedule and added St. Anthony's Prep, Bob Hurley's team from Jersey City, New Jersey. Against the better competition that season, Kobe averaged 31.1 points, 10.4 rebounds, 5.2 assists, 3.8 blocks, and 2.3 steals. Rapidly approaching six-foot-six, Kobe pushed his team to an elite level. The Aces finished 26–5, and they managed to unseat rival Ridley, the six-time defending champions of the Central League. In the game that finally pushed Ridley aside, Kobe scored 42 in a 76–70 Lower Merion victory.

In the AAAA playoffs, the Aces' run ended in the second round with a late Kobe turnover. Even in 1999, five years after it happened, he considered that outcome one of the most painful experiences of life. It was a valuable lesson but one he hoped never to revisit, he said.

The emotion washed over him in tears as he apologized to his teammates in the locker room afterward, never mind that he had scored 33 points with 15 rebounds. "He blamed himself for the playoff loss," Treatman said. "The only reason we were even there was because of him."

Treatman considered Bryant a clear choice as Philadelphia-area high school player of the year for 1994, but the writer learned that the *Inquirer*'s preps editor, who had yet to agree to a full-length story on Kobe, was about to designate Howard Brown, another area phenom. To avert what he considered a mistake, Treatman said he intervened with the *Inquirer*'s sports editor to make sure Bryant got the award.

By the 1994–95 season, Treatman had begun working on a

local TV show covering high school sports in addition to his duties as a correspondent for the *Inquirer*. In that capacity, Treatman said, he produced the first TV feature on Kobe and was immediately awed by the player's obviously innate media skills. "He was perfect, just a natural," Treatman recalled. "He knows what to say and how to say it. He listens to the question. A lot of people don't do that. He listens."

It was becoming imminently clear just how much Kobe Bryant would need those media skills. Another summer of nonstop basketball awaited him, along with a special treat. He had worked his way into playing pickup games with some members of the 76ers and other NBA players at the St. Joseph's University gym.

"He blended with the rest of us," veteran center Rick Mahorn would later recall for *Newsday*, "and if you can blend with us as a high school player, that says something right there. That says you belong. Dude even tried to 'poster' me. He tried to dunk on me."

In one game Kobe guarded journeyman pro Willie Burton, who had managed to score 53 points in one game during the previous NBA season. According to various accounts, Burton scored over Kobe and followed it up with a little trash talk. Kobe answered with a 10-basket scoring spree while allowing Burton just one more basket. The veteran stormed out of the gym in anger and never returned. He later wound up playing in Europe the next season.

Kobe, meanwhile, was elated. For years he had dreamed of going directly to the NBA from high school. It wasn't a dream he shared with many, but he knew that for such a move to be possible he would have to show tremendous promise by his senior year at Lower Merion. He hadn't known how he was going to accomplish this goal, but he spent hours each day turning over the various scenarios in his mind.

With his showing in pickup games against the pro players at St. Joe's, he had gotten his first big sign.

His appearance at the prestigious Adidas ABCD camp that summer brought the next indication that his dream just might unfold. He went into the camp as a highly regarded player, but there were numerous others considered as good or better. "He dominated the ABCD camp," Treatman recalled. "That clearly established him as the number-one player in the country. Every recruiting service had had Tim Thomas or Jermaine O'Neal listed as number one until that 11th-grade summer. Mike Bibby was up there, too. But Kobe became number one after that summer circuit of camps."

When Kobe appeared at the Adidas Big-Time Tournament in Las Vegas, Houston Rockets coach Rudy Tomjanovich and a host of other NBA scouts were in the audience. At an NBA players' camp for high schoolers, Kobe came from behind to block the shot of seven-footer Loren Woods, who would later play for Wake Forest and the University of Arizona. "Kobe came from nowhere and just swatted it off the backboard," Treatman recalled.

The scouts visibly squirmed at such displays, and word soon spread among NBA circles that Kobe was considering making himself available for the draft. Just a year earlier, seven-footer Kevin Garnett had bypassed college to find success in the NBA, which meant that pro executives hungry for talent began reconsidering the idea of drafting high school talent.

Pro basketball had always considered itself a business for men, players with mature bodies and hard-driving appetites. Yet as far back as the 1940s, exceptional teenagers had found a way to survive and thrive in the "business." Paul Seymour, for example, got his start in the game as a 17-year-old do-everything guard back in the old barnstorming days during World War II, when teams traveled from town to town looking for games. He was young and smart and quick and managed to dart his way around the old, two-fisted game. His teammates smoked in the locker room at halftime and shared a six-pack or two after the game. Then they'd get back in their cars and drive to the next town.

After the war Seymour settled in with the Syracuse Nationals as pro basketball found some stability in league play. There was the old National Basketball League, and the new Basketball Association of America. Before long they merged to become the NBA. Most of the players were veterans in the truest sense of the word. Many of them had served in World War II. They knew how to fight for a roster spot, which meant there wasn't much room for youngsters.

But Seymour proved he was as smart and tough as they were—so smart and tough, in fact, that he would play for years in the NBA and then become a coach. Looking back on it, that was quite an accomplishment.

Pro basketball was a risky business back in the late 1940s and early '50s. There were few fans and hardly any press coverage, maybe a paragraph on the back pages of local newspaper sports sections. When the NBA started, it had 17 teams, but that number soon dwindled to 9 struggling clubs.

In those days you played college basketball with the idea of earning a free education. Giving up that education to chase the limp dream of pro basketball was a foreign idea to the college players of that era; they would just as soon have planned a stroll on the moon. Besides, the college game was the glamour game. It got all of the media attention.

Even so, there was the rare exception like Joe Graboski, who entered the league right out of high school in 1948 and averaged 11 points per game over the next 13 years. For the most part, though, pro basketball teams didn't want young players.

The NBA soon adopted a rule that if you left college early you had to wait until your class graduated before you were eligible to play. How solid was this rule? Wilt Chamberlain, the master post player of his era, left the University of Kansas after two seasons in 1958 and wasn't allowed to play in the NBA. Instead he spent a season yukking it up with the Harlem Globetrotters before his class graduated and he was allowed to join the old Philadelphia Warriors.

The NBA kept that attitude toward youngsters until the American Basketball Association jumped into the competition in 1967 with no rules preventing players from leaving college to join the pros. The next season Spencer Haywood, a talented rising junior at the University of Detroit who had just competed on the Olympic team, decided to leave school to play for the ABA's Denver Rockets.

The problem came when Haywood was invited to switch to the NBA's Seattle Super Sonics the next season. Citing their rule against signing underclassmen, the NBA's other owners would not allow Haywood to move to the Sonics, which prompted the player to file a lawsuit. A federal judge ruled in his favor, saying that the NBA could not prevent an underclassman from leaving school to play pro hoops.

That ruling opened the door a bit wider. Soon a range of young players declared themselves "hardship cases" and ditched college to take some of the big cash the ABA teams were waving around. The best of these was Moses Malone, who left Petersburg (Virginia) High School in 1974 and proved he was man enough to play for the Utah Stars.

But there were also heartbreak stories, like that of Skip Wise, a phenomenal six-foot-four guard out of Baltimore's Dunbar High School who wound up at Clemson University. He became the only freshman in the history of the storied Atlantic Coast Conference to make the All-Conference first team. He had size, and he could shoot and handle the ball. He also had a rare charm. Clemson fans loved Skip Wise. But when his college coach, Tates Locke, was fired for recruiting violations in 1975, Wise made a rushed decision to sign a contract with the ABA's Baltimore Claws.

Just months after his freshman year in college, Wise learned the hard lessons of pro hoops. The Claws folded during training camp, and suddenly he found himself cast on the open market, scurrying about from camp to camp, trying to find a roster spot. His total pro career ended up being two games with the San Antonio Spurs. His skills simply weren't refined enough, his experience not deep enough, for him to make a team. Sadly, there was no turning back to college.

"Skip was left with nothing—no basketball and no education," Locke wrote in his confessional, *Caught in the Net*. "It wasn't long before he got into trouble with the law, then into drugs. It was a sad, sad ending to a youngster who had more pure basketball talent than any kid I've ever coached."

Wise ended up spending much of his life in prison, and his story was a sour reminder to NBA executives in their constant search for talent. By and large they came to consider most young players too risky, except for 6-foot-11 giants like Darryl Dawkins, the Florida high schooler who came to the NBA in 1975 as a 76ers rookie with Joe Bryant. All Dawkins seemed to lack was emotional maturity.

The tragedy, said former teammate Doug Collins, started when Dawkins struggled to get playing time as a rookie. Forced to sit on the bench, he settled into the role of a comedian. He had great wit to match his physical abilities, but soon Dawkins was drawing his identity as a comedian. Thus he never quite took himself seriously, and neither did others. The wacky, offbeat Dawkins had a career that spanned 14 NBA seasons, but he could have been a truly great player. Longtime

NBA observers have always wondered how good he could have been had he spent three or four years in college, learning the game and growing up.

By and large, pro teams shunned young players during the 1980s, especially those who wanted to come into the league directly from high school. But the National Collegiate Athletic Association decided to adopt tough new academic eligibility rules in 1983 and then toughened those rules again five years later, meaning that more and more athletes from disadvantaged backgrounds struggled to find a place in college hoops. Many of them wound up going to junior college, shoring up their grades and games, then moving on to two years of Division I finishing school.

Those circumstances affected Shawn Kemp, a promising prospect of Concord High in Elkhart, Indiana. He graduated in 1987 and made the unpopular decision to bypass the Hoosiers in favor of the University of Kentucky. But he couldn't play basketball that first year because he failed to qualify academically. Then, as the season was set to open the next fall in Lexington, he was questioned by police for his alleged involvement in pawning stolen jewelry that belonged to the son of coach Eddie Sutton. Although he was never charged with a crime, the circumstances resulted in Kemp's leaving Kentucky in the middle of the school year and enrolling at Trinity Junior College in Texas, where he played pickup ball, attended some classes, and decided higher learning just wasn't right for him. That spring of 1989 he announced that he would enter the NBA draft at the tender age of 19.

"I realize now I should have done more schoolwork," Kemp said at the time. "That might come later. But that's over for now. Basketball is what I do for a living."

The move was met with immediate skepticism. Too young, too immature, observers said. Any team that drafted him was taking a tremendous gamble. Yes, he was talented, but could a teenager, especially one who had been in trouble, handle the NBA life? Many scouts didn't think so.

Despite all the questions, the Sonics decided to take him with the 17th pick of the first round in 1989. "We saw things in a 19-year-old kid that you just don't teach," Bob Whitsitt, then president of the Sonics, said after watching Kemp work out before the draft.

"He made some mistakes," Bernie Bickerstaff, Seattle's coach at the time, said of Kemp's troubles in Kentucky. "But everything checked out on Shawn. If you go by what you hear instead of what you see, you're in trouble. After talking to the people who really knew him and talking with him ourselves, we were convinced Shawn was a good kid."

Seattle had a veteran roster and wouldn't need him right away. He could develop slowly. A shadowy figure on the Sonics bench that first year, he averaged 6.5 points and showed tons of promise. Around the league he became known as Kid Kemp.

It wasn't a name that would live for long. Over the next few years Kemp developed into quite a man, and pro basketball executives began to revise their thinking about young players.

Even with Kemp's success, there was no rush by NBA teams to sign teenaged players. The risks were still too great, many NBA executives figured. But then, in 1995, the situation was right for Kevin Garnett to move to the NBA right out of high school in Chicago. After a rookie year of adjustment, it became clear that Garnett was an emerging star.

Pro basketball certainly needed talent anywhere it could be found. Riding on the wake of Michael Jordan's stardom and the brilliant marketing efforts of commissioner David Stern, the league had expanded steadily through the late 1980s and early '90s, to the point that there were 29 teams in 1995. The established NBA owners loved this expansion because it brought them hundreds of millions in expansion fees to share. From its days as a backwater sport, the NBA had seemingly overnight become the hip new entertainment form. The problem was that expansion stretched the talent base in the league to pitiful levels. To add to the talent base and to expand its global marketing base, the league had begun pulling in European players as the 1990s opened. That helped a bit, but the talent base in Europe was also thin.

Which meant that it was only logical that pro basketball would begin scouring the high school talent as the NBA's contract values soared. Even the best high schoolers had little grounding in the fundamentals, and the NBA was clearly not a league set up for teaching and nurturing young players. But the draw of the money was huge. Suddenly the top college freshmen and best high school players began eyeing guaranteed NBA rookie contracts that would make them instant millionaires.

For Kobe Bryant, a child of affluence, the money was a factor but far from the main focus of his consideration. He had continued to pore over videotape of NBA games and had become infatuated with the idea of competing against Michael Jordan someday. When Jordan returned to the NBA in the spring of 1995 after an 18-month hiatus, Bryant knew that the star might not stay long. If he hoped to compete against Jordan, Kobe knew he would have to push the schedule.

As it turned out, there was plenty of help for him in doing that. He returned from his appearance in the Adidas tournament in Las Vegas to find an invitation from Sixers coach John Lucas to work out with the team. Kobe arrived at the gym and discovered that Lucas had special plans.

"He came up to me," Bryant recalled, "and said, 'Kobe, I've got a surprise for you.' I turned around, and Jerry Stackhouse walked in the door. We went head-to-head. It was great, a lot of fun."

Fun, indeed. Playing one-on-one, Bryant defeated Stackhouse, Philadelphia's top draft pick out of the University of North Carolina.

In a matter of days, Kobe received a recruiting letter from UNC coach Dean Smith. It was nice, but the evidence that he could turn pro was rapidly stacking up, and thoughts of college grew dimmer by the day as he spent the summer going against pro players in pickup games.

"I felt real comfortable all summer with the guys," Kobe would explain to *Newsday* that fall. "I had no butterflies, no nothing. Never felt intimidated. I could get to the hole, I could hit the jumper, I could score, although not at will, but I could get some shots. I was able to create for my teammates and rebound. Plus the guys respected me, and when they respect you, that must mean something."

Late in the summer Kobe led a team from Delaware Valley to a surprise championship in the scholastic division of the Keystone State Games while averaging 38 points a game. His high school coach served as coach for the Philadelphia team, which Kobe toasted in the title game with 47 points, all good enough to earn him the MVP award.

Finally it appeared that the *Inquirer* was ready to do a story on his rapid rise. A reporter from the paper phoned Treatman and said, "I know you know Kobe, and we'd like to talk to you."

Treatman wondered if he should tell the *Inquirer* just how far Kobe had traveled in his thinking over the summer. "You know he's the number-one player in the country," Treatman said, an opinion that took the reporter by surprise.

The reporter asked what college Kobe was considering.

"Do I tell him?" Treatman asked himself before finally replying, "Well, he's considering LaSalle, Villanova, North Carolina, Duke—and the NBA."

Treatman had thought he was giving the paper a big scoop.

"He laughs in my face, literally laughs in my face," Treatman recalled.

"I'm not kidding," Treatman told the reporter.

The writer said he waited a month for the story about Kobe to appear in the *Inquirer*. Instead, the rival *Daily News* ended up getting the scoop first with a headline that said "LaSalle or the NBA."

A week later, the *Inquirer* assigned a reporter the task of writing a follow-up to the *Daily News* story. Shortly thereafter, Treatman gave up his duties at the *Inquirer* when both Gregg Downer and Joe Bryant asked him to serve as an assistant coach for Lower Merion for the 1995–96 season. He would assume a range of chores for the team, including serving as something of a public relations liaison to help handle the crush of media interest generated by the revelation that Kobe was considering becoming a professional.

"I've never seen a kid get more attention than Kobe got his 12th-grade year," Treatman said.

"He's the most complete player in the country," Tom Konchalski, a New York–based talent expert, told reporters. "He has great skills but also great instincts. He plays with a poise that belies his tender age. He's kind of reminiscent of Grant Hill, although he's more physically developed at this stage than Grant was."

The news accounts of his feats and his potential created something of a Kobe craze in basketball-savvy Philadelphia. His parents had tried to prepare him for the mixed reception he would receive as an affluent, successful African-American.

Once he began driving his father's BMW, Pam Bryant made sure Kobe always kept his driver's license and vehicle registration with him. He would be stopped by police because of his complexion, his age, and his vehicle make, she told him.

"And you know what?" his mother later revealed. "Two weeks later he was stopped. The cop told him, 'You look too young to be driving a car like this.' And then he looked at his license, saw it was Kobe, and before you know it he wanted an autograph."

His growing fame also brought a rush on tickets to Lower Merion games as fans across the region came to see him play. "Everybody wanted to see him play," recalled James Franklin, an assistant football coach at Idaho State who at the time was a college student who had grown up in Philadelphia. Although he was more of a football player and not a particularly intense basketball fan, Franklin said that he, too, was drawn to see Kobe play a half dozen times. "He had a flair for the game, and most people wanted to get a little taste of that. He was just electric. The stands were packed, and the whole time people were whispering Kobe this and Kobe that, 'I saw him do this last game,' or 'I saw him do that.' 'Did you see that?' He was just always electric, always trying to do something to top something else he had done and to have people talking for the next game. It was his presence; he would look at the fans as he ran back on defense after a big play—that kind of stuff. He just had a flair. It wasn't one of those things where you see young players with an attitude. He just had an air about him. You could just see he was intelligent, carried himself well. You could just see it. You didn't have to be a major sports fan or a coach or a scout or anybody like that. You could just see it in him."

At first Franklin hadn't even planned to go watch him, but some friends were going one night and Franklin decided to go along. "It wasn't even my idea," he recalled. "They said there was this guy Kobe Bryant that I needed to see. I had nothing better to do, so I just jumped in the car with them and went. You know, I had heard of him, but then I went and saw him. And it was just addictive. He was a man among boys. You knew he could just take over the game at any point. And he was having fun out there. It was electric. We all wanted to go back and see him again."

That kind of response characterized Kobe's senior year, Treatman recalled, especially when Lower Merion played in the Palestra, Philly's ancient basketball temple, which seats about 9,000. "There were people filling the Palestra to see games. People standing in the aisles. It was crazy."

Also typical of every game that season was the line of autograph seekers stretching through the venues where Lower Merion played. "There were long lines waiting for tickets, cameras everywhere, national news people coming into our place on a daily basis, phones ringing off the hook," Downer recalled. "It was very exciting, though, playing in front of huge crowds. . . . Traveling with Kobe was like traveling with a rock star."

The intense pressure alone should have been enough to sink any 17-year-old, but Kobe had begun learning to shoulder his pretensions at an early age. It helped tremendously, Treatman said, that Downer stepped up to take as much of that pressure as possible. And he did so with a full acceptance of the circumstances. "Gregg felt a lot of pressure," the writer turned assistant coach recalled. "He laughed about it and said, 'If we win, people will say it was because we had Kobe. If we lose, people will say, "How could you lose with Kobe?" ' "

The fact remained that Lower Merion was a suburban school, not a traditional power, facing a tremendous challenge. Not surprisingly, the signs of difficulty appeared early for the

Aces that season, many of them related to the fact that point guard Emery Dabney would be academically ineligible for the first few games of the season, which left put a greater burden on Kobe. "He had to do too much," Treatman said.

As a result, Lower Merion broke out to a disappointing start with four wins and three losses. The schedule for this super-hyped senior season showed part of the problem. In the second game of the season against powerful Philadelphia Roman Catholic (where Kobe had been rumored to transfer), Kobe used his power to draw defenses to get his teammates a variety of open shots. But by the second half Roman Catholic's talent edge had the Aces down by six. Kobe answered by shaking off double and triple teams to score on eight consecutive possessions. Out of necessity he tried to take on the opponent single-handedly. He wound up scoring 30, but Lower Merion lost.

The game had attracted a range of reporters, as interest grew in a young player seemingly brash enough to consider turning professional *before* his senior year of high school.

"Kobe has choices," Joe Bryant told them. "He can do whatever he wants. Our family will support Kobe with whatever he decides to do."

Asked if he would attempt to change his son's mind, Joe Bryant replied, "Why would I do a thing like that? If Kobe feels he's ready, then he goes with my blessing."

"It's been my goal ever since I started high school," Kobe acknowledged. "I always wanted the option of going to the NBA. My father played, but that's not the reason. My decision has nothing to do with him. And I'm not studying Kevin Garnett. I wish him the best and hope he exceeds expectations, but what he does really doesn't have any effect on me.

"I can't give an answer now. Maybe later on this year. Then I'll look back to see what I've learned as a player. That's when

I'll decide. And if I make the decision to go, I'm going. I'm not going to change my mind."

Serving as a backdrop to Kobe's increased notoriety was Kevin Garnett's performance in the NBA that November. In just his second season out of high school, Garnett was demonstrating in game after game with the Minnesota Timberwolves that he was surprisingly well equipped to meet the competition. Garnett, however, was a seven-footer. The NBA media remained hugely skeptical that Kobe, a six-foot-six player, was ready to meet the physical and emotional demands of pro competition. He had added about 15 pounds over the summer to boost his weight to 200. Still, the doubt was substantial.

"I've heard a lot of people say I don't have the maturity yet for the NBA," Kobe told *Newsday*. "Well, I've seen things in my lifetime that ordinary kids my age haven't seen or experienced. I've been all through Europe, to France, Germany, lived in Italy, been around professional basketball players my whole life. Growing up the way I have, I think I've matured faster than the ordinary person my age."

"Talking to Kobe is like talking to a 23-year-old, not a high school kid," agreed his father.

Certainly Lower Merion's schedule was a test of that maturity. Next the Aces went to the Beach Ball Classic in Myrtle Beach, South Carolina, a tournament that drew the best high school teams from around the country. The Aces won their first game, beating a team that featured prep star Jason Collier. Next up, though, was a team from Jenks, Oklahoma. Kobe fouled out late and watched his teammates get outscored 21–2 in overtime.

Kobe and his Aces soon recovered from those early struggles and embarked on a 27-game winning streak that would propel Kobe right into the eye of his dream. For most of his young life he had spent hours employing the psychological technique of visualization in terms of learning moves and being successful, trying to visualize himself doing those things before he did them. In the same way he had visualized himself and his teammates in an elevated level of play.

His fine postseason that year would be foreshadowed in a January game against Marple Newtown, a 95–64 win in which he registered his first 50-point game. That and each of his succeeding performances only goosed the crowds to higher levels of Kobe mania.

During a midseason showdown with Central District rival Chester, the fans had chanted "Overrated! Overrated!" at Kobe. The Aces had lost to Chester by 27 the season before, so each player had the number 27 on his jersey to keep the memory of that embarrassment fresh. Down 8 at the half, Lower Merion charged back, energized by a Kobe dunk and won, 60–53.

The Aces won the District title and rolled into the divisional playoffs against Coatsville, a team that featured future University of Connecticut star Richard Hamilton, who had played AAU ball with Kobe. The venue for the meeting was the Palestra, Jeremy Treatman recalled. "With just a second to go before the half, Kobe caught the ball in front of the basket and executed a reverse dunk over his head. It was sensational. I've been in the Palestra for 20 years. I don't think I've ever heard it louder than that moment. There was a standing ovation from both sides of the stands as we were walking off the floor for halftime. It was just so loud that you had to look up at the crowd. It was like this Kobe hysteria."

The playoffs also featured a second-round game against Academy Prep in which Kobe registered another 50-point game, including 31 in the first half. "He hit six 3-pointers in the first half alone," Treatman recalled. "He was on inside and out."

The *Inquirer* editor who had turned down Treatman's story requests for three seasons had come to that game. Treatman remembered him standing wide-eyed during the half, just as caught up in the performance as the fans.

Such performances made trying to get a ticket for Lower Merion playoff games nearly impossible (there were reports of $1,000 prices from some scalpers), Treatman said. "It was insane. They broke all the fire codes in the Palestra trying to fit all the people in."

Against rival Chester in the state semifinals, Kobe struggled through the first three quarters, making only 8 of 25 from the floor. In the fourth, though, he erupted for a dozen points, and the Aces battled into overtime, where he added another 8, Treatman recalled, "and Kobe had this monster dunk to clinch it."

Each and every outcome of that special playoff run seemed to twist its way down to the final seconds, Treatman recalled.

The win propelled the Aces into the state AAAA championship game against Erie Cathedral Prep at Hersheypark Arena in Hershey. Erie immediately seized control of the tempo, held Kobe to just 8 points in the first half (all in the second quarter), and took a 21–15 lead at the half. The Aces seized a 6-point lead in the third, but Erie again gained control of the tempo and managed to move up 41–39 late in the game. With a flurry of fouls, Erie sent Kobe and his teammates to the line, which provided just enough edge to give Kobe the championship he had talked about since his first days in the school as a freshman.

The outcome was the reward for his thousands of hours of work. "When I was partying, he was out playing basketball," high school friend Matt Matkov recalled. "When I was waking up, Kobe was playing basketball before class."

With the state championship victory, Kobe decided to alter his modus operandi, even if it was only briefly.

"I'm going to party," he told reporters.

At best, the evening was a temporary interlude from the main issue that had been cooking on Kobe's agenda for months—his decision about his future.

Throughout the season, rumors persisted that he was headed to college, that Joe Bryant was leaning on his son to attend LaSalle. Then speculation jumped to Duke, where it was said that Joe would go as an assistant coach and Kobe would play.

As close as he was to the situation, even Treatman couldn't get a clear read on the Duke angle, which seemed tantalizing for father and son.

Asked his college preferences, Kobe replied, "First, LaSalle; my dad is the assistant coach there. I like North Carolina because of Dean Smith and Michael Jordan. They have a tremendous program. I like Duke quite a bit because of Grant Hill. Lastly, I like Arkansas because of Nolan Richardson and their style of play."

"Quite naturally, Kobe has attracted a lot of national attention," Joe Bryant told reporters. "This is a big year for him, but he hasn't let the recruiting and all the publicity change him as a person. He's been able to handle things quite well. I'm really happy for him."

The bottom line, for Kobe, was that he had gone into the season looking for additional evidence that he was ready to turn professional. In his mind, he had found it. Over his four years at Lower Merion, he had scored 2,883 points, making him the leading high school scorer in southeastern Pennsylvania history, greater even than the legendary giant, Wilt Chamberlain, who had racked up better than 2,300 points playing for Philly's Overbrook High. As expected, Kobe had been named to the prestigious McDonald's and *Parade* high school All-America teams. But then came the final crowning factor in Kobe's decision. He was named USA *Today*'s High School Player of the Year.

Beyond all that, there was another emotional reason for looking to the pro game. His old hero, Magic Johnson, had returned to the NBA in an attempt to reignite his competitive battles with Michael Jordan. The thought of going against both of them provided Kobe a whole new realm of visualizations. "I wanted to get in the league and play against those guys," he would later reveal.

In the weeks before he announced his decision, the debate heightened over his choices. Chris Carrawell, who had played against Kobe and later signed to play at Duke, told reporters Kobe had made "a bad decision. I understand the money, but it's better to go to school. At least for three years. I don't think they're ready mentally or physically. I played against Kobe Bryant and Jermaine O'Neal in some All-Star games. Kobe's good, but I don't think he's good enough to go to the pros out of high school."

Rick Mahorn, on the other hand, who had witnessed Kobe operating in those summer showdowns with pro players, had no problem with the move. "He's ready if that's what he wants," Mahorn said. "There's no question about it."

On April 29, Jeremy Treatman helped the school set up the press conference in which Kobe would announce his decision. Set in Lower Merion's gymnasium, the event attracted quite a range of regional and national media. "There were a lot of people in that gym," Treatman recalled with a chuckle.

The *Washington Post*. ESPN. The *New York Times*.

His shaved head glistening in the TV lights, Kobe, still just 17, stepped to the bank of microphones and announced, "I have decided to skip college and take my talents to the NBA.

I know I'll have to work extra hard, and I know this is a big step, but I can do it.

"It's the opportunity of a lifetime. It's time to seize it while I'm young. I don't know if I can reach the stars or the moon. If I fall off the cliff, so be it."

"We were going to support him no matter what he chose to do," Pam Bryant told reporters afterward. "Whether it was college or going to the NBA, we're always going to support him. That's what we always do. This was Kobe's decision. He has goals, and we're always here to support him."

A reporter wondered if Joe Bryant wasn't allowing the move simply because he needed to live vicariously through his son.

"If that were true, then Kobe would go to LaSalle for two years, find a wife, have three kids, and raise a family," Pam Bryant said. "That was Joe's dream, and it's worked out pretty well for us. Joe played in the NBA. He doesn't have to live through anybody."

"I thought that was the perfect answer," Treatman said later.

"I've been fortunate in the sense that I've been around and know the water he's about to tread," Joe himself replied. "There are a lot of parents who would have no clue. I don't think you can fault me for having an understanding of what's going on. I've talked to all kinds of people, and I've touched a lot of bases. I think Kobe is lucky to have someone who's been there.

"Hey, I would have liked to have seen Kobe go to school for four years and go to Harvard. But is that reality? Would he have stayed in school for one or two years? This was Kobe's dream. This is his life, so it was his decision. . . . I don't have any doubt in my son. No doubt, just support and a lot of love."

Bryant reminded reporters that his son had a unique maturity. "Living in Italy was the key," the father said. "The maturity and responsibility our kids learned over there. The people who have made negative comments really just don't know Kobe. He's a super kid, and he knows what he wants to do and can accomplish.

"My wife and I have been married for 22 years," he added. "We've been through ups and downs, but that's a part of life. But the most important thing is that we wanted to raise our kids to be stronger and better people than we are."

In the wake of Kobe's decision, Joe Bryant announced his own resignation from the coaching staff at LaSalle so that he would be free to support his son's endeavors in the NBA.

The family had tried to prepare for the negative reaction that had been building to Kobe's decision. But in the end there was perhaps no way to anticipate the depth of anger, Jeremy Treatman said. "It was like the media took it personally. It didn't make any sense."

Columnist Mike DeCourcy in *The Sporting News* went right for the family. "I'm not sure why anyone cares if he's ready for such a life, because his folks apparently didn't."

Those words stung, but even worse was the yammering of Howard Eskin on Philly's all-sports talk radio, WIP, Treatman said. "He ripped Kobe, and he had never even seen Kobe play. He came up with theory after theory as to why they were doing it. He thought the dad was all behind it."

"They don't know me," Kobe told Treatman. "They don't know how bad I want it."

"I think it stunned him," Treatman said. "I think the negative stuff out in L.A. later about the draft stunned him, too. He was mature enough then to realize that the nature of publicity wasn't gonna change. He said he wasn't gonna care, that he would use it to motivate himself to work even harder."

Fortunately, the family network that had stood him so well over the years was there to help ease the blow. "He had supporters, too," Treatman said. "The people that really mattered supported him. He had uncles, grandparents and parents, friends. The coaching staff at Lower Merion and his teammates supported him, too."

The time between the announcement and the draft allowed the briefest respite of personal time, although Kobe would be consumed with predraft appearances. But socializing was not an activity with which he was entirely familiar. Pam Bryant acknowledged to reporters that she had "concerns about drugs, alcohol, and fast women, but kids are exposed to that in high school. Kobe's a well-balanced young man. He's always stayed focused on what is important. I don't worry with Kobe or any of my children, because we have a good family foundation."

Just like his basketball, Kobe set his social sights on the top. He had met the teenaged singer Brandy, who also starred in the TV show "Moesha," during the televised 1996 *Essence* awards in New York. Afterward, he got the idea that she would be his dream date to the Lower Merion prom.

"I got my friend to ask her, and then she asked her mother," Kobe explained later. "It's crazy, isn't it? I just kept thinking, Damn, that's Brandy."

Suddenly, Lower Merion administrators found themselves trying to find means of managing the paparazzi who descended on their prom, in addition to the line of autograph seekers. Kobe's big night out with Brandy snared coverage from *People* and *Jet* magazines.

In one short year he had joined the entertainment elite, and the price for that was the forfeiture of his privacy. As the draft neared, the questions centered on speculation as to where he would fall in the order of the talent-rich 1996 draft.

Georgetown's Allen Iverson, Georgia Tech's Stephon Marbury, Massachusetts center Marcus Camby, University of California freshman Shareef Abdur-Rahim, Connecticut guard Ray Allen all went ahead of Kobe, who was finally selected with the 13th pick by the Charlotte Hornets. The course of events brought yet another shock to the Bryants. The Hornets had been one of the few teams that Kobe hadn't worked out for in the weeks before the selection.

Then, less than an hour after his selection, the trade rumors circulated through the media assembled at the Meadowlands in East Rutherford, New Jersey, the NBA arena hosting the draft.

Charlotte coach Dave Cowens had described Kobe as "a kid" and questioned his age and inexperience. Cowens had doubts as to how much Kobe could help an NBA team as a rookie. Those comments were soon followed by word that Kobe had been traded to the Lakers for Vlade Divac, which in turn was followed by word that Kobe's agent, Arn Tellem, had forced the trade because Kobe wanted to be in a bigger market, with more media opportunities.

Again the media were swift to attack.

"Apparently Cowens had not received a copy of the Kobe Bryant marketing plan," *The Sporting News* blasted. "That is the state of David Stern's NBA these days. The brats are running the day-care center. It isn't about basketball anymore. It's all about image."

Not even 18, and already at the heart of so much turmoil, Kobe Bryant withdrew even further into the protective embrace of his family that summer. In a swirl, the Bryants made plans to relocate their lives to Los Angeles. The first hazy webs had slipped from Kobe's dream, revealing a world of even greater fantasy and greater peril, enough to make the heart race and the mind wander, leaving Kobe with the same old question, only now it was magnified many times over.

"I knew I was going to make it," he would explain to me later. "But I didn't know how. How was I going to make it happen?"

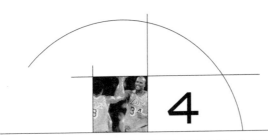

4

LAKERSVILLE

"Every night was something new."
—Kobe Bryant

Several years ago I happened into an empty gym just in time to catch Jerry West renewing his lonely, long-term relationship with the basketball goal. He stood at the far end of the gym delivering a series of carefully crafted 16-footers. After each shot the ball would settle through the net and hit the floor with just enough spin to go bouncing back to him. He hardly had to move to retrieve it. Then he would start the process over, studying the rim for a long pause before each attempt, then dropping in another swisher.

I did some quick math and figured that West, then in his early fifties, had sighted the goal probably no fewer than two million times since his grade-school days, when he first began lofting a ball at a hoop suspended above the dirt outside his Chelyan, West Virginia, home. Yet here he was, a half century later, pausing and studying, as if he were seeing something for the first time, discovering something that the rest of us couldn't see.

"Why were you spending so much time studying the rim between shots?" I later asked.

"Because every goal is different," he replied.

Each of his releases had produced a perfectly elliptical arc that concluded just where he intended. When he first came into the NBA in 1960, the shot was flat, and people noticed it, because they notice everything about rookies (or they think they do). It wouldn't do to have a flat shot. So Jerry West set out to fashion the perfect ellipse.

People also noticed that as a rookie he seemed to have trouble going to his left. That wouldn't do either. So West worked at that, too. He went left so much that people guarding him forgot there was a right.

All of it was accomplished with long hours working alone, just West and the hoop. It's a relationship that tugged at him long after he had retired as a player. "I wonder, what the hell am I doing this for?" he said of his shooting, sounding a lot like somebody who had just bumped into an old, irretrievably lost love. "It's a part of my life that was there at one time, and it's not there now."

I first interviewed West years ago in Dallas, while he was on a scouting trip. It struck me then that you didn't have to spend too much time with him, perhaps a matter of minutes, before you sensed his anguish. It wasn't a flaming pain, rather a deep, slow-burning one, a complicated anxiety, some form of unrequited yearning. Years later I would spend an afternoon rebounding free throws for Kobe Bryant and be struck by how much his hunger reminded me of West's tightly wrapped anxiety.

He should be happier, I thought after interviewing West. After all, he has been one of the most successful executives in the history of American professional sports. Prior to that, he was one of the greatest basketball players ever. He averaged 27.1 points over his 14-year career and 29.1 points in the playoffs; only Michael Jordan has finished his career with a higher playoff scoring average. That would be enough for anybody, you would think. But it obviously wasn't enough for Jerry

West. Which made me wonder why. How can one person demand so much of a competitive life?

"Jerry always seems like he's having a terrible time or something bad is impending," Kareem Abdul-Jabbar told me several years ago. "He's always worried."

The great Laker center chuckled and said West reminded him of the pilots in the film *Catch-22* who are about to fly off into combat. His sense of foreboding has always seemed to keep his angst spinning.

"Jerry is the most impatient man I've ever met in my life," John Black, the team's public relations director, once explained. "I love the guy. He's hilarious. He and I had lunch with Mitch Kupchak [the Lakers' GM] the other day. We're only a quarter of the way through our meal, and Jerry's already done and drumming his fingers on the table. Everything he does is done at hyper speed. You should see him play golf. It's hilarious. He walks up to the ball and whacks it. Never takes a practice swing or anything. He used to play a lot of golf, but now he plays only a few times a year. And he always shoots 70 or under. If he shoots a 71, he's pissed."

That competitive impatience, that demand for excellence, is the key to understanding both West and the Lakers. For most of four decades his rather complex competitive nature has driven this franchise, first as a player, then as a frustrated coach, finally as an executive, working, as he explains it, "in my own weird way." He is the club's past, present, and future, the compass that has allowed his team to proceed with a purpose across the strange landscape of the NBA.

"The bottom line is, my number-one priority in life is to see this franchise prosper," West once said. "That's my life. It goes beyond being paid. It goes to something that's been a great source of pride. I would like people to know that I do care. It's not a self-interest thing. I do care about the winning and the perpetuation of the franchise. That's the one thing I care most about. I don't care about the pelts and the tributes. I like to work in my own weird way, working toward one goal, a winning team here."

As an executive, West still travels like a player. A single road bag. His crisp white dress shirt neatly tucked inside with his other belongings. No hangers. No suit bag. He remains a spartan, still moving unencumbered as he did when he ran the backcourt for the Lakers for 14 seasons. Still gliding through his tasks with a proficiency that startles the opposition.

Yet his every move remains haunted by the same old questions. What would it take to close? What would it take to finish? What would it take to win? Most people are happy for a partial answer. But life had taught West a different lesson. Six times in the 1960s he and the Lakers faced the Boston Celtics in the NBA Finals. Six times they lost. On their seventh try for a championship, the Lakers met the New York Knicks. They lost again. They finally won in 1972, then lost an eighth time in the Finals the next year.

"I don't think people understand there's a real trauma associated with losing," West said. "I don't think they realize how miserable you can be. Particularly me. I was terrible. It got to the point with me that I wanted to quit basketball. I really did. I didn't think it was fair that you could give so much and play until there was nothing left in your body to give and you couldn't win."

Yet the more elusive it proved to be, the more the championship came to have an almost mesmerizing hold on him. "The closer you get to the magic circle, the more enticing it becomes," he said. "I imagine in some ways it's like a drug. It's seductive because it's always there, and the desire is always there to win one more game. I don't like to think I'm different, but I was obsessed with winning. And losing made it so much more difficult in the off-season."

As a six-foot-two junior forward at West Virginia University, he led the Mountaineers to the 1959 NCAA championship game where they lost by a point. "I had my hands on the ball about midcourt with no time left on the clock," he recalled, "and I said, 'If I could have just gotten one more shot . . .' But it wasn't to be. Those are the things frankly that stay with you more than the wins. Those are the things that really are wearing.

"My basketball career has sort of been on the tragic side of everything. It hasn't been on the positive side. It was so close, yet so far away."

The worst loss by far was the 1969 NBA Finals, where the Lakers, highly favored to win the title, lost the seventh game to the Celtics at the Forum. It was their sixth and final loss to Boston. West was named the MVP, the first and only time in NBA Finals history that the award has gone to a member of a losing team. The gesture was nice, but it didn't address his agony.

"It was like a slap in the face," he said. "Like 'We're not gonna let you win. We don't care how well you play.' I always thought it was personal. It got to the point where I didn't think I was doing enough. I was searching everything that I had ever done in my life for a reason, looking for an answer why. Why couldn't we win it? That's why it became so personal. It almost controlled my life."

The championship failures only embedded his superstitions more deeply. Before each home game he would take the same circuitous route to the Forum, using the same back streets. Once in the locker room, he would tear a stick of gum in half, placing the pieces on each side of his locker in exactly the same place. He would try anything to alleviate the curse of the

Celtics. "Jerry couldn't even wear a green sportcoat or a green shirt for a lot of years," Bill Sharman, his friend and former coach, once revealed. "Green really rubbed him the wrong way."

It is said that when he won the Finals MVP honor, *Sport* magazine presented him with a green Corvette.

West insisted the enemy wasn't the color green or even the Celtics. In his mind there was no enemy. There was only the obstacle, and that was the game itself. His unfortunate compulsion was perfection in a sport that never allowed it. Yet he came as close as anyone. One great night as a player, he made all 12 of his free throws and 16 of 17 field goal attempts. He also had 10 rebounds, 12 assists, and 10 steals.

"I had nights where you just couldn't guard me," he said.

At times, though, West tended to brood over the flaws in his game, said Fred Schaus, who coached him in both college and the pros. "When he was not playing well, he'd kind of go into a shell. He wouldn't talk to anybody, not the coaches or his own teammates. If he wasn't playing well, he was tough to live with."

"I was nervous all the time," West said. "But then again, I was a nervous player. That's where I got my energy from."

In 1971, the Lakers held a Jerry West appreciation night at the Forum, and Boston center Bill Russell paid his own plane fare to Los Angeles to address the crowd. "The greatest honor a man can have is the respect and friendship of his peers," Russell told West that night. "You have that more than any man I know. If I could have one wish granted, it would be that you would always be happy."

Strange, this coming from Russell, the dominant Celtic center, who had more to do with West's unhappiness than any other single human being.

Finally, in 1972, the Lakers powered their way to a championship. But for West the finish was rife with irony. After years of losing, his emotions were nearly empty, and when the Lakers got it, the title seemed anticlimactic. "I played terrible basketball in the Finals," he said. "And we won. And that didn't seem to be justice for me personally, because I had contributed so much in other years when we lost. And now, when we won, I was just another piece of the machinery. It was particularly frustrating because I was playing so poorly that the team overcame me.

"Maybe," he said after a moment's thought, "that's what the team is all about."

It seemed logical that at least part of his lifelong anguish stemmed from those long-ago frustrations. But only West knew for sure. Or maybe nobody knew. But West did know this: no matter how great he was way back when, he had accomplished things as a Lakers executive that he never accomplished as a player. In the 1980s his team won five NBA World Championships, two of them over the Celtics, thus vanquishing the curse of the green. But that proved a paradoxical knowledge for West. It both increased and lessened his anguish all at the same time.

The pain, it seemed, was a central ingredient to his approach. "I hope these things stay with me," he said of his anxieties. "If I weren't like this, I probably wouldn't work."

Former Laker GM Pete Newell once explained that to understand West you had to factor in that he was from West Virginia, the land of Appalachian poverty and coal mines. That part of the equation posed no problem for me. My father was an old set shooter who played in the semipro industrial leagues across southern West Virginia. From my earliest memories West was a deity in our household. When I was six, my old man packed up the family and took us to see West play in the Southern Conference tournament in Richmond, Virginia. I don't remember a whole lot about it, except that West and his Mountaineers were victorious and that the trip seemed long and I got carsick along the way.

My father was a fierce observer of West Virginia basketball, and West was the pride of the state. The son of a mine electrician in a little hamlet not far from Charleston, he led East Bank High School to a state championship as a senior, then listened as more than 70 colleges across the country begged him to come play for them. His home was the hills, though, and he chose to stay and play for the beloved Mountaineers.

Drafted by the Lakers, he came to Los Angeles in 1960 with a flattop haircut, skinny legs, and a high-pitched mountain twang. It was the age of "The Beverly Hillbillies," and the shy, serious country boy found a Hollywood eager to lampoon him. Teammate Elgin Baylor first called him "Tweety Bird" because of the high-pitched voice and the skinny legs. West hated that.

Then Baylor came up with another name. "Zeke from Cabin Creek." He hated that one, too. "I've never seen Jerry walk by an autograph yet," Newell said of West. He signed because he believed he owed it to the fans. But when they asked him to sign Zeke from Cabin Creek, West refused.

Catchy as the name was and eager as the team was to build a following in Los Angeles in the early years, Chick Hearn constantly referred to West as Zeke on game broadcasts until West's first wife, Jane, quietly asked him to quit using it.

"Jerry was never a very secure kind of person," Newell said. "Believe it or not, he has never had a great self-esteem. Everybody thinks more of Jerry than he does of himself. That's the West Virginia in him."

His background was also the root of his stubborn streak, his ability to persevere as an NBA executive, a complicated job that very few do well. Most people who have tried running pro basketball teams soon find themselves sunk in confusion and despair. West, though, was clearly tougher and more determined than his peers. Anyone dealing with him on trades and other NBA deals soon learned that underneath the courteous exterior he possessed a toughness hardened by his coalfield upbringing. More than that, however, he seemed to view everything as a function of his high competitive standards. There was a right way to approach every facet of the game. In Jerry West's mind either you adhered to that standard or you failed. Most people in the NBA never seemed to recognize or understand that standard, much less be concerned about adhering to it.

West, the player, operated exactly that same way, Newell said, explaining that he succeeded because "he was driven for it. The drive was greater than the fear of not succeeding."

West acknowledged that the competitiveness that drove him as a player also pushed him as an executive. "But it's so different," he said. "Being a player, it's a wonderful feeling to win an important ball game, to compete against the best players. Being a general manager is so much more subtle, so much more frustrating. It's a completely different feeling. Every once in a while, when you get something done as a general manager, you really feel good about it. You really do. Finding and drafting players and watching them develop—that's where you get your satisfaction."

West's relationship with Lakers owner Jerry Buss had been punctuated by disagreements over the years, sometimes followed by West considering attractive offers to take over other franchises. But he could never bring himself to leave. Since his rookie days he had been a Laker in one capacity or another, except for two seasons of bitter feuding with then-owner Jack Kent Cooke in the 1970s.

Throughout his tenure he had been possessed by one relentless goal, winning each season's championship. He suffered from ulcers and sleepless nights in the early 1990s, particularly after games, when he would twist and turn, running over every play in his mind. At the end of the 1989 season a spot mysteriously appeared on his lung, frightening West and his family. It later went away, but doctors weren't sure what it was. The fear made him appreciate his family more, but it didn't dull his drive.

"I do think this job is wearing," he said at the time. "There's a lot of pressure on you."

The translation, of course, was that he put tremendous pressure on himself and indirectly on the coaches and players.

"Maybe I'm spoiled," West said. "Maybe the success of this team has spoiled me a little bit. I try to be objective. It makes no sense that I'm not happy. I should be happy. The reason I tend not to be happy is goal setting. You want to stretch yourself. You want to stretch your players and make them try to take that last step, and that's to end their season with a win. If you do that, you're gonna have a fun summer."

The Tradition

Evidenced by his manic approach, it was obvious that West took tremendous pride in the running of L.A.'s grand old franchise. He was mindful of a team tradition that stretched back to the very essence of pro basketball.

The Lakers began life in 1946 as the Detroit Gems in the old National League, a forerunner of the NBA. No one recalls exactly where the first training camp was held, but it seems likely they had one, probably at Detroit's Holy Redeemer High School gym. The Gems had been started on a whim by a Michigan jewelry store owner named Maury Winston, a rabid fan who figured a basketball team would be a good promotion for his business.

That logic quickly proved flawed because even the good pro teams had few fans and got no press in 1946.

The Gems were terrible. They finished 4–40, the worst record in modern pro basketball, and Winston lost thousands of dollars. One night a mere six paying customers showed up to see the Gems play, and Winston later resolutely issued each of them a refund. "Maury Winston seemed like a real nice guy, but he didn't know too much about basketball," recalled Sid Goldberg, a sports promoter of that era. "He was in over his head."

Thoroughly whipped by season's end, Winston quickly sold the franchise for $15,000 to an enterprising group of investors from Minneapolis. They, in turn, renamed the club the Lakers (Minnesota being the land of cold, clear lakes), thus setting in motion a curious and wonderful curriculum vitae. From its meager beginnings, the team has gone on to win 13 league championships, or nearly a fourth of the pro titles since World War II. On another 13 occasions they have lost in the NBA Finals, a league record.

And when they didn't win, the Lakers still remained competitive. Seldom in their 46 seasons of existence have they failed to make the playoffs.

But the story is about more than winning. With their verve and style, the Lakers rescued pro basketball from its plodding pace and laborious nature. They've always been at the vanguard of the sport's western movement, at the cusp of its innovation, at the hot spot of whatever star quality the NBA could muster. In its early years pro basketball was an eastern game, played in underheated gyms in cold cities. The Lakers were the force that tugged the game west and into the new age. To pro basketballers in 1947, Minnesota seemed like the far reaches of the universe, until the Lakers once again expanded the horizon and relocated in Los Angeles in 1960.

To Hollywood.

To basketball as entertainment. To Showtime.

It was the perfect place for a team that had always understood the preciousness of star quality. Long before they arrived in Tinseltown, the Lakers were the league's main gate attraction. They brought pro basketball its first dominant giant, George Mikan, and its first jumping jack, Jim Pollard. The Minneapolis Lakers teams they anchored won six pro championships and rated marquee billings at Madison Square Garden, where they were the regular centerpiece in the double-headers that the NBA sponsored in its early seasons.

Despite the success in Minneapolis, the team's tenure there ended badly, in near financial collapse, and the move to Los Angeles in 1960 was a desperate gamble for survival. "Call me for anything, but don't call me for money," Lakers owner Bob Short told Lou Mohs, the team's general manager, when he sent the club packing west.

Once there, the team boasted two of the game's most exciting young players, West and Elgin Baylor, who led the Lakers to one playoff battle after another. Their performances attracted the early Hollywood crowd, Doris Day, Danny Thomas, and Pat Boone, who sat courtside in the L.A. Sports Arena and brought pro basketball its first real taste of glamour.

Then in the midsixties came new owner Jack Kent Cooke, who built his own arena, the Fabulous Forum, a building with a studied ambience intended to attract the city's wheelers and dealers. The game's first self-declared sex symbol, Wilt Chamberlain, arrived in 1968, and after losing in seven league championship series, the Los Angeles Lakers finally won the 1972 title, with West and Chamberlain as aging superstars.

Chamberlain departed in '73 and West in '74, and Kareem Abdul-Jabbar arrived a year later, only to endure four frustrating seasons until the team drafted Magic Johnson. On the brink of the Showtime era, Jack Kent Cooke grew weary of ownership. He was buffeted by a stormy divorce and agreed to sell out to real estate whiz Jerry Buss in 1979. With Johnson in the backcourt and Abdul-Jabbar looming inside, the Lakers evolved into a sleek, powerful machine. They won five NBA titles in the 1980s and could have won another four if not for injuries and miscues. Their style attracted the affections of a new generation of Hollywood stars, led by emperor of L.A. cool Jack Nicholson, perched next to the proceedings in his courtside seat.

With their success came money. Lots of it. The Lakers became the glitter on the National Basketball Association's pot of gold. The financial growth has been astounding to witness, said Sid Hartman, a Minnesota newspaper columnist who ran the Lakers in their early years. "We paid Maury Winston $15,000 for the franchise in 1947," he recalled. "Bob Short bought the Lakers in 1957 for $150,000. He in turn sold them to Jack Kent Cooke in 1965 for $5.2 million. Cooke sold it to Jerry Buss in 1979 for $67.5 million."

By the late 1990s the franchise was escalating toward a worth of more than $300 million. *Los Angeles Times* columnist Mark Heisler projected that Buss and his associates annually pulled as much as $80 million in profit from the team, the Forum, and the associated sports ventures.

How had the franchise maintained this lofty perch over the years? The answer seemed simple—by having star players and winning championships, a mix of star quality that attracted Hollywood's and the world's interest.

The tentative nature of that formula made itself known abruptly in November 1991 when Magic Johnson announced his retirement due to his HIV infection.

"Since I came here in 1960," West said at the time, "the Lakers have always had one or two players that have been at the top of the league in talent.

"In perpetuating this franchise, our next move is, where do we find another one of those guys?" he asked.

With Johnson's departure and subsequent failed attempts at a comeback, West embarked on what would prove to be an extended period of maneuvering to pull together another championship chemistry.

Admitting that any franchise would be lucky to have one Magic Johnson in a lifetime, West nevertheless became obsessed with finding the next great one, "that one unique player who can get through the tough losses and come back and compete the next night. Those players are rare in this league. They'll play hard every night. They'll play in every building. They'll play in every circumstance. That kind of person is the most difficult to find."

Seeing the athletic talent would be easy, he said. The hard part would be identifying what couldn't be seen. He knew this would be nearly impossible, particularly when he didn't see it in Johnson the first time around.

"I felt he would be a very good player," West said of Johnson. "I had no idea he would get to that level. No idea. But see, you don't know what's inside of people. You can see what they can do physically on the court. The things you could see about Magic you loved. But you wondered where he was gonna play in the NBA. But just through hard work he willed himself to take his game to another level. I don't think anyone knew he had that kind of greatness in him."

Identifying that player, seeing the unseeable, was just the first part of West's impossible task. After that he had to manipulate the NBA's byzantine personnel structure so that the Lakers could get the rights to that special player. That had become nearly impossible with the league's salary cap and expansion. "The problem is, it's like a poker game," he explained. "Any team that has a player play 10 years is probably going to be out of chips pretty soon. So you have to try like crazy within the scope of this league to keep your team young and productive. In the past we've been able to bring in younger players and phase out older players at the end of their careers."

Despite his determination, that replenishing process stalled after Johnson's retirement, as the franchise sorted through an array of players and coaches, trying to find a competitive mix.

For five long seasons, the circumstances dragged on with West torturing himself looking for answers. Meanwhile the Lakers plodded through one unproductive season after another. Always a bundle of nervous energy during games, he grew into a picture of anxiety, often retreating to the Forum parking lot during games while the outcome was being settled. Or he could be seen standing near section 26, peeking past the ushers at the action, his body twisted with tension.

Usually he could determine in the first three or four minutes how the Lakers were going to do. If the prognosis was bad, he would slip from there to his office, where he would watch the rest of the game on television. There he could express his disgust in solitude, taking offense if the game wasn't played right.

The circumstances pushed him to search harder around the league, looking for a sign that some supremely talented young player would emerge from the amateur ranks or that some impressive veteran from another team would find the contractual freedom to become a Laker.

While the situation stretched his patience, West busied himself by acquiring the finest complementary players he could find so he would have the pieces in place for adding the prize talent for which he was searching.

The Art of the Deal

Finally, early in the 1996 off-season, Jerry West found that two very special opportunities presented themselves. Both a talented young amateur and the most impressive of veterans were available. But getting them would require a huge gamble, meaning that if he miscalculated all of his hard work of the last five years would be wasted. It was a risk that would cost tens of millions, but after years of yearning to compete for a championship both West and Jerry Buss were willing. That the two developments converged so nicely almost made them seem preordained.

Because he was 17 and there were so many concerns about his suitability for NBA life, Kobe Bryant agreed to perform an unusual number of workouts for teams as the 1996 draft appeared. He jetted from point to point on the NBA map, hoping to show teams just why they should take a chance on someone so young.

In Los Angeles, Bryant found an organization that immediately understood his potential. His workout left West raving. The Laker scouting staff may have questioned Bryant's willingness to involve teammates, but West watched him move and shoot during the workout, then saw him battle assistant coach and former Lakers defensive star Michael Cooper. There was length, there was strength, there were physical talents, but to go with them was a beautifully polished set of skills, the kind of skills that a 17-year-old could possess only after long hours of dedicated work. The skills themselves said much about work ethic and that hardest-to-read factor, the player's heart.

It was the single best workout West had ever seen. "He has the potential to be an All-Star," he excitedly told people within the organization.

Even so, there didn't seem to be much of an immediate opportunity for Kobe to become a Laker. Joe Bryant had done his research and figured that his son would go somewhere in the top 15 picks. The Lakers were drafting much lower than that.

Unbeknown to the Bryants, a very large development was already bringing a shift in the course of events. Shaquille O'Neal had grown disenchanted with his team, the Orlando Magic, and had filed for free agency. He presented an intimidating package of strength and athletic ability and seemed certain to net an offer worth tens of millions as a free agent.

Some observers were stunned that O'Neal would think of leaving Orlando and the opportunity to play with gifted young guard Anfernee "Penny" Hardaway. ESPN declared that there was no way O'Neal would be foolish enough to go, because playing in Orlando presented the best opportunity to win championships.

Other observers, though, began to question the Magic's chemistry. There were whispers that Hardaway's immensely successful "Li'l Penny" marketing campaign had created a persona so large that it crimped even O'Neal's style.

Another factor was his team's losses in the '95 and '96 playoffs. In Orlando it was O'Neal, not Hardaway, the coaches, or his teammates, who bore the pressure for those losses, both sweeps. In '95 the Magic fell 4–0 to Houston in the NBA Finals. In '96 it was the Bulls who took them 4–0 in the Eastern Conference championship series. O'Neal wept after both of those series, the only times in his life he had cried over basketball other than a loss in the state championship game his junior year that abruptly wiped out an unbeaten season.

The losses, the negative publicity in Orlando, his rumored differences with coach Brian Hill, his ill feelings about Magic management—all would later be added to the financial opportunities and listed as the reasons for his free agency.

Much later O'Neal himself would pinpoint a perceived lack of support from Orlando management in his having to deal with what he saw as negative media. "The media in Orlando are very small-minded," he said. "Very stupid. For example, when I was having a baby, instead of asking me, you know, who the girl was—it was my girlfriend for five years, and we were planning on getting married—they tried to flip it. They asked, 'Is it a white girl?' Stupid shit like that. 'Is it a girl he met on the road?' they asked. 'Is it a whore? Is it a stripper? Because we know those guys go to strip clubs.' Just stupid shit like that.

"Nobody upstairs [in the team's front offices] really ever stuck up for me," he said, explaining that the team should have helped ease the tension between him and the media. "I did the Shaq's dinner for the city. I went to the hospitals to visit children, gave kids clothes. I did a lot for the city on my own. Nobody upstairs ever said, 'Leave Shaq alone.' They treated me like I was one of those young prima donnas that was always getting in trouble, drinking and driving, doing drugs, bullshittin' around. And I wasn't. I was a model athlete. Do the right thing. Stay out of trouble. Yessir. Yes, ma'am. Very respectable. Listen to the coach. Listen to the organization. Never was in trouble. Never got fined. Never talked back to the coach. Still, they let the media treat me like I was one of those type players."

Whether Orlando management could have exercised much power over the media wasn't clear. What was clear was that the Lakers were a team with a history of taking special care of players. West, in particular, had been a superstar himself. He knew the pressures, the misunderstandings, the problems that players of stature face. It could be argued that no NBA executive went to the effort that West did to protect and nurture young stars.

Then there was the Lakers tradition. Their Hollywood affiliations, their aura in the Forum were real attractions to O'Neal. Working in Los Angeles meant he could take advantage of the Hollywood connections to his off-court interests, his rap music production and feature film making.

West and his staff saw that they had a shot at signing O'Neal but that it could cost them as much as $100 million, a figure large enough to frighten off most suitors. The situation left West struggling to find room under the salary cap to sign the big center.

"If you have to give up your entire team for a cornerstone player such as Shaquille, you'd consider it," West said.

It soon became clear that he could have a shot at both players, Kobe Bryant and O'Neal, if he could trade center Vlade Divac and his $4 million salary to Charlotte for the rights to Bryant. The only problem with that strategy was that the Lakers would be sunk if they traded their center for Bryant only to later discover they couldn't swing the final deal for O'Neal. "It really was a gamble," said Lakers owner Jerry Buss. "We could have been left high and dry. We laid it out there and could have lost just as easily.

"From the time we traded Vlade we were out on a limb. We were either going to be very sorry or ecstatic."

West figured he would have to come up with a $95 million offer to get his prize. But ultimately that would prove to be many millions short of what was needed. To create more room under the salary cap over seven seasons, West practically gave away guard Anthony Peeler and reserve forward George Lynch, sending them to Vancouver.

"The Lakers could have folded," said O'Neal's agent, Leonard Armato. "They may have been on the verge of it a few times. But Jerry West wouldn't do that. He was Mr. Clutch as a player and again in these dealings."

The Orlando offer jumped to $115 million, then a little more. The anxiety climbed to unbearable levels for West and his staff. To push their offer to $123 million, they renounced seven players, including Magic Johnson and Sedale Threatt.

Dumping their roster of players seemed to border on lunacy. If O'Neal stayed in Florida, the Lakers would be forced to bring in a host of low-rated talent to fill the gap.

The Magic could have paid more to sign their own free agent, well above the Lakers' $123 million. But it became apparent that, as O'Neal claimed, money wasn't the key factor. Actually the Orlando deal was frontloaded with as much as $20 million in cash the first year, but O'Neal looked west.

"They're a basketball organization," the center said of the Lakers. "When I made my decision to move, it wasn't on money, it wasn't on movies, it wasn't on rap. I just wanted to feel appreciated, that's all. That's what it really comes down to. Not money. Who cares about money? Man, I mean I got money."

For the fourth time in the franchise's illustrious half century of history, the NBA's glamour team had managed to snare the game's most physically dominating presence by signing the 24-year-old O'Neal.

"Los Angeles, shorn of Magic Johnson and Wayne Gretzky, torn by earthquake, riot, and the murder case of the century, took a giant step in its comeback in the size 22-EEEEE shoes of Shaquille O'Neal," declared columnist Mike Downey in the *Los Angeles Times*.

"If this had gone much longer, we were dead," West, who bordered on nervous exhaustion following days of anxious maneuvering to get O'Neal, told reporters after announcing the deal. "To get this prize," he said, "I think is something that when I look back on history and the time that I've spent with this team, this might be the single most important thing we've ever done."

If his efforts had failed, the tightly wound Laker executive said he might well have jumped out of the window of O'Neal agent Leonard Armato's high-rise offices.

A similar sentiment settled on the executive suites of the Orlando Magic. "I think he had a better chance to win here than in L.A." said Magic executive Pat Williams. "It came down to the aura of Los Angeles."

By moving from Orlando to Hollywood, O'Neal stepped into a long line of great Laker centers. In 1947 the prize for the Minneapolis Lakers was the original center, Big George Mikan, who was obtained with swift front-office moves in a player dispersal after the Chicago American Gears folded in the old National Basketball League.

The result for the Lakers? Six pro championships over the next seven seasons, during which Mikan was so overpowering that he forced rule changes widening the lane.

In 1968 the Lakers coup was getting Wilt Chamberlain in a mammoth trade. The results included four trips to the NBA Finals over the next five seasons, although the Chamberlain-led Lakers won only one title, and that didn't come until 1972.

In 1975, Kareem Abdul-Jabbar of the Milwaukee Bucks was available in a trade, and the Lakers outbid the New York Knicks to get his prized services. The result was five NBA titles and eight trips to the league championship series. But Abdul-Jabbar spent four miserable seasons in L.A. before the arrival of point guard Magic Johnson, who teamed with the big center to put together the great Showtime teams.

Another little-known fact was that the Lakers came very close to snaring rookie center Bill Russell until the Boston Celtics backed out of a 1957 trade. Russell went on to lead Boston to 11 titles over the next 13 seasons, but those could have been Lakers titles if the deal had gone through.

If nothing else, history had shown NBA teams just how important it was to have a dominant big man. More than 75 percent of the championships in league history had been won by clubs that relied on power games featuring big, bad post players. Having such a player was particularly important in

Los Angeles, where marquee value ranked at the top of the food chain. Certainly O'Neal had plenty of that with a budding career as an actor, movie producer, and rap recording artist. But it was his backboard-shattering play in the post that mattered most to the Lakers.

With the team's tradition came the expectations in the Great Western Forum, where Hollywood stars paid $700 nightly for courtside seats to be entertained by basketball's best. With O'Neal's contract those ticket holders knew prices were headed up.

The size of the deal brought an immediate gasp.

How, critics asked, could one player command so much money, particularly one with 54 percent free throw shooting in four NBA seasons? O'Neal's clunkers at the line had allowed opponents to defend his slam dunks with fouls that dared him to make the foul shots. This characteristic—and the fact that he had never led his LSU club to an NCAA title—drove comparisons to Chamberlain's star-crossed career.

The Lakers did admit to being concerned about O'Neal's free throw shooting. But, as veteran Los Angeles sportswriter Mitch Chortkoff pointed out, "Del Harris coached Moses Malone, who made the most free throws in league history. He also coached Jack Sikma, the only center to lead the league in free throw percentage."

Harris was understandably ecstatic and characteristically understated. "This will be better," he told reporters.

The coach's sentiment clearly matched O'Neal's perspective that he had come to Los Angeles to team up with Kobe and Eddie Jones and Nick Van Exel and Elden Campbell, all of them young and talented and seemingly poised on the verge of greatness, immediately if not sooner.

That certainly was the hope in Los Angeles, where happy endings were concocted daily in the celluloid screening rooms of the film industry. Making them happen on the court, however, proved to be a bit more problematic.

First Blood

Days after announcing that he would go to the NBA directly from high school, Kobe Bryant signed a promotional contract worth approximately $10 million with Adidas, the shoe and clothing giant. That money made it possible for him to add a Range Rover and a BMW to the growing Bryant family fleet. Jerry West and his staff, meanwhile, engaged in a bit of fretting over how the organization would deal with having an 18-year-old in the fold. Having seen what the Hollywood life had done to Magic Johnson, the Lakers tried to think of ways of softening his adjustment to pro life. But that proved to be very little trouble initially. Shortly after their son's being drafted and traded to the Lakers, Joe and Pam Bryant packed up with younger daughter Shaya, who withdrew from LaSalle, and moved to Los Angeles to inhabit a six-bedroom seaside home in Pacific Palisades with Kobe. They were there to provide the support he needed in this period of adjustment to life in pro basketball.

Sharia, the older daughter, remained at Temple, where she was a budding volleyball star and rapidly nearing completion of her undergraduate degree in international business administration, the field of study that Kobe said he, too, would like to pursue someday.

With their quick departure, the Bryants decided to keep their house in the Philadelphia suburb of Wynnewood, with the understanding that grandparents would cut the lawn at the vacant property.

Sometime later, Sharia would get her first view of her brother playing on television and would be surprised to see how much he had grown. "He's got more money and lives in California," she would tell USA *Today*. "But he's just Kobe to me."

Just who that was would long remain a mystery to his Lakers teammates. From his first contact with the team, he presented an aloof front, leaving them to guess at exactly who he was. In his early days in Los Angeles, he accepted an invitation from O'Neal to go out to dinner. "It was good," Kobe said of his first sit-down with his teammate. "It was cool."

But it wasn't a scenario that would be repeated. The 24-year-old O'Neal enjoyed the L.A. club scene and nightlife, something that held little appeal for his workaholic younger teammate. "I just didn't like to go out that much," Kobe explained when asked why he and O'Neal hadn't pursued an off-court friendship. Instead, he enjoyed time with his family or spent hours alone in his new room. There, in his retreat filled with stereo equipment, video game gear, a computer, and video monitors, he could study basketball to his heart's content or even write poetry. If he tired of his virtual nightlife, he could get up and gaze out on the silvery Pacific or cast his thoughts to the sparkling lights of L.A.

Mostly, it was clear that Kobe was intent on saving himself for his relationship with the game. Beyond what he gave to his family and his video games, he kept his entire focus on playing and the limited promotional appearances necessary to support his business interests. With a new rookie salary structure in place, he signed a standard three-year, $3.5 million contract with the team, then made a brief appearance on "The Tonight Show" with Jay Leno.

From there his focus turned to playing for the Lakers' developmental team in the Fila Summer Pro League, one of several leagues that NBA teams use for summer work. "Nobody knew what to expect when he came in," recalled Larry Drew, the

Lakers assistant who had the chore of running the team. "Everybody knew he was a talent."

Many observers suspected that O'Neal's high-profile arrival in Los Angeles would help to obscure Bryant's introduction, thus taking some of the public pressure off the young rookie. But hopes of that evaporated with his first appearance at the Long Beach Pyramid, the 5,000-seat arena where the summer league held games. Usually there were plenty of empty seats, but his first night brought an overflow crowd, and 2,000 fans were turned away.

"I remember the first day he arrived," Drew recalled, "all the media and all the people that were there chanting his name. It was a packed house. The first day he came he didn't even get to dress to play, but there was a lot of electricity in the air about him being there."

Usually the Lakers used the league games to help prepare their rookies and young players for adjustment to the team, Drew said. "But there wasn't a lot done early the first few days he was there. We didn't get a chance to practice. In summer league we normally get five or six days to practice and to get the players used to what we want to do. He came in right as the games were being played, so he was just kind of out there, kind of playing on instinct. He was like a little puppy let out of a cage. He was bouncing all over the place. Everybody could see that he was gonna be a special talent. You could see the swagger about his walk. He was a confident kid who didn't shy away, who had no fears about going against pro players."

In fact Kobe showed that he had no qualms about stepping in and taking charge, even to the point of directing teammates on what to do, where to go on the floor. Even his rookie teammates were four and five years older than he, but if that gave him reason for pause he didn't show it.

"I just want to get out there and win," he told the *Los Angeles Times*. "If Coach needs me to be a leader, that's what I'll be. And no matter what, if I see something wrong, I'm going to give my input, just like Shaq would give his input. But it's important for me to stay within the concept of the team."

More important, the star quality that West and Jerry Buss were desperate to see made itself known immediately. He scored 27 in his first game, 36 in another, and over the four-game schedule averaged 25 points and 5 rebounds.

Like West and Buss, Kobe was looking for proof that he could star, and the summer league games provided him all the evidence he wanted. "I felt that I could always do what I did in high school, that it wasn't that hard," he explained later.

To do that, however, he would need playing time, which would require that Del Harris have as much confidence in him as Kobe had in himself. Harris, however, concluded that Kobe was a kid who needed a more realistic view of the team and his role in it. "Del was a prophet in this," a Lakers staff member who worked closely with Harris would explain later. "Del saw this coming and tried a long time ago to get Kobe under control."

Harris would later explain to some Lakers staffers that the team's management had given him directives that Kobe had to receive playing time so as to learn. The staff member got the distinct impression that Harris would have preferred to keep the 18-year-old on the bench.

The issue was one that West cared deeply about because it reflected his own career. He came to Los Angeles in 1960 and was joined by Schaus, his college coach at West Virginia, who promptly kept him on the bench for a few weeks. West steamed the entire time and never forgave Schaus for keeping him out of play.

Young players, especially good young players, have to play, was West's dictum. There's simply no other way for them to get better.

"The main thing Kobe Bryant needs is experience," the Lakers executive would say during the season when reporters asked about Kobe's playing time. "He doesn't need to work on anything. He just needs to play more."

Regardless, Kobe's plans for immediate stardom suffered a setback. In early September he was injured while playing an outdoor pickup game at Venice Beach. "The first thing I heard about Kobe was that he had injured his wrist playing at Venice," recalled Derek Fisher, the Lakers' other first-round pick in 1996. "I just couldn't believe that a guy would be playing up at Venice Beach. That was my first experience with how excited and enthusiastic he was about just playing the game. He truly had a passion for playing, regardless of where it was, what time of day—he was gonna play."

Publicly, some Lakers staffers offered admonishment for Bryant's stooping to pickup ball to fix his hoop jones. West, though, could see true passion in a player. "This guy will play in a Little League tournament," he said of Kobe. "It doesn't bother me. He loves to play basketball. He's one of the more dedicated players I've ever seen."

Asked about the injury, Kobe said, "I went up to tip-dunk the basketball. The ball was bouncing on the rim and dropped in. I made the mistake of not holding on to the rim, grabbing the rim and coming down slowly. I just tried to back off in the air."

Suddenly he tumbled to the pavement and banged his wrist. Immediately three knots appeared, and he knew it was broken. Fortunately, the injury didn't require surgery, but it meant that he wouldn't be ready for the opening of training camp in

October. For a rookie to miss training camp was a huge blow, especially as the Lakers adjusted to their new center. "This will set him back," Lakers GM Mitch Kupchak told reporters. "He's an 18-year-old player, and the first training camp is very important."

Complicating the situation was the fact that Kobe had no one position but was viewed as a combination of a point guard, off guard, and small forward and would play at all three positions during parts of the season. His size and quickness were the core of a tremendous versatility, but missing training meant that he would develop it at a slower pace.

Beyond that the camp brought an adjustment for rookies and veterans alike, now that the Lakers had their new post weapon. "Everybody had to learn to play with Shaq, to face the basket and when to cut," recalled Travis Knight, who was also a rookie that fall.

"That first day of training camp Kobe was injured and everything," Fisher recalled, "but he still wanted to be out there, trying to do two-line layups and do everything that he possibly could to still be involved with practice and be a part of the group."

Establishing himself as part of the team was clearly important to Kobe, yet as time went on his teammates found that he kept them at a distance, answering questions about anything not related to basketball with one- or two-word replies. He seldom initiated any personal conversations at all, Fisher recalled, an approach that Kobe would maintain in the months and years that followed.

Finally, over the summer of 1998 and later as practice began for the shortened 1999 schedule, Fisher would decide that he needed to break through Kobe's standoffish manner with teammates. "I had never just had a personal conversation with Kobe or anything to get a better feel for who he is and what makes him tick as a person," the Lakers point guard explained.

Over time Kobe's silence had mystified, then irritated teammates, leaving some with the impression that he considered himself above them. "He really is to himself," Fisher explained in a 1999 interview, "so you don't know exactly how he feels. You don't know what makes him happy, what makes him sad. So it was hard for us early on to understand what he was going through, what he was trying to do, and that he was really trying to be a part of the team. But the way he played was just the way he knew how to play."

As the situation wore on and the hard feelings deepened, Fisher decided that as a point guard he should try to break through to Kobe. "I just kind of started thinking about both of our situations, and knowing his potential for growth in the future, I thought that he was going to be here for several years," Fisher said. "The type of season that I had in 1998, I thought that I was going to be here for several years to come. I just kind of started thinking that we possibly could be the backcourt of the future for this organization and that it was going to be really important for us to have some type of bond. We may not raise each other's kids and be godparents and do things like that for each other's families, but we have to have a working relationship. And that's when I kind of started. Even though he wasn't necessarily reaching out, I kind of started reaching out, trying to be more talkative, just trying to maybe spark conversation about anything just to get to know him a little better."

Over time Fisher came to the conclusion that Kobe's silence was merely a defense mechanism. It was almost as if Kobe feared that taking a more personal approach with his teammates might open him up to being swayed away from his dreams and his goals. "From day one, he knew the things that he wanted to accomplish in his career," Fisher said. "Things that he's wanted to achieve, he already had that in mind. Because of his talent level, it's almost like a self-fulfilling prophecy for him. If he sees something, he can go and get it."

Most other players, even most stars, didn't have that power, Fisher said. "When he entered the league, he had all of these things in mind, that he wanted to be an All-Star, that he wanted to be a starter, that he wanted to average 20 points a game. All of these things that eventually happened for him, he saw them. He wanted to come in and do those things, but he didn't want to come in talking about them. He has a certain confidence that other people don't have and can't carry."

From the very start, Kobe's Laker teammates didn't know how to take his extremely high confidence, which was unusual for even a veteran player, much less an 18-year-old. Only when he began to break through Kobe's barriers two years later did Fisher begin to see that the confidence wasn't arrogance so much as it was Kobe's means of protecting himself and his goals. "The more you experience time around him and get to see him in different situations, the more you understand that that's all it is, is confidence," Fisher explained. "It's not arrogance. It's not his personality. He's not a selfish person. He's not a guy that only thinks of himself. He's just a guy who has an immeasurable amount of confidence in his ability to play the game."

In the fall of 1996, however, that information wasn't available to his Lakers teammates. And later, even when it was available, some still struggled to see him as more than arrogant. Without question Kobe's decision to have minimal personal relationships with his teammates would factor heavily into the team's chemistry for the next three seasons and would serve to vex players, coaches, and staff members alike.

Clearly, though, Kobe's rookie season proved to be the best in terms of relationships with teammates. First, the Lakers had brought longtime veteran Byron Scott back to the team, and with his warm personality and vast experience he proved to be a solid mentor.

Scott took to Bryant because the rookie was very different from the majority of young players passing through the league. First of all, Kobe was familiar with basketball history and wanted to soak up everything he could about Scott's days with Johnson and the Showtime Lakers. He also politely pushed for information and advice on training and pacing oneself to be successful in the game. Scott got the immediate impression that what he said was being listened to and filed away.

"Byron told me how important it is during the season to keep your work habits," Kobe later explained. "You have to keep working on your jump shot, your physical preparation. At this level you always have to be working to improve your game, or you'll get left behind."

Scott, who would move on to become an assistant coach with the Sacramento Kings after that season, saw that many young players coming into the league had acquired such a veneer of cool in their short lives that they would never have risked appearing so childlike by asking such questions. Kobe, however, didn't seem to give such notions even a thought. If there was information about the game, he wanted it.

"I'm just very curious about the game," Kobe said in explaining his approach.

It also helped that first year that Kobe had a friendship with Lakers guard Eddie Jones, whom he had first met five years earlier in the Sonny Hill League. Then 23, Jones was heading into his third season with the Lakers after an outstanding start to his career. He had been ready with friendly advice when he learned Kobe was going to be his teammate. "Eddie said I had to prepare myself mentally because L.A. can be very distracting," Kobe said.

O'Neal, too, stepped forward with a good-humored friendship. "There's clearly a looking-after-him attitude on this team," Kurt Rambis, a Lakers assistant that season, explained. "Not because he's a little baby and can't look out for himself, but because everybody has a real feel for what he's going through. We all lived away from home for the first time. He's in this setting where almost every other person is a couple of years significantly older than him."

But in time each of those relationships would become strained by the circumstances. Kobe's intensity simply burned with an all-business approach.

One longtime Lakers staff member explained it this way: "We weren't sure if Kobe was just quiet or if he literally thought he was better than everybody else, if he thought he was this supreme athlete and everybody else was playing their roles just to make him better."

Given no evidence to the contrary, Kobe's teammates concluded he was far more interested in his own personal accomplishments than he was in team goals, Fisher said. "That's why people really misinterpreted him a lot of times as a guy who really thinks only of himself."

Nearly three years later Kobe would be asked if he had any kind of personal relationship with any of his teammates. "Not really," he replied. "All that matters is what we do on the court."

Into the Breach

If training camp brought the initial difficulties of Bryant's pro career, it also brought the first comic relief. Veteran hazing of rookies had long been a staple of Lakers life that began each season with the opening banquet of training camp. As called for by tradition, West would begin the proceedings after the meal with his sparse comments about the upcoming season. He reminded the players about league policies concerning gambling and fighting and how they should conduct themselves as Lakers. His speech was usually devoid of talk about Lakers tradition. The task, as West saw it, was simply to live up to the tradition, not talk about it.

After West spoke, trainer Gary Vitti and equipment manager Rudy Garciduenas spoke to the group about routine procedures. In past seasons it had been the task of Magic Johnson to step up next with an indoctrination session for rookies in which they were ordered about the room, asked to introduce themselves, and required to sing their school anthems. Johnson always conducted these sessions like a drill sergeant, and there was a purpose to them. One year one of the team's top draft picks couldn't manage in 11 takes to announce his name, school, hometown, and academic major. The players and coaches had howled with each successive screwup. But underneath the hilarity developed a hard edge of worry. Something had to be wrong. And it was. The player would later reveal an inability to remember even the simplest plays. Despite impressive physical talents, he had to be cut.

Beyond that opening night frivolity, the veterans required the rookies to spend much of the season in servitude, carrying the bags off the team plane and doing other basic chores. In recent seasons much of that ritual had dissipated, especially with the retirement of Magic Johnson. The last Laker to rule the rookies, recalled Eddie Jones, was hard-nosed James Worthy, who hadn't been with the club in more than a year. Everybody else on the team was too young, Jones said, to do too much veteran harassing.

Most of the rookie festivities in 1996's opening team dinner were saved for Kobe. "They didn't make everyone sing a song," Travis Knight recalled. "They made Kobe sing because of the Brandy thing. He did a good job, put a little effort into it. He knew most of the words. It was funny."

The veterans made Kobe stand and sing one of Brandy's soulful ballads. "They thought it was funny," Bryant would confide later. "I didn't find it too funny. They made me sing 'I Wanna Be Down.' I knew most of the words 'cause I hear it all the time. The guys gave me a hard time about that."

On the floor it proved hard for his coaches and teammates to get a good read on Kobe in his first weeks as a Laker, with the injury limiting his involvement. "He didn't play for a lot of training camp," Travis Knight recalled. "But he was running, doing a lot of sprinting drills—things like that. You could tell he was in good shape. He wasn't at all intimidated by the situation, though."

He snared his first playing time that October 16 in a preseason game played in Fresno and responded with 10 points and five rebounds. Two nights later the Lakers played their first game of the preseason in the Forum against Kobe's hometown 76ers, which certainly factored into his hyper approach. Late in the game he tried to force a dunk and collided with Philly reserve center Tim Kempton. The impact sent Bryant plummeting to the floor and left him with a badly strained hip flexor and yet more downtime.

It was obvious that Bryant took special delight in getting to the basket to dunk in the face of taller players, but in the aftermath Eddie Jones advised him to ease up on trying to dunk so often and so spectacularly, especially when a three-foot bank would do the job. Once he healed, Bryant responded by revising his dunking technique. From then on when he attacked the basket through a crowd, he would seek to initiate contact with a defender to brace himself and protect against free falls and other crashes. Often the officials would give him the foul call, an added benefit to his penetration. Sometimes, though, they would whistle him for the offensive foul for initiating the contact. That was annoying but still far better than more injuries.

The hip flexor meant that he got no playing time in the home opener, a Lakers win over Phoenix. The next game, against Minnesota, he played briefly, had his shot blocked, and racked up a turnover. "I'm sure he would have liked to make a more auspicious debut," Harris told reporters. "It's OK. We already know he can play."

In all, five games would pass before Bryant finally got that first pro bucket in Charlotte. Like most pro coaches, Harris took a wait-and-see approach with rookies. Kobe was no different, except that Harris took even more caution because of the age factor. Besides, the coach had plenty of other problems on his hands. Stripping the roster to get O'Neal meant that the team had undergone the largest single turnover of players in franchise history. Of the 16 athletes on the training camp roster only 5—point guard Nick Van Exel, center Elden Campbell, forward Cedric Ceballos, forward Corie Blount, and Jones—had been Lakers the previous season.

As a result Harris would spend most of the season searching for the right mix around O'Neal. The situation was complicated further by the fact that halfway through the schedule Cedric Ceballos was traded to Houston for Robert Horry. Then West decided to add another veteran forward by trading for George McCloud.

Even with the headaches the Lakers started 3–0, including an impressive road win over New York, the start of their first extended East Coast trip. But soon their losses would include an unfathomable defeat at the hands of Toronto and the loss to Charlotte.

The situation, to some degree, meant that Kobe would be overlooked. More of a factor, his injuries meant he had had little practice time in the preseason, and with so many new players there was much work to be done.

Of his team's problems, coach Del Harris said, "We're just totally out of rhythm offensively, and our execution is very weak. We don't set or use screens very well, and we have a tendency to bog down in our ball movement. Those are things, hopefully, gradually we'll work our way through, but we're gonna have to do it in games, because we're playing four games a week the first six weeks of the season. So we don't have the practice time."

The other unspoken factor was that Harris didn't hold marvelously organized practices. Traditionally the Lakers had been a franchise that prized practice, with Pat Riley conducting the sessions with a tightly packaged fervor. Yet even Harris's defenders would later concede that he had that old-style NBA attitude of just rolling out the ball for the veterans. There were days where the team accomplished much in practice. But there were also far too many times where Harris would stop the proceedings to drone on and on about things that left the players banging their heads against the wall to relieve the agony.

Having been raised on Gregg Downer's expertly organized sessions at Lower Merion, Kobe was shocked at the lax approach. "Practices were very structured at Lower Merion. Very intense," he would later confide. "But a lot of times with Del people just did what they wanted. Guys wouldn't even practice at all."

Because West made every attempt not to intrude on the coaches' domain, the team VP never attended practices unless the Lakers were undergoing a brief pregame shootaround at the Forum, so he wasn't aware of the circumstances, explained a team staff member. But in that regard Harris was hardly the ideal coach for developing a young player. The other side to that argument was that the NBA was never meant to be a league for developing talent. With a schedule that called for three or four games a week, there wasn't the time. The circumstances presented a harsh reality that grew more worrisome to Kobe with each passing week. Over the course of the season he would play in 71 games and average a little better than 15 minutes a game of playing time, good enough to rank him only 11th on the roster.

Joe Bryant had spent much of the first months of Kobe's career involved in promotional duties for a shoe company. But the senior Bryant counseled his son to be patient about playing time. "My father tells me, 'Your time will come,'" Kobe told me at the time.

"He's gonna be fine," O'Neal said, "once he gets a chance to go out there and shine and do his thing. He's gonna be fine."

The coaching staff could see that Kobe's progress would be important to his team's playoff hopes, although his coaches were quick to defray any pressure. Still, the first month of the season found the Lakers bench struggling to score. Kobe clearly understood and hoped that he could expand his role by providing scoring off the bench. "I think of me stepping in there and being young and just having so much energy coming off the sideline, hopefully I can be a spark plug," he said.

But it would take time and experience for him to earn a more effective shot selection. Plus, with many of his minutes coming at the two-guard position, the nuances of defending the pro-style high screen and roll were a challenge to learn.

Even with their growing pains, the young Lakers moved forward with a sense of progress over the first five weeks of the 1996–97 season. After a win over Orlando on December 6, their record stood at 14–7.

"We're gonna be fine," O'Neal said of the Lakers' start. "Even if we had gone 21–0 this month, we're not gonna win or lose anything the first month, as long as we satisfy ourselves. Our formula is to win about 50 or 60 games, get home-court advantage, and take it from there."

Even young Kobe knew it wasn't going to be that easy.

The Lake Show

With the franchise searching for an identity in the wake of the great Showtime teams, the new young group of Lakers had taken to calling themselves "the Lake Show." Despite the newness of their relationships, they found a groove that December of 1996, winning seven of their first eight games that month. O'Neal in the post presented a troubling problem for their opponents. At the point, left-hander Nick Van Exel displayed an unbridled bundle of moxie and quickness. Eddie Jones was a defensive terror on the wings. And Elden Campbell provided power and flexibility as either a forward or backup center.

Little did anyone realize at the time that this promising group would peak so short of expectations. In retrospect the Lake Show would come to be viewed as a misdirected lot, and when the members were later shipped out of town one by one, the veteran sportswriters covering the team would be happy to bid them good riddance.

Even with the obvious rough edges, hopes and expectations grew that December as they rolled past Detroit, Denver, Seattle, Orlando, Minnesota, Sacramento, Indiana, and Portland on their way to a midmonth meeting with Michael Jordan and his Chicago Bulls. The Lakers had settled into a blitzing, open-court style, pressing and slamming opponents into submission. It was a fun style to play, one that suited Kobe's skills as a finisher, meaning that the limited minutes he got were usually eventful.

Each game on the schedule offered a sense of excitement as he made his first stops around the NBA map, but the visit to

Chicago sent his hopes soaring. One of his main reasons for moving directly to the NBA had been the opportunity to compete against Jordan, but Kobe hardly stirred from the bench in that first meeting. His personal disappointment was soon exceeded by the entire team's.

Using their young legs and up-tempo style, the Lakers quickly moved ahead of the Bulls that night and appeared on their way to domination through three quarters. Early in the fourth quarter they still held a plump 19-point lead. Then, the Bulls' pressure defense began forcing turnovers. Chicago's Toni Kukoc got hot from 3-point range, quickly accelerating a momentum shift.

"I saw it coming," Eddie Jones would say later. "We knew it was coming. We knew we weren't going to get any calls down the stretch; we weren't going to get anything given to us."

With every turnover the Lakers slipped deeper into trouble. The Chicago pressure defense kept shoving the issue, possession after possession. With their long arms Jordan and Scottie Pippen fed off the passing lanes, sending a surge through the United Center crowd. Kukoc kept hitting threes, enough to allow the Bulls to break back to even by the end of regulation, then win in overtime. The Lakers walked away in shock.

"The only thing is, we have lapses," Jones said. "We can go out and play a half where we look so confident, we look like we're so into the game mentally that we know what's going on in every aspect. But it's a thing of consistency. Against the Bulls we looked like we were the best team in this league that first half. But then we faltered down the stretch. We're not consistent."

"You know we're not gonna make excuses for the way we played," O'Neal said. "We played like shit the last quarter. We had three excellent quarters, but then the last quarter we just folded up. And that's why we lost."

Added to the Lakers hurt was the fact that the game drew one of the largest national cable television audiences ever. They had faltered before millions of witnesses. "Everyone who saw that game knows that we beat ourselves," O'Neal said. "I didn't take any shots in the last 25 minutes because we couldn't get the ball past half court. If we just come out and do everything right and play well, we can beat 'em. We match up with them better than they match up with us."

The Lakers were still smarting from their anguishing Bulls collapse two weeks later when I joined them on a quick road trip to Vancouver. No one was more burned by the turn of events than Harris, who had set his sights on a February rematch with Chicago in Los Angeles. His team had answered the disappointment in Chicago by winning six of its next seven games, including a five-game winning streak heading into the matchup with the Grizzlies. Even so, the game still sat in their craw.

The Lakers opened the 1997 portion of their schedule by winning a game in Sacramento, then beating the Kings again in the Forum on Friday night, January 3. From there they slipped into Canada in the wee hours of Saturday. Less than eight hours later they were dressed and ready to practice at General Motors Place, the Grizzlies' arena. With the hectic travel schedule, practice time had been negligible. Harris used a brief Saturday morning session to focus his team on defending the high screen and roll, a reminder for the veterans and a key lesson for Kobe.

Then the players broke into informal shooting drills, big men at one end, guards at the other. With O'Neal at a safe distance, Eddie Jones, ever the prankster, donned the center's long mink coat, which had been folded over a sideline chair. Looking like a munchkin out of *The Wizard of Oz*, he stepped on the court to shoot a three. The sight of Jones in the massive coat brought a chuckle from the group (Shaq, at the other end of the floor, didn't see it), but Shaq's muscle-bound body-guard sitting courtside glowered in irritation, prompting Jones to take off the coat and drape it back over the chair. After Jones moved off to resume shooting, the bodyguard got up and refolded the coat carefully.

Moments later assistant coach Larry Drew challenged Van Exel to a shooting game with a small wager. Shooting threes from left to right, Van Exel advanced to the top of the key before missing, then waited to see how far Drew would go. "I'll be there," the coach said, smiling and nodding to the victory spot in the far corner, and sure enough he ran the table, leaving Van Exel very long faced.

"Five . . . four . . . three . . . two . . . one," Shaq counted loudly before launching a shot from midcourt, an air ball that missed by a good five feet as practice ended.

On the surface the Lakers were a loose bunch. They led the Pacific Division with a 24–9 record. Behind the scenes, though, both coaches and players were tinkering with a tenuous chemistry. "I feel they are making progress as far as maturity goes," Byron Scott said of his young teammates. "Everybody understands where we're going, where we're headed, where we want to get to. Each month I think we've improved in every aspect of the game."

A big part of this development centered on the growth of Van Exel as a point guard. He had been forced to alter his game with the arrival of O'Neal. "I think Nick's growth is getting better each game," Eddie Jones said. "I think the acquisition of Shaquille O'Neal has made Nick expand his game more than ever, because Nick is really passing the ball super. Everybody knows Nick not for being a passer; everybody knows Nick for his crunch shots, his three-point shooting, him creating his own shot. But now he's creating shots for everybody.

It's a transformation in the sense that Nick is growing as a player out there on the court."

O'Neal agreed, saying that the development of his relationship with Van Exel would be a key to the Lakers championship potential. "Nick is a fierce competitor," Shaq said. "He shoots the ball well, plays hard, is very, very unselfish. When I first talked with him, he told me his goals. He said, 'Look, I don't care about scoring. I don't care about anything. I just want to lead the league in assists, and I want you to lead the league in scoring.' "

Then in his fourth NBA season, Van Exel's development had come at the constant pleading and fussing of Harris, leading to some flashes of anger between the two. "They've got problems there with Nick and Del," former Laker George Lynch, who had been traded to the Grizzlies from the Lakers over the summer, had alleged that morning in a Vancouver newspaper interview. "These two guys don't get along, and I have to say I don't blame Nick. He's a free and open type of guy, and he needs space to be his best, and maybe they've had problems with too much control. When you get in a tough game down the stretch, you've got to have your coach and your point guard get along. If they don't, it's not going to work."

"All teams have these things happen," assistant coach Larry Drew explained when asked about the relationship, "and George was around when some of them went on. But Del and Nick have ironed their differences out, and they have a good working relationship now. Most of these young point guards are very competitive. Everybody wants to win. There are gonna be some times when coach and player get into it. These guys are highly competitive. Take Nick for example. Nick has a tremendous will to win. Sometimes he may overstep his boundary, but he's extremely competitive. That's good, and as a coaching staff we understand it. And Del has done a tremendous job with it."

During the previous weeks the Dallas Mavericks had sought to trade point guard Jason Kidd for Van Exel, but it was Harris who didn't want to make the trade because he didn't think Kidd could shoot nearly as well as Van Exel. Later the failure to make that deal would leave some Lakers insiders shaking their heads.

Harris, though, seemed to relish the challenge of making Van Exel harness his game to blend with O'Neal. It was the same transformation that he hoped to see Kobe make, once playing time became available.

In the interim Kobe had taken to using pregame shoot-around time to make up for the lack of real practice time. That Sunday night before the game in Vancouver, for example, Kobe worked with Larry Drew, focusing on his crossover move and handling the ball in the half court. As the schedule wore on and playing time for Kobe became harder to find, the coaches had settled on the idea of developing him as a backup point guard, which would allow him some extra minutes on the floor. Kobe was eager for any opportunity and jumped at the idea. Focusing intently while working with Drew that night, he executed his crossover move, got rid of the ball in the high screen and roll, then got it back from Drew in the deep left corner, where he dropped in a smooth trey. From there, the coach and player shifted to the right side of the floor, where they again ran the high screen and roll and again Bryant completed it with another swished three.

Veteran Lakers beat writer Mitch Chortkoff, watching nearby, talked about Bryant making a key play in a recent defeat of Sacramento. "Kobe stole the ball from Billy Owens, looked around, saw nobody was near him, so he did a 360-spin for a dunk," Chortkoff said with a smile. "That brought the crowd to its feet. That's an example of why Shaq made up the name 'Showboat.' The night before Kobe blocked a shot by Mitch Richmond at the end in a close game, and then at the other end the Lakers missed, but Kobe got the rebound with his back to the basket and put it back in over his head."

Chortkoff also pointed out that Bryant had had a key turnover that cost the Lakers in a game against Portland, which made Harris anxious about playing him. Chortkoff had advised Harris that he would just have to live through those things as Bryant developed.

That night in Vancouver wound up being special for the Lakers. O'Neal dominated the Grizzlies inside, and Van Exel doled out 23 assists feeding him the ball, just one assist shy of Magic Johnson's team record. The game was Del Harris's perfect vision of the way things ought to be for the Lakers.

"He crossed the 20-assists barrier for the first time in his career, and he's very happy about that," Harris said of Van Exel. "I like his points when he gets them, but I don't care if he scores a lot of points."

Van Exel admitted that the offense had sputtered during the team's adjustment to playing with O'Neal. "I think at times we're too stagnant," the point guard said. "Everybody is standing around and watching when we throw the ball into the post. There's no movement. Everybody's watching to see what the big guy's gonna do. Then there are a lot of times when we're just careless with a lot of turnovers."

That assessment would become a refrain among Lakers players over the coming months. The circumstances would trouble no one more than Kobe, who wanted playing time badly, only to realize once he got that playing time that he was trapped in a stagnant offense.

With Van Exel playing so well, the Vancouver game offered little opportunity for Kobe. "You can see the pressure I'm under as a coach," Harris explained. "You got Kobe Bryant who's got such a tremendous game, and yet ahead of him at his normal position are both Eddie Jones and Byron Scott. So I don't know where I'm going to get all the minutes for these guys. We've got some tremendous two and three players."

On the issue of his playing time, Bryant said, "I just sit there on the bench, trying to stay loose, and if he calls me I'm going to go out there and try to give it my all. It's nice to get in there and mix it up with the guys when it really counts. I'm starting to understand the flow of the game a little bit more. I'm starting to feel more comfortable out there on the floor. Now that we've had a little opportunity to practice, I understand all of this a little more."

Part of his strategy for keeping his disappointment at bay was to focus on others who had faced far more difficult circumstances. "I read the autobiography of Jackie Robinson," Kobe said. "I was thinking about all the hard times I'd go through this year and that it'd never compare to what he went through. That just kind of helped put things in perspective."

Still, with his personal expectations so huge, it was hard to keep the negative thoughts at bay. "My rookie year I had no clue," he would tell me later. "I figured it would work out and I would realize my dream, but I didn't know how. I kept thinking about it all the time and wondering, 'How? How is it going to happen? How are the pieces going to fall in place?'"

What wore on him most was Harris's seeming inconsistency. Kobe never knew when the coach was suddenly going to decide to play him major minutes. He would play well, and just when it seemed like he would get more time, Harris would hold back. "I felt like I was playing with one hand tied behind me," Kobe said of the experience. Joe Bryant would caution patience in these hard times. It was the strength of their relationship, plus Kobe's religious faith, that helped keep him on track and set him apart from other young players. "I had that much trust in my father," Kobe explained. "I had that much trust in the Lord in the special situation He had put me in."

He decided that he would see Harris's approach as a positive. "One of the hardest things this year was not knowing whether you're going to play or how many minutes you're going to play," he would explain at the end of the season. "But at the same time that kind of helps you, because you just have to be ready every night."

The other relief was the sheer joy and wonder of his rookie experience. "It's fun," he told himself. "I'm in the NBA." The pace itself was a blur of hastily grabbed meals, of jetting from one section of the continent to the other on a weekly basis. Tuesday in Minneapolis, Thursday in Sacramento. Friday back to L.A. for one of Pam Bryant's home-cooked meals. Then back out on the road again five days later. Since childhood he had been used to five-star hotels and in-room dining, so the hermitlike existence of an NBA rookie seemed to his liking, as long as room service could deliver the apple pie à la mode he craved and the hotel TV offered TNT games. On buses and the team plane, he read or tuned the world out by stuffing his head between earphones.

There were other adjustments for an 18-year-old in the land of big paychecks. One of the most challenging was Los Angeles itself. "Because of the lifestyle," Bryant said. "With there being so many distractions. But I think that if you can remain focused on your goal and what you're there for and what got you there, you should be OK."

Asked about off-court entanglements, he said, "Sure, the groupies come after you. Living in L.A., how could you not be approached by women like that? They tend to be older, but some are younger. You have to handle it in a professional manner. I've learned all about that growing up."

His family helped tremendously in that regard. Asked if he had phoned his parents often during road trips, he said, "Off and on, yeah, we've been talking. My mother calls me all the time."

Setback

The Lakers, meanwhile, continued their much needed adjustment to O'Neal's hulking presence in the lane. Asked if anything had surprised him about the big center in their first few months together, Van Exel replied, "The surprises come in practice, because he does a lot more there than he does in the game. A lot of people don't really get to see him in practice. But he has a lot of skills, a lot of talent. He works hard every day, in practice, in the games. Whatever he does, he works hard at."

In Orlando, O'Neal had acquired a reputation for shirking team leadership, but in his first months in Los Angeles his coaches and teammates saw little evidence of that. "He's much like Magic," Mitch Chortkoff, who had covered the Lakers for three decades, said of O'Neal. "He works hard every day and expects his teammates to do the same. He practices when it's optional and dives for balls in scrimmages. Players pick up on that. He had to show me, too, because I covered Magic and know the example he set. I didn't know much about Shaq. He had to show me, and he has. That part of him doesn't come through much because of the moviemaking—people get the image of him as maybe a part-time player. But he doesn't do any of that movie stuff during the season. And he is all business."

"He's a better leader than I was informed," Del Harris agreed, acknowledging the reputation from Orlando. "Again, maybe that was because he was young. Perhaps it's a function of maturing, but whatever, he's a nice leader on our team."

Earlier in the year I had covered Jordan and the Bulls during a preseason game in Las Vegas. At the time Jordan had made a point of telling reporters, "Everybody knows that Shaq is going to have to make his free throws. He knows it, too. I'm pretty sure the Lakers know it. They're gonna have to find someone else they can go to in the fourth quarter that can knock in the free throws, because if he can't knock in the free throws and he's in there in the fourth quarter, they're going to foul him. And that's a good call, looking at the dominance that he can orchestrate. That's the easy play, the easy way out, to foul him. You hope you don't hurt him. I don't think anyone's going to try to hurt him, but they're gonna try to send him to the free throw line."

Jordan, of course, was playing mind games with O'Neal. The Bulls star knew the contingent of Los Angeles reporters present would get the message to the Lakers center, who spent time grieving over his free throws.

In Vancouver, I reminded O'Neal of Jordan's statement. "That's all right," he said. "The year that I sent Michael home [when O'Neal's Orlando Magic beat the Bulls 4–2 in the 1995 playoffs] I made my free throws. I can hit 'em. I'm not worried about all that. If people think that's the way it's gonna be, that's a challenge to me. Bring it on."

As far as the mental challenge Jordan had issued him, O'Neal said, "I will never let any man, no matter who it is, try to talk me out of my game. He can say what he wants to say. That's fine. It's a challenge. My time is now, though. My time is now. Not two years from now, not next year. I want it done right now."

O'Neal paused, then he forecast that the Lakers would win the title. "I'm going to send Mike home this year," he said with determination.

At the time it sounded strong, but a little less than a month later O'Neal would suffer the first of two knee injuries that would cause him to miss a total of 30 games. In early February he strained his right knee, causing him to miss the second game against the Bulls and the NBA All-Star game. While O'Neal rested, his teammates managed a 106–90 whipping of the Bulls in the Forum. Then, immediately after the All-Star weekend, O'Neal returned to action in a road game in Minneapolis. There he injured a ligament in his left knee, causing him to miss 28 games.

Suddenly, just as the team had begun to adjust to playing with the big center, it had to shift back to its old identity, built around Campbell on offense and its pressure defense. The situation expanded Kobe's role only slightly. Even so, he had found a means of reaching the spotlight, in snowy Cleveland of all places.

He, Travis Knight, and Derek Fisher had all been invited to play in the rookie game at the NBA's annual winter carnival, the All-Star weekend.

In the past, the All-Star weekend had featured an old-timers' game, but a series of serious injuries had forced the league to drop that event. The need to promote its future stars prompted the NBA to replace the old-timers with a rookie game, East vs. West. What made the 1997 event so special was the fact that the league was celebrating its 50th anniversary that weekend and honoring the game's 50 greatest players over its first half century. The rookie game presented an opportunity for young players to show their stuff before the game's legends, and Kobe took every advantage during the 30-minute exhibition. Philadelphia's Allen Iverson used his quickness to score 19 and led the East team to victory. But Kobe led the charge from the West with 31 points, many of them delivered with his trademark flash.

About an hour after the rookie game he was scheduled to participate in the slam dunk contest. First devised as an attraction during the last ABA All-Star game in 1976, the event had been revised by the NBA in 1984 and was used to showcase some special high flying by Jordan, Dominique Wilkins, and a host of other players. By the late 1990s, however, the event had been able to draw only hungry young players and had lapsed into a sense of sameness season after season. As a result the league had decided to phase it out after the 1997 event. For this last event the league selected an All-Star panel of judges that included Julius Erving, Walt Frazier, and George Gervin. Kobe's sense of the game's history gave him more than a little extra buzz for the event. After the rookie game he kept on his uniform and stayed in the locker room, waiting nervously for the dunking competition to begin. He seemed to welcome the opportunity to answer a few questions to help him pass the time.

I asked him about being a public figure and a role model at his age. "You have to remind yourself at times that you are a role model, that kids are looking up to you whether you want them to or not," he said. "You have to accept that and handle yourself in a professional manner. All I'm doing is just living my dream. If people want to look at that as if I'm a role model and they want to add to my responsibility, that's fine."

I asked if there was any problem adjusting to the 82-game schedule and the seductive atmosphere of the NBA. "A lot of times 18-year-olds," Kobe said, "we have so much energy, we want to go out all the time. In the NBA you have to learn how to manage your time; you have to learn how to rest and take care of that rest. You have to take time out to let your body recuperate.

"With me it's pretty simple," he said earnestly, "because there's a lot I want to accomplish in my life. Particularly in L.A., there are a lot of things that can tempt you. So you just have to keep your mind on your long-term goal and think more objectively. It's really easy for me."

From there Kobe left the room to join a slam dunk field that included Michael Finley of the Dallas Mavericks, Chris Carr of the Minnesota Timberwolves, Bob Sura of the Cleveland Cavaliers, and Darvin Ham of the Denver Nuggets. His nervousness apparent, Bryant barely made the round of four finalists for the event, but from there he trotted out a spectacular finish, good enough to claim the slam dunk trophy. From the left side he attacked the basket, switched the ball between his legs, and whirled in to find the rim, a finish that ignited the building, bringing Dr. J. and the other judges to their feet. Spurred by the outburst, Kobe rushed to centercourt and flexed hotdog style for the judges.

"The crowd got me real pumped up, and I just felt like flexing," he explained later. "I don't have much, but I flexed what I have."

The many eyes on Kobe began to decide that, like Kevin Garnett before him, Bryant had handled well the challenge of coming to pro basketball from high school. The road had been a little more troubled for Portland's Jermaine O'Neal, a seven-footer from South Carolina who had joined Bryant in the '96 draft. O'Neal's experiences in Portland had led to some midseason misgivings about bypassing college, which he later recanted. Fifty-one days younger than Bryant, Jermaine O'Neal said he and the Lakers rookie spoke twice a month by phone. "We've been friends," O'Neal said of Bryant. "But we've gotten even closer since we came into the league. We understand the situation we're in. We talk to each other and let each other know what's going on in each other's lives."

The young players were very aware that they were part of a high-dollar experiment, one that worked by this simple equation: The NBA's owners received $125 million in franchise fees every time they agreed to expand the league. The owners liked that money very much. They wanted to expand frequently, but Commissioner David Stern and others who cared about the game cautioned them about getting too greedy and expanding too quickly because it stretched the talent base too thin, meaning that the quality of play in the league would decline dramatically.

The only way to keep getting those $125 million deals was to expand the talent base. One way to expand the talent base was to lure in European players. The other was to offer big contracts to the best high school and college talent. If more 18-year-olds could be brought into the league, the NBA could expand and the owners could rake in more money.

However, the league could face a big public backlash if it brought in young players who failed dramatically as Skip Wise had failed back in the days of the ABA. So the league set up support and guidance programs for young players to make sure they adjusted to the pro life.

Despite the adjustment of Bryant and others, the circumstances had led CBS college basketball broadcaster Billy Packer to declare that the NBA had become "the enemy" of basketball, a comment that angered league officials.

Packer, however, insisted that the NBA's grab for young players would eventually destroy the quality of the game in both college and the pros.

Utah Jazz president Frank Layden offered this perspective on the tension between pro sports owners and their greed: "They are short range," Layden said of the owners. "They're not concerned with quality. They are concerned with the effective making of money. One owner said to me, 'We are not in the horse racing business.' Guys who own horses are constantly trying to better the breed; they're constantly trying to enhance the sport. In football, basketball, and baseball, no, they are not trying to do that. They don't care. But somehow the game goes on without them and improves."

While nowhere near as great as he had hoped, Kobe's progress was enough to convince others that they, too, would be able to make that jump. That March, 17-year-old high school senior Tracy McGrady announced he would forgo college and make himself available for the draft. A six-foot-nine, 200-pound guard, McGrady said he felt ready to follow Garnett, Kobe, and Jermaine O'Neal.

"I thought it'd be the best decision for me and my family, so I will make myself eligible for the 1997 NBA draft," McGrady said at the press conference announcing his decision in Durham, North Carolina, where he attended a private high school. "I feel like I can do some things like the other young guys." McGrady added that he's a "guy that can handle the ball, run the point, and hit the three . . . somebody possibly like another Penny Hardaway."

McGrady had passed the standardized tests for college admission and had thought of going to Kentucky or Florida State until he got assurances that he would be one of the top players drafted, thus guaranteeing him a contract worth a million or more, although he said the money wasn't his reason for bypassing college.

"My dream is to make it to the top," he said. "And I have a good chance to do that."

Kobe's dream, meanwhile, continued to circle in the holding pattern of rookie purgatory, with Del Harris managing the traffic control tower. Bryant's All-Star splash was good for the sale of his new shoe, the Adidas KB8, but it didn't help him pry much playing time out of his coach.

"You can learn only so much by watching," Kobe, sounding a lot like Jerry West, told a reporter. "You have to get out there and make some mistakes to really grasp what you're trying to do."

"We brought him along a little slowly during the regular season—very slowly, actually—because we had a 50-plus-win team and he did not have training camp and was injured twice," Harris would explain later. "But his progress was gradual and obvious and definite."

Harris's approach, however, seemed absent of logic to Kobe's family and friends. Over the remainder of February and March, he played sporadically. And it seemed that Harris had given up on his plan to use him as a backup point guard. When Van Exel was injured in April, the replacement chores fell to rookie Derek Fisher. Harris clearly didn't trust Kobe's decision making with the ball or his defense.

Yet in the six games that Kobe started at two guard as a rookie, the Lakers were 5–1, and he clearly presented problems for opponents with his ability to score. Although he ranked 11th on the team in minutes played, he was second on the team in offensive production, ranking only behind O'Neal in points scored per minute played. In games where Harris allowed Kobe to play 20 minutes, he averaged 13 points, and if he was given 25 minutes or more, his scoring average jumped to better than 16 points and his field goal percentage went to .500, the kind of numbers that West knew he could produce after watching him work out that day months earlier.

Whenever he went into the game, his ball-handling skills and scoring ability meant that he was going to draw a swarm of defenders. What he did once he drew those defenders was critical to his and his team's success. "It's a lot easier when you have guys like Eddie Jones and Byron and Elden and Shaq around you," he said. "It makes the job a whole lot easier. You just go in there and try to create things, whether it's scoring opportunities for yourself or your teammates."

"I've seen the kid come a long way in a very short time," Byron Scott said. "He understands a lot of things that are going on out there now that he didn't at the beginning of the season."

Finally, over the final weeks of the regular season, Harris let him play a little, and Kobe responded by averaging 11 points per game. Still, it was too little too late in the eyes of Kobe's family and friends. Strangely, Harris chose the playoffs to shove the young rookie into pressure situations with the season on the line. Kobe himself would never complain about the circumstances. He was glad for every opportunity to learn.

But Jeremy Treatman watched the situation unfold and was dumbfounded. "It was almost like Del Harris was setting him up to fail," the writer said. "He hardly played him during the year, then put the ball in his hands with the season on the line."

O'Neal returned from his knee injury April 11 and immediately helped the Lakers to a win over Phoenix, bringing L.A.'s record to 53–25. Three days earlier Kobe had come off the bench against Golden State and scored a career-high 24 points. The late-season playing time had brought a surge in his confidence. Asked to look back on his decision to turn professional, he told a reporter, "I definitely had a lot of fun," he said. "I wouldn't change it for the world."

With O'Neal's return the Lakers won four straight, bringing the regular season down to a final meeting with the Portland Trail Blazers. If the Lakers won, they would claim the Pacific Division title. Jordan's eerie prediction from the start of the season came to pass. The Lakers sent the ball to O'Neal, who was promptly fouled. He could have tied the game with 1.2 seconds to go but missed both free throws. With the loss the Lakers finished at 56–26, their best record in seven seasons.

To prepare for the playoffs and their first-round matchup with Portland, they repaired to the College of the Desert for a minicamp. Asked if Kobe would be a factor in the series, Harris told reporters that the matchups would be difficult for the rookie. The Blazers featured the strong and wily Isaiah Rider at two guard and Cliff Robinson at small forward.

"We'll just have to see," the coach said.

Regardless, Kobe had done "an amazing job, I think," Harris added. "Particularly when you consider that not only did he not have the college experience but he did not have a training camp, and then he had a couple minor injuries that kept him from getting kind of a foundation built. But, throughout the season, he developed his game and came through with some big games for us. Obviously at age 18, he's still in the process of development and will be for some time."

With O'Neal scoring 46 points in Game 1, the Lakers quickly took control of the series against Portland, then did the same thing in Game 2. Kobe played a total of six minutes over the two games, but his team owned a 2–0 lead. In Game 3, with Portland's crowd shoving the Blazers back into contention, the Lakers could find no punch until Harris inserted Bryant. Immediately aggressive, he began driving to the basket and drawing fouls, creating offense for himself and his teammates. On that day he would finish with 22 points, but that wasn't enough to bring the rest of the team alive. Portland won, 98–90 and closed the gap to 2–1 in the series.

His reward for the effort was hardly any playing time in Game 4. Nevertheless, the Blazers had no means of contending with O'Neal and fell by the wayside, 3–1.

The next round brought the veteran Utah Jazz, routinely a tough matchup for the young Lakers, but in their late-season run the Lakers had dispatched the Jazz 100–98 with 39 points from O'Neal. The outcome was enough to give Harris and his staff hope that they could turn the circumstances around in the playoffs. The Jazz, though, wasted little time in dispelling those notions with a 93–77 win in the Delta Center. For Game 2 the Lakers managed to mix their post and perimeter games, with O'Neal scoring 25 and Robert Horry finding his range with seven consecutive 3-pointers. The effort earned the Lakers a shot to win it at the buzzer, but Karl Malone blocked Van Exel's shot for a 103–101 win and a 2–0 series lead.

Game 3 in the Forum brought a Lakers blowout, 104–84, fueled by 17 fourth-quarter points from Kobe. In all he would finish with 19 for the game, the team high. He made 13 of 14 free throws, a tremendous display of poise down the stretch for an 18-year-old.

Unfortunately, the afterglow lasted only briefly. Malone answered furiously in Game 4, scoring 42 points to give his team a 3–1 series lead with the venue returning to Utah. There, in Game 5, the Jazz jumped to an 11-point lead and seemed set to cruise. The Lakers had lost Horry to a third-quarter ejection, weakening their defense. Still, they managed to roll back into contention and even held a 1-point lead with about nine minutes to play. From there the lead shifted back and forth until O'Neal fouled out with just under two minutes to go. Then Utah's John Stockton managed to blow past Kobe for a tying layup.

With the score knotted at 87 with just under a minute left in regulation, the teams went into a final flurry of fruitless possessions. Eddie Jones had a shot blocked; Malone missed a jumper. Then, with 11 seconds to go, Van Exel got a steal, which set up a last possession for Los Angeles. During the ensuing time-out Harris decided that the ball and the shot should go to Kobe. The plan? Spread the floor and let him attack.

Questioned repeatedly about the decision later, the coach explained that Kobe's one-on-one skills made him the best choice to get off a solid shot. "I spent over half of the year being criticized for not playing Kobe," Harris said. "Now I'm getting criticized for playing him."

According to plan, Kobe got the shot, a decent look at the basket from 14 feet, with the defense in his face and the Delta Center crowd pounding down the noise. The building exploded when it fell an air ball. Overtime would only extend his nightmare. With O'Neal out of the game and with an offense that offered little structure or little plan, the Lakers found themselves putting the extra period in Kobe's hands. Each of his three deep air balls goosed the home crowd to delight. The loss sent the Jazz on their way to the conference championship and effectively ended Phase 1 of Kobe Bryant's NBA education.

After the debacle, he sat quietly for a time, composed himself, then answered reporters' questions. Sure it hurt, but he would keep the memory as motivation, he said. "You've got to put it behind you. But, yeah, you have to pull it out at the appropriate time. When it's summertime and you're a little tired, a little down, you're hurting and you don't feel like working out, you pull it out of your memory bank and remember the situation.

"Hopefully, that can give me a little boost."

"He's a young guy, and this is all new to him," Stockton told reporters. "He's played with a lot of confidence in this series, but he was asked to make some tough shots at the end, and he just didn't come up with them."

Already there was word that Kobe planned to take a course in advanced Italian in summer school at UCLA.

Asked what he planned to do with the rest of the time off, Kobe explained that he would proceed to practice.

"I've still got a lot of energy left, man," he said.

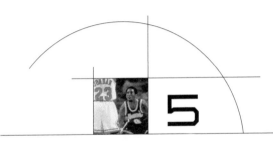

5

THE MIKE ALIKE

> *"Every play, you look at him and you wonder, What's next?"*
>
> —EDDIE JONES

Given the opportunity, Del Harris would have slowed things down for Kobe Bryant's second NBA season, but the playoff embarrassment spurred the player to work even harder over the summer of 1997. His drive surging, Kobe had his foot on the accelerator, pushing every moment to maximum learning opportunity. He burned up the rest of his 18th year doing everything possible to get better. It would soon become clear that at times he went too far.

The effort began with his flight home from Utah after the Lakers' Game 5 exit and his passel of air balls. He sketched out what he planned to do, which would begin early the next morning at Pacific Palisades High, where administrators allowed him to work out on his own schedule. Never mind that the team plane hadn't landed in L.A. until the wee hours, he was up the next morning in the gym, shooting shot after shot, attacking the visualization of his failure, erasing the negative evidence, pushing himself toward a positive mind-set. Then he returned to do it all over again the next day.

He punctuated these efforts with trips to Gold's Gym for sessions with his trainer. The goal was relatively simple: Refine technique, working the muscle memory of each made shot into a granite groove, something so chiseled into his fiber that it would never leave him. Then add strength so that no matter where he was on the floor, he had the power to exercise his will and the muscle to protect himself against injury.

When his body wearied, he shifted to mind work, memorizing Italian for his UCLA summer session or poring over film from the season, studying his team, himself, other teams, other players, looking for a competitive crease, for a place that he could shove his will and make his power grow. He also reviewed his failure at the end of Game 5 at Utah, the 14-foot air ball, and asked himself why he hadn't just gone to the basket and torn the rim down with a jam or forced the Jazz to foul.

"I can beat that buzzer anytime," he told himself. "Gimme the ball in the last 10 seconds; I can wait till decimal time, I'll still hurt you, tick, tick, tick, tick. . . ."

Later, as training camp opened, he would have to view the sequence again. He laughed at it. The only thing that would have hurt, he later told a reporter, is if he had chickened out and passed the ball, if he had not taken that pressure on himself.

"I wanted those shots," he said. "I just didn't make them. If I had it to do over again, put me in the same scenario, I'd take the shots again. I have no problem with that. Regardless of what anybody says."

He knew the great ones wanted the ball at the end of the game. Jordan had set a standard for that. Soon it would become common belief that he wanted to be the next Jordan. That wasn't his goal. Rather, he viewed Jordan's achievements as a landmark on the way to his goal, an imposing landmark but a landmark all the same.

Nick Van Exel later joked about lending Kobe a Jordan highlight videotape. "I gave him a highlight tape of Mike, and I ain't seen it yet. That was last year," Van Exel said, laughing.

Over the first few months of the 1997–98 season it would become clear that Bryant had spent quite a bit of time studying the tape, because he had just about all of Jordan's moves down pat, even the famous post-up gyrations where Jordan would twitch and fake his opponents into madness.

"He's got a lot of 'em," Jordan himself would admit later.

A lot of Lakers fans had come to the same conclusion and wanted to see Harris play him more. So did NBA photographer Andrew Bernstein, who had spent the better part of two decades training his lens on the stardom of Magic Johnson and Michael Jordan.

Bernstein had watched Kobe's difficult rookie year and found himself pulling for Harris to play him. "He had a difficult transition from being this huge, huge phenom out of high school to having to sit on the bench," Bernstein said. "There was a lot of pressure and things written in the paper, pressure for Del Harris to put him in immediately and start him and give him his 30 minutes a game of playing time. I was one of the guys who would have loved to see him in there more."

The reason, Bernstein said, was Kobe's star quality, a special presence before the camera that only a select few NBA players had. Kobe obviously had it, the photographer said. "When he was in there playing, it was like Michael was in there.

"It was amazing with Michael and Magic," the photographer recalled. "You just put them in front of the camera, and that charisma comes out, that charm. Kobe has that, too. He's got that look; he's got that twinkle that Michael had, that Magic had. You can see it on film."

The NBA has to have that Jordanlike star, Bernstein said. "And it's obvious how desperately Kobe wants to be like Michael. He's taken a lot of Michael's game and Michael's mannerisms and sort of adapted them to himself. You can see it when he comes into the basket and he's up in the air and he does his little dipsy-doo. Sometimes he'll react like Michael did when he has a great dunk or he hits three threes in a row. He'll give you that Michael face. It's wonderful."

Like Jordan in his early years, Kobe had made his mistakes, Bernstein admitted. "But you can't keep the guy in a box. You gotta let him out. He has that much talent."

The Lakers coaching staff, however, wanted Kobe's thinking to run in another direction during the 1997 off-season. He was directed to play again for the Lakers team in the L.A. summer league, where he was told to put his focus on improving as a team player and learning where to send the ball when he drew double teams. Larry Drew again coached the team, and Kobe again turned to his instincts, using his superior conditioning to blow past the competition. Neither Drew nor West liked what he saw. On one occasion Kobe crossed words with Drew, who accused him of "playing like the old Kobe." He was still approaching the game in terms of himself, not the team, the assistant coach said.

And West emphasized that the demands were going to be greater with the upcoming season. To help meet those demands, Kobe employed the services of a private shooting coach, who began the process of helping him rebuild his shot. The results were disastrous. When training camp opened in Palm Desert in October, Bryant brought out a stiff and mechanical form, one that sent shots clanging in every direction. The Lakers coaches, stunned to hear that Kobe would think about altering his seamless form, hooted about the results and pushed him back to his old approach.

Privately, though, the Lakers organization was worried. In conversations about Kobe some staff members began to sound a refrain, "He listens to his father too much."

No one seemed to have direct evidence of this, only Kobe's intransigence in the face of their demands to play the team game. Perhaps Joe Bryant was counseling his son contrary to team wishes, but the father had seemed determined to remain in the background. Still, some Lakers staff members had become skeptical despite his friendly manner. It seemed that Joe Bryant had also generated resentment in Philadelphia basketball circles during Kobe's transition to pro basketball. In particular he was said to have fallen out with his old friend and protector Sonny Hill. Their differences began the spring of Kobe's senior year in high school. It was Hill who had helped Joe get the job at LaSalle in the months after his return from Europe. Hill had had him on his radio show and reintroduced him to the Philly basketball community.

But in the spring of 1996, "Joe burned his bridges with LaSalle coach Speedy Morris," explained an associate of the Bryants. Some in the LaSalle basketball office came to believe that instead of doing his duties recruiting for the program, Joe Bryant was spending his time trying to arrange his son's future in pro basketball and to secure a shoe contract for Kobe. As a result, much-needed recruiting work wasn't done. The LaSalle basketball office made repeated attempts over several weeks to contact Bryant, but he failed to return calls.

Feeling partly responsible because he had helped Bryant get the job, Sonny Hill tried phoning Kobe's father and also had trouble getting a return call.

Some time later, Hill was able to get Bryant to phone into his radio show as a guest, the result of which was a very uncomfortable segment in which Hill first questioned and then upbraided Bryant for his behavior.

At least some of those involved in the tightly knit circle of Philadelphia basketball came to the conclusion that his son's success had changed Joe Bryant. In Los Angeles he had not come close to generating any such hard feelings, just a growing suspicion that he was behind Kobe's stance. Others, though, scoffed at such notions.

"You'd never see Kobe's dad at practices," Andrew Bernstein said, "and sometimes he would come on the road to see games, but that was mostly during the playoffs. He was never obtrusive or anything that would be detracting from his game. Just very much in the background. His father is very down to earth and supportive of Kobe, but not to the point of putting him on this huge pedestal."

In Orlando, Shaquille O'Neal's stepfather had done just the opposite, becoming such a pain in the neck that he eventually was ejected from an NBA game for an outburst about officiating. Joe and Pam Bryant may have agonized at the high-profile lessons their son was learning, but the vast majority of their efforts were aimed at counseling him not to get discouraged, to continue working hard, to make every effort to get along.

Kobe would shake his head. "You don't have to tell me those things," he would tell his parents, adding that he knew how to exercise good judgment.

As mysterious as it seemed, Kobe's main reluctance in following the Lakers plan was that he didn't trust Del Harris's offense and was never quite sure what to make of Harris himself. Yet rather than confront him or speak out about the issue, Kobe simply kept working, picking his way along, trying to grow and survive without coming into unnecessary conflict.

Asked later why he didn't say more, why he didn't complain, Kobe confided, "I decided just to leave it alone. He was the coach."

Harris, though, faced increasing questions about his young player. "It causes a rift between us because I'm trying to get him to give up the ball, and he feels that his game is to take on the world," Harris told reporters.

Kobe was aware that he needed to fit better within the team, but his efforts to do that were often frustrated by turnovers. He considered the offense unorganized. The ball usually went first to O'Neal in the post. If the center was impossibly double-teamed (which he often was), he then sent it back out to the perimeter, where things often seemed to break down for the Lakers.

And there was another factor. Like a young Jordan, Kobe always considered himself the best opportunity for his team to score. That mind-set was a product of his confidence and his upbringing. The Lakers staff considered it a habit that needed breaking.

Kobe, however, saw it as much more than a habit. He saw it as the essence of who he was as a basketball player, and that was why he vowed, "I will not let them break me."

Some observers considered this the height of selfishness. Other observers thought back to a young Jordan, fiercely determined to establish his own dominance. Was Kobe that once-in-a-lifetime kind of player? Many of his teammates and several members of the Lakers staff considered such notions narcissistic if not preposterous. For Kobe it was the dream that he was determined to make into reality. He had the talent, and he had the drive, and he was willing to gamble everything to make it happen.

Although few people understood it at the time, because the circumstances gathered momentum so quickly, Kobe Bryant really didn't have much choice. To explain that, Detroit's Grant Hill recalled how former heavyweight champion Larry Holmes had described his own experiences trying to be the next Rocky Marciano. "If you don't do what he did, you're not going to be appreciated for what you've done," Hill recalled. "That's what you have to be careful about. Kobe's a great player and has a great team. But if he doesn't do what Michael does, he's going to be a failure."

For the time being, though, Kobe accepted that his station in life was to come off the Lakers bench and provide scoring whenever it was needed. Harris had given up on the notion of using him as a backup point guard and decided his minutes would come spelling Eddie Jones at the two guard or as a backup to newly signed free agent Rick Fox at the small forward.

Fox had turned down a multiyear offer from the Cleveland Cavaliers for better than $20 million to come to Los Angeles for a one-year, $1 million contract. He did so for two reasons, because he thought the Lakers had an excellent chance of winning a championship and because the team located him near Hollywood to help his young acting career. West liked Fox, a University of North Carolina product, because of his complete skills. He was bulky, but could shoot, pass, defend, rebound, and even work off the dribble a bit. Plus Fox had a little age on him at 28, something the Lakers needed. Their roster boasted the youngest team in the league, with Van Exel and O'Neal at 25, Derek Fisher at 23, and Jones at 26.

Having just turned 19, Kobe was the epitome of the Lakers youth. High-profile. Precocious. Challenging authority in his quiet, determined way. In a culture gone gaga over youth and celebrity and money, Kobe possessed all three in dangerous quantities yet seemed quite capable of coping with them.

"It's nice to finally meet someone younger than me," Tiger Woods, who had faced a similar challenge, had told him upon meeting him in the Lakers locker room the previous season.

Even Kobe's sternest critics were hard-pressed to find examples of his mishandling the circumstances. His Lakers contract had two more seasons to go at about $1.2 million, and his Adidas deal and limited but growing list of endorsements had left him with a fat bank account. The outward signs of this were the finely crafted suits he wore to games and his black BMW 740i. Otherwise, money was something to be left in the bank, something that was to be treated with care and pride, he said.

By and large, though, he was all about basketball.

A constant critic of the NBA, CBS college basketball analyst Billy Packer liked to recite an example he'd heard from a church sermon. There are situations in nature, Packer said, where a butterfly begins to emerge from its cocoon, but the fiber of the cocoon is not strong enough, meaning that the insect can break through the walls without working very hard. As a result the young butterfly fails to develop enough strength to break all the way out of the cocoon. Instead the insect stalls halfway out of the cocoon. Lacking the strength to break all the way out, the young butterfly then drowns in its own mucus, Packer said. He likened the situation to that of college underclassmen and high school players going into the NBA to receive large contracts before they had developed their skills.

Michael Jordan said that he had seen those very circumstances among many of the NBA's new generation of well-paid young players. "I'm concerned that this league can be marketed to be, or misunderstood to be, spoiled kids with a lot of money, with no effort, no motivation, paid off of their potential, never reaching their highest potential because of the spoiling of athletes," Jordan said, adding that the problem stemmed from young players mistaking their wealth for achievement. The achievement comes only after hard work, but many young players fail to see that, he said.

Kobe didn't appear to be one of them. His cautious approach with wealth had begun when he signed the Adidas contract right out of high school. "I hadn't earned it yet," he said, "so I used it as an incentive to work harder."

His parents had not only schooled this approach but were elated to see it. It was hard not to let their pride shine through. "If Kobe wasn't a basketball player, he'd still be successful," Joe Bryant told *Rolling Stone*. "It's not just about his athleticism. It's about his personality and how he handles himself. That's why he's always going to be successful—because we're going to try to separate the two. But if his basketball impact and personality come together, you're talking about a megastar, just out there—Michael Jackson level."

The double entendre of that quote was exactly what concerned some people and spurred some critics. The *New York Times Magazine* published a story about the Bryants that portrayed Kobe as largely unhappy, someone who might become a prisoner of his celebrity and circumstances, much like Michael Jackson. The Bryants and their friends, including Jeremy Treatman, considered the *Times* story a hatchet job that misinterpreted the circumstances.

From all outward appearances at least, Kobe was a picture of 19-year-old wholesomeness. No earrings. No tattoos. No alcohol. No drugs. Just his ambition. It's a good guess that any number of parents across the United States would covet the opportunity to see those circumstances in their own late-teen children. As summer became fall in 1997, Kobe seemed to be quite comfortably settled in his Pacific Palisades home with his parents and his 20-year-old sister, Shaya, who had begun attending Santa Monica City College. His other sister, Sharia, 22, was advancing nicely toward a December graduation from Temple.

One Philadelphia friend described the Bryants as the Brady Bunch, and Joe sought to confirm that, saying that the family enjoyed piling onto a bed to watch a movie together. His new-found wealth meant that it was Kobe who occupied the master bedroom in the house, a status he liked to emphasize with jokes about his parents having to take out the trash.

"He's obviously the star of the family," Andrew Bernstein said, "but he's still one of the three kids. He's still the baby in the family, and they pretty much treat him that way. They're like any other family. His sisters are still his big sisters. And he's still a little brother."

With his living arrangements Kobe decided to bring a Siberian husky puppy into his life and even fancied adding a tiger, an idea he got after meeting Mike Tyson, who had three of the big cats.

Like his relationship with Tyson, few of his acquaintances matured into friendships because of concerns that someone or something might influence his focus on his goal. "My parents raised me to be an individual," he told Bill Plaschke of the *Los Angeles Times* as the 1997–98 season was getting ready to open. "The key to success at anything, I think, is avoiding peer pressure."

Avoiding peer pressure meant avoiding peers, perhaps the greatest price of his drive to master the game. "I'm very selective of who I hang out with and who I let in my inner circle," he explained.

If the circumstances meant that he had to spend time alone, he was certainly secure enough and comfortable enough with himself to do that. His late-night reading list included autobiographies of Arthur Ashe, Michael Johnson, Evander Holyfield, and Jerry Rice, and when he wearied of that he would dial one of his small circle of friends from Philadelphia at midnight, which meant the phone back east would ring at 3:00 A.M. In some conversations he would write rhymes with Anthony Bannister, a high school friend and leader of the spiritual rap group the Cheizaw. Bryant's music name—he called himself Kobe One Kenobe the Eighth—had *Star Wars* origins. The group, of which Kobe was supposedly a member, even recorded a single during Kobe's first year with the Lakers, although he decided to hold off on releasing it, just as he decided to hold off on a book with Treatman.

"I blitz through offensive lines, sack your rhyme, blindside your mind, intercepting your dime, I cock with a deep breath, the game ends in sudden death, Hollow tips for field goals to end the context," read one set of Kobe's lyrics.

He and Bannister would usually close their phone conversations by praying together.

Even though his clean living remained a constant, Kobe was changing dramatically during those days leading into his second season. For starters, he had added another inch in height, sprouting to six-foot-seven over the course of his rookie season, and his training had pushed his weight up another 10 pounds. Then there was the new hair, a sign that like many youths he was searching for an identity.

"Look at me," he told a reporter as the season opened. "I have hair now." And facial fuzz.

"When I came to the Lakers last year, I wanted to get a clean start," he said of the shaved dome he had sported as a rookie. "But this year, this is me."

Although he spoke little to his teammates, Kobe accepted the fact that Fox would start in front of him and set his mind on doing everything he could to help the team coming off the bench. Mainly he made it his mission to score and score some more, the only problem being that O'Neal was the Lakers weapon of choice. The center led the league in the number of shots per minute played. Jordan was second in that category. Harris was stunned to discover that Kobe, his team's sixth man, held the third spot.

And if Harris had graded each of those shots for style, Kobe might well have ruled the league. Every breakaway seemed to carry the potential for a spiraling slam. Every trip through traffic brought a nifty shifting of the ball from hand to hand, the eyebrows arched in anticipation, the lower jaw sagging as he instantaneously measured distance and float time to the rim. In a preseason contest with the newly renamed Washington

Wizards, Kobe showed his defender a crossover dribble and found room enough to launch his dunk attempt just past the foul line. Washington's Ben Wallace, a muscular six-foot-nine, stepped in to provide help defense, but Kobe somehow rose over him, like a Piper Cub clearing a water tower, and got to the goal for a dunk. "He jumped right the f—— over him!" one Lakers staff member recalled.

"I would pay money just to watch Kobe play for 10 seconds," Eddie Jones said, adding that he would want the 10 seconds to come at the end of every quarter. "Because you know he's getting the ball. And you know he's doing something with it."

"People talk about him being the next Jordan," Shawn Kemp said of Kobe. "But when you see him dunking on people or flying through the air, that's not Michael. That's Kobe doing that. No one else."

His air shows became such a routine feature of Lakers practice that his teammates would often stop and ask themselves, Did I just see what I think I saw?

Blastoff

The regular-season schedule opened with the Lakers entertaining Utah and Kobe entertaining the crowd. He scored 23 in a confidence-boosting win. But he didn't play up to Harris's team standards in the next two games, both wins. It wasn't until the fourth game, yet another win, that he broke out again with 25 points against Golden State. A late ankle sprain kept him out of action for a three-game road trip to Texas, where the Lakers racked up three more wins, bringing their start to seven straight victories. Kobe returned for a romp over Vancouver, then put the exclamation mark on the month in his team's first visit back to Utah since the playoff debacle.

This time he blocked a 3-point attempt by Utah's Bryon Russell in the closing seconds and sailed in for the clinching dunk. With that the Lakers were 9–0 and Kobe was the talk of NBA players and executives, a buzz that sizzled among the local media in every city the Lakers visited as Thanksgiving came and went and November gave way to December.

"I don't want to sound blasphemous," Kings director of player personnel Jerry Reynolds told reporters, "but he really can be like Jordan."

"He's not a kid anymore," an ecstatic Harris had said after the Utah win.

The Lakers had run their record to 11–0 when O'Neal pulled an abdominal muscle against the Clippers, an injury so painful that it would keep him out for weeks. Suddenly the team needed Kobe's scoring even more, and he was happy to oblige, upping his average to better than 19 a game, big numbers for a nonstarter. The Lakers, though, saw a dip in their fortunes as they adjusted to O'Neal's absence. Their 11–0 start soon sagged to 15–5. It was obvious that Kobe was too aggressive many times, too far away from team concepts. "I don't think he's aiming for triple-doubles yet," Rick Fox told reporters in reference to Kobe's paucity of assists. "He definitely sees himself as a scorer. His mark on the court, as he sees it, is giving [his team] 30 points in 20 minutes and then walking off with the win."

Kobe realized that vision of himself on December 12, scoring 27 in a win over Houston, followed by 30 points, his career high, against Dallas two days later.

Looming on the schedule was a road trip to the Midwest and a matchup with Jordan, a development that sent a tingle through the Bryant family and boosted the buzz about Kobe into a small-scale media frenzy. The matchup attracted reporters from virtually every magazine and news show, all of them sensing some sort of coronation.

Next?

Over the years Jordan had entertained a succession of young players touted as the next apparition of his greatness. The media heralded the coming of one after another until the role itself took on a name—"Heir Jordan." As the original rebuffed each and every one of the imitators and successors year after year, the process took on a strange feel, sort of like a convention of Elvis impersonators in Vegas.

Still, from its earliest days the NBA had been a business that survived on star power. Even before the Jordan era there had been a mentality of "Who's next?" As Jordan neared the end of his magnificent career, that question only intensified.

In the early 1990s Southern Cal's Harold Miner had the sad misfortune of being labeled the "Baby Jordan" and believing it. Grant Hill, too, labored under the hype as a Detroit Pistons rookie in 1994, although time revealed he was a player more along the lines of Scottie Pippen. Jerry Stackhouse followed Hill into this mire of embarrassment in 1996, and in December 1997 it was Kobe Bryant's turn.

"It's every year," Hill said of the phenomenon. "There will be another one next year. It's part of it, the hype."

This time around, though, Jordan himself did a double take at the similarities. Chicago reporters noted that Kobe even had the demeanor of a young Jordan in his interview mannerism. But the real comparisons came from Bryant's game itself. Not the defense, and certainly not the competitive maturity. But the offensive moves were another story.

How would Bryant do matched up against Jordan? That question offered a bit of comic relief to a Bulls team laboring to win games with All-Star Scottie Pippen out after foot surgery and feuding with the team's management. The real issue for the Bulls was their difficulty scoring. The Lakers were a young, athletic team that flaunted a wicked running attack.

The Bulls, meanwhile, still lacked the transition game that Pippen's defense brought them. As a result Chicago had struggled over the first six weeks of the season, getting few easy baskets and few easy wins.

Then, just before the Lakers arrived, Chicago got a preliminary test against another running team, the Phoenix Suns, and promptly whipped them in the United Center, one of the first signs the Bulls had begun to find a way to adjust to life without Pippen. It was obvious they would never get near championship level without the star forward, but they could still compete.

The Lakers made that discovery just moments into their meeting with Chicago. Van Exel admitted there was a certain look in Jordan's eyes that told them the contest would be decided early. Indeed the Bulls controlled the tempo, established a limited transition game, and iced the Lakers by the end of the first quarter, which was fine with the United Center fans, because it meant they could sit back and watch the individual duel between Jordan and Bryant.

"Michael loves this stuff," Bulls guard Ron Harper said of the meeting between the two. It was a scenario that Harper knew well. As a young, high-flying star for the Cleveland Cavaliers in the late 1980s, Harper was considered an early Jordan heir until a knee injury forced him to remake his game. "[Bryant] is a very young player who someday may take his throne," Harper said, "but I don't think Michael's ready to give up his throne yet. He came out to show everybody that he's Air Jordan still."

While the outcome was a 20-point win for the Bulls, the contest between master and student generated a few sparks. Jordan scored 36, and Bryant produced a career-high 33. It was a night for highlight clips with both players dancing in the post, draining jumpers from the perimeter, and weaving their way to handsome dunks. "I had that same type of vibrancy when I was young," Jordan told reporters afterward. "It's exciting to match wits against physical skills, knowing that I've been around the game long enough that if I have to guard a Kobe Bryant . . . I can still hold my own."

Jordan did attempt to show restraint. "It was a challenge because of the hype," he said, "but it's also a challenge not to get caught up in the hype, not to make it a one-on-one competition between me and Kobe. I felt a couple of times that it felt like that, but I had to refrain from that, especially when he scored on me. I felt a natural tendency to want to go back down to the other end and score on him. . . .

"It's a natural thing to want to get back at him. But you can't. It takes a lot of discipline not to get caught up in that individuality of our games. You stick close to the system, and you think team first and try to do your job."

It was especially fun for Jordan because the Lakers showed a disinclination to double-team him. "The urges were there tonight," he admitted. "Mentally I think I'm tough enough to take on those challenges because I know so much about the game and I can make the adjustments. I feel if they're not going to double-team me then I have the advantage. Defensively I just have to get used to playing against a player who has skills similar to mine. I try to pick a weakness and exploit it."

Bryant's specific weakness was his defense, no surprise considering his age and experience, Jordan said.

"It's definitely a lot of fun playing against Michael," Bryant countered. "I just accept challenges. I want to guard Mike. If he goes around you, he goes around you."

If nothing else, the circumstances revealed that Bryant possessed certain Jordanlike qualities, namely aggressiveness. The observations sounded hauntingly like Bulls coaches talking about Jordan in 1985–86. Jordan, though, came to the NBA after three years of undergraduate study under Dean Smith at North Carolina.

Jordan himself admitted to being a bit awed by the aerial talent on display. His Airness confided, "I asked Scottie Pippen, 'Did we used to jump like that? I don't remember that.' He said, 'I think we did, but it's so long ago I can't remember it.'"

The situation left Jordan feeling a little like he had been forced to play defense against himself. "I felt like I was in the same shoes of some of the other players I've faced," Jordan explained. "He certainly showed signs that he can be a force whenever he's in the game. He has a lot of different looks. As an offensive player you want to give a lot of different looks so that the defense is always guessing."

Jordan pointed out that just like himself as a young talented player, Bryant had to learn to make sure that his "taking over" didn't take away from team effort.

"Man, that's the hardest part about ball," Bryant agreed, saying that the urge to challenge Jordan individually was gigantic. He admitted that the power to score was something he had to learn to control. "You have to just hold it back sometimes," he said. "It's so maddening. I just read how the defenses are playing me. Right now, they're playing me for the jump shot. They don't want me driving to the basket."

Going to the hole was obviously his delight, and like Jordan, he seemed fearless, despite that fact that Bryant learned the hard way about the injury time that comes from getting slammed while trying to jam.

"You just gotta go hard," Bryant said. "I look forward to that. I learned my lesson on that last year in the first couple of games. Went to the rack, landed on my back, and was out. I pretty much learned how to take it to 'em, jumping into their chest, not trying to avoid contact. That's when you get hurt."

"As a rookie he had the chance to kind of grow up a little bit," Larry Drew said. "It was a tough year for him last year, but he handled it well. He's got that one year under his belt. There was a little bit of maturity that goes along with that. He got to see what the whole NBA life was about. He made a good adjustment. He's not surprised by many things anymore. And I try to stay in his ear as much as I can about things that happen out on the floor.

"He absorbs it, and he very much wants to learn. That's what makes this kid unique. He's always willing to learn."

Indeed, in the fourth quarter of his game against Jordan, Bryant stopped the Chicago star to ask a question about posting up.

"He asked me about my post-up move, in terms of 'Do you keep your legs wide? Or do you keep your legs tight?'" Jordan said. "It was kind of shocking. I felt like an old guy when he asked me that.

"I told him on the offensive end you always try to feel and see where the defensive player is. In the postup on my turnaround jump shot, I always use my legs to feel where the defense is playing so I can react to the defense."

Jordan added that Bryant's biggest challenge would be "harnessing what he knows and utilizing what he's got and implementing it on the floor. That's tough. That's experience. Those are things that Larry Bird and Magic Johnson all taught me. There's no doubt that he has the skills to take over a basketball game."

Bryant said his answer to Jordan was to "try to play my heart out. Michael loves challenges. He loves to answer the bell. But at the same time, my father always taught me growing up that you never back down to no man, no matter how great of a basketball player he is. If he's fired up, you get fired up. You go out there, and you go skill for skill and you go blow for blow."

In fact Joe Bryant made a special trip to Chicago to see his son take on Jordan and was elated afterward. "Good game," the father told the son with a smile.

"He said it was exciting," Kobe revealed later. "My cousins were watching it on TV. They know I'm not scared. They know I won't back down. I'm just going to keep going and keep going."

Given Bryant's abilities, Jordan quipped that the next time instructional questions came up in the middle of a game he would charge Bryant for the lessons.

"That just comes from competitiveness," Bryant explained about asking Jordan for the tips. "You want to learn as much as you can. He told me a lot of things. I'll use them."

What else did he learn from his first major encounter with Michael?

"He does a great job of initiating the offense, making the proper cuts, getting his teammates open, whether it was with back picks or moving without the ball," Bryant said of Jordan. "Even when he doesn't have the ball, he makes himself visible, makes himself a threat, allowing guys like Luc Longley and Steve Kerr to get open. Those are the things that I learned from him, how to be a threat without the basketball."

Chicago reporters were amazed at how nonchalant Bryant was about the media attention. His calm before the cameras and microphones suggested maturity. "Everything that comes along," Bryant said, "the media attention and things of that nature, you just put it in perspective by understanding what got you to that point. That's hard work. That's the game itself. Pressure? There is no pressure."

The comparisons to Jordan he seemed to take in stride. "It doesn't matter to me. When Doc came out," Bryant said of Julius Erving, "people compared him to Elgin Baylor. When Michael came out, people compared him to Doc. People are gonna make comparisons. I just go ahead and play. Sometimes the competitiveness surges, and I just wanna go and take over the game. But I just have to relax, because we have so many weapons."

Perhaps the main lesson for Bryant was that the little things add up. In the second period, Jordan caught the young Laker off balance, went up for a jumper, and drew the foul. It was a classic case of the veteran schooling the understudy. But Bryant went right back at him.

"That's the whole purpose of the game," Kobe said. "If somebody scores on you, you go right back at 'em and try to make 'em work back down on the other end. Michael's just another basketball player. But he's the top basketball player.

"Obviously when he comes into the game, you want to play your hardest against him. You want to play your best against him. When he makes comments and comes into the game and you're guarding him, you just have to answer the bell. That's the ultimate challenge. I relish that.

"He's a very smart competitor," Bryant said of Jordan. "I could tell that he thinks the game, whether it's the tactical things or little strategies he employs on the court. I'm checking him out and analyzing him so that I can do the same thing. But he's just better at it, because he's been doing it a while. He's very smart, very technical. You just don't naturally acquire that. You can go into the NBA and be in the league awhile and play games, but if you try to learn and really push yourself to learn the game, not just from a physical standpoint but from a mental standpoint . . ."

Bryant paused at that thought. "When you have the talent to go along with that," he said, "that's what you call the whole package."

Unless, of course, your coaches want to rewrap that package. Then your endeavor becomes a lonely process. Of his entire experience playing against Jordan, the most important thing was the insistent advice from the great one. Stay aggressive. You've got to stay aggressive, Jordan told him.

Those few words were just enough to help Kobe hold on in his battle not to be broken. In the lean times ahead he would harbor them like jewels.

Frenzy

It's strange the way stories gather momentum on the media agenda. Buzz begets headlines, which beget more headlines, which beget TV feature packages, which beget magazine cover stories, which beget a bubbling pot of interest. In Kobe's case the whole situation begat All-Star votes.

The heart of it all began with the opinion within the buzz. Dennis Scott, then playing for the Dallas Mavericks, had told reporters that within a matter of a couple of years Kobe "could be the man of this league."

Scottie Pippen agreed, saying "The more you watch him and see some of the spectacular things he can do, you realize how great a player he is. You have to sit back and say, 'He's only [the equivalent of] a sophomore in college.' He's going to turn out to be a great pro."

Hundreds of thousands of fans agreed with that assessment as the votes for the All-Star game stacked up in the final days of December. It would prove to be an unprecedented response, with fans choosing a 19-year-old substitute as an All-Star starter. With their votes the fans said they preferred Kobe's potential to the accomplishments of a whole range of established veterans, including Sacramento's Mitch Richmond, Utah's Jeff Hornacek, Portland's Isaiah Rider, Seattle's Hersey Hawkins, Houston's Clyde Drexler, Dallas's Michael Finley, and the player who started in front of Bryant on the Lakers, Eddie Jones. Before Kobe's election to the game, the youngest All-Star starter in league history had been a 20-year-old Magic Johnson.

Clearly it helped Kobe's cause that the Lakers were a team afire, even without O'Neal. Coming out of the Chicago loss, L.A. won four straight with Kobe leading the team twice in scoring with 19 points. After a loss to the Celtics, the Lakers ripped through another streak of five wins against one loss. By the first of January, O'Neal had returned, sending Kobe back down the Lakers list of offensive priorities. Regardless, they rolled through January at a 9–4 pace with O'Neal averaging 29 points a game and earning NBA Player of the Month honors. That momentum brought them right up to February and a Forum visit from Jordan and his Bulls.

The good news was that the Lakers won this time, even with Jordan scoring 31 to Kobe's 20. He had virtually hyperventilated in anticipation and failed to play well, despite the fact that the Lakers needed him with both Van Exel and Horry out with injuries. Eager to please, he found himself serving up bad shots instead. "In the first half of that game, I let my emotions dictate the tempo of my play," Kobe would admit later. "I played with my emotions and not my head. That's something I didn't want to do."

Instead, L.A. used 25 points from Fox to help power a third-quarter blitz that the Bulls couldn't contain. Blue from his early ineffectiveness, Kobe went home to find his family celebrating the victory. "They had just beat the Bulls," Joe Bryant recalled, "and he came home and everyone was happy. And Kobe's response was 'Michael was using my own guys to pick me off.' He's always trying to learn from the experience. What he can become is scary."

Once the Western Conference coaches had decided on the substitutes, the Lakers found themselves with four All-Star representatives, with Van Exel, Jones, and O'Neal joining Bryant on the roster.

Reporters asked Harris if Kobe would be ready to meet the competition at the All-Star game in New York. "You're going to find out soon enough," the coach replied. "I have total confidence in Kobe Bryant that he will not embarrass himself. All I can tell you is he will play well in the All-Star game. There won't be any second-guessing."

Held at New York's Madison Square Garden, the 48th NBA All-Star game opened its publicity assault by drawing hundreds of media representatives from around the world to a hotel ballroom for the opening interview sessions on Friday afternoon. Each All-Star player was positioned at a table around the massive ballroom, but it was Kobe's table that immediately attracted a major throng of reporters, all squeezing in around him to videotape or record his comments.

"Kobe has taken the league by storm," Orlando's Anfernee Hardaway said as he watched reporters crowding around the Bryant table.

"All this is incredible," Kobe said into the bank of microphones in his face. "My body's numb. My heart's racing. I don't know what to think. It's cool."

Asked to compare himself and Jordan, he replied, "There aren't any similarities, other than we're both six-six and we rely on athletic ability. I mean, he's Michael Jordan."

Just outside the gathering, Joe Bryant spoke to a smaller group of reporters. "I don't think his work is over," he said of his son. "There's still a lot to achieve. And the thing is, he knows it's out there and wants to go after it."

It seemed as if overnight Kobe's image was everywhere. In full-page newspaper ads promoting the All-Star weekend and its broadcast events. On magazine covers and international news feeds. On cable sports shows.

Then, on Sunday morning before the game, he appeared on "Meet the Press" with NBA commissioner David Stern and other players. And later, when NBC broadcast a promotion for an upcoming Lakers/Rockets game, it was Kobe's image, not O'Neal's, that got top billing.

Watching the swirl of Bryant mania, Detroit's Grant Hill shook his head. "It makes you mature fast," he said. "It's good, but it's also a curse."

In retrospect it would clearly be viewed as a Cinderella moment. "I'm a little sad because it's over," Kobe would say afterward, sensing the stroke of midnight. Later he would look back and prize his role in what appeared to be Jordan's last All-Star game, which proved to be quite a show while it lasted.

Starting the game matched up against Jordan, Kobe flashed his creativity with an array of first-quarter aerials that included a 360-degree slam and an alley-oop dunk on back-to-back possessions. Jordan replied with a pair of fallaway jumpers, one of which caught Kobe in a fake and earned an added free throw.

"I came down being aggressive," Bryant told the assembly of reporters afterward. "He came back at me being aggressive. That's what it's all about. All I want to do is get a hand up, try to play him hard, try different tactics on him, see how he tries to get around me. I can use it for my knowledge in the future. He hit those two turnarounds. I was like 'Cool, let's get it on.' "

Bryant's enthusiasm for the individual matchup, however, was not something that pleased Seattle coach George Karl, who was in charge of the West team. In particular it was the third period that seemed to inflame his vexation. On one possession with about four minutes to go in the quarter, Kobe led a fast break and decided to finish on his own, first hiding the ball behind his back with his left hand, then bringing it out for a falling-down hook that dropped in as he tumbled to the baseline. The crowd exploded in delight, but Karl frowned on the bench.

Kobe also left Karl Malone fussing by motioning him off when the Utah veteran stepped up to set a screen. " 'I got it,' " Malone, shaking his head in disgust, later quoted Kobe as saying. Caught up in the fun of the moment, Kobe would later be stunned by Malone's comments and the ensuing media commentary. "I probably waved him off, but I really don't remember the play," Bryant explained later. "But it probably happened. I'm sure Karl isn't going to lie about something like that."

Also in that third period Bryant dropped in a 3-pointer to pull the West within 12 points. At the end of the quarter the East held a 101–91 edge. In the personal showdown Jordan had 17 points, 3 rebounds, and 4 assists in 24 minutes. Kobe's numbers were 18 points, 6 rebounds, and 1 assist in 22 minutes. It was Karl, however, who promptly ended the battle by benching Kobe for the entire fourth period while Jordan continued playing to claim game MVP honors with 23 points, 6 rebounds, 8 assists, and 2 turnovers, all good enough to propel the East to a 135–114 victory. After the game Kobe walked over to give Jordan a congratulatory hug.

"I didn't come out here to win the MVP, actually," Jordan, who had been battling a flulike head cold, told the media. "I just wanted to make sure Kobe didn't dominate me. The hype was me against him. I knew I wasn't feeling 100 percent because I've been in bed for three days. He was just biting at the bit. I'm glad I was able to fight him off."

Later some West veterans expressed surprise that Karl kept Kobe out of the game, and one even wondered if the decision wasn't a function of Jordan's and Karl's University of North Carolina connection and the closeness they shared. Others pointed out that Karl was known for using the All-Star setting to teach young players a lesson. In 1994 the Seattle coach had sent a swarming defense at Shaquille O'Neal, then playing for the East, to prevent him from having an impact on the game. Such a defensive effort was highly unusual for the All-Star game, and it left O'Neal fuming.

Asked about his decision to bench Kobe, Karl explained, "An All-Star game is a mix of excitement, entertainment, and fundamentals. I thought we tried to be too entertaining. The East made good basketball decisions and shot well. If it had been close at the end, Shaq and Gary [Payton] and Kobe probably would have been in the game."

Of the Bryant-Jordan matchup, Karl said, "I have trouble visualizing an individual challenge. It's a team game. Kobe made some great plays, but Michael and the East made better basketball decisions. Kobe will probably have the opportunity to come back here and add more 'simple' to what he's doing."

It was as if Karl and Del Harris were of one mind.

"It's tradition," Kobe responded, masking his disappointment. "You let the veterans go in and do their thing. I was kind of happy. I just wanted to sit back, observe the whole thing, and soak it all up. This is the most fun I've ever had—

Michael Jordan, my first All-Star game in New York City. This might be his last All-Star game. That made it incredible."

"It was a 25-point blowout," Karl said. "I felt it was much more important to reward everybody than to focus on an individual situation."

"I think Jerry West was happy," Bryant said, hinting at his frustration with the Lakers organization. "I got a chance [in the fourth] quarter to sit back and relax and be ready for the rest of the season."

Seeking to soften his chastising efforts, Karl said of Kobe, "There was a lot I liked about him in my short period of time with him. When you talk to him, he seems to listen. He seems to want to learn. He seems to want to hear about experiences and situations that could help him. If he keeps that attitude, he then will continue to go forward and prosper."

"I think it's a little bit unfair to Kobe," Cleveland's Shawn Kemp remarked. "What happens is, you have a young guy that comes into this league, and people start comparing him to Michael. When he doesn't perform to that level, time after time, then they start to discredit him as an athlete and as a person. So if I were Kobe, I'd just try to stick to my main game plan and worry about myself, my own game, and not worry about Michael."

Harsh Lessons

The dark clouds wasted no time in descending on Bryant's career after the All-Star weekend. The excitement and non-stop media interviews had left him exhausted, but there was no time for rest. The Lakers first game after the break was in Portland, and Eddie Jones was out with the flu, meaning that Kobe would get his first and only start of the season. The Lakers immediately fell into a hole, then battled back to within 4 at halftime, only to see Portland open the third quarter with a 20–4 run to take a 78–59 lead. From there the Trail Blazers stretched their advantage to 104–75 with about 8 minutes left in the game. Then Kobe, who had struggled much of the game, came alive with 10 points to lead a 28–4 Laker spurt, to pull within 108–103 with 2:28 remaining. The Blazers, though, pushed on from there to win 117 to 105.

Although Kobe finished with 17, Harris was incensed at what he considered selfish play and poor defense against Portland's Isaiah Rider, who scored 24.

Two nights later, back in Los Angeles, Jones remained ill, but Harris chose to start little-used Jon Barry rather than Kobe. Owner Jerry Buss appeared to be infuriated by the move and had heated words with Harris in front of reporters after the game, but the message got through clearly to Kobe. The coaching staff and his teammates were ready to "show him" that he needed to be brought back down to earth after his All-Star experience. Although he downplayed his feelings publicly, the circumstances only deepened Kobe's sense of alienation and resentment, feelings that threatened long-term repercussions for everyone involved with the Lakers. "I don't start him," Harris said in explaining his approach, "and I take him out when he doesn't play team ball. Everybody everywhere wants to see him play more. He will when he's more effective on a full-time basis. Everybody should be on the same standard. You have to play team basketball."

Beyond that, opponents began showing him extra defensive attention, leaving him feeling as if the entire NBA was coming down on him at once. "Early in the season, if I got by one guy, I was free," Kobe explained. "Not anymore."

Not surprisingly, the team as a whole also spiraled into trouble, losing seven out of the first dozen games on the schedule after the break. After the loss to the Blazers came disappointments against the Sonics, the Houston Rockets, and the Phoenix Suns. To make matters worse, on February 18 Van Exel was sidelined by a knee injury that required surgery.

Officially Kobe became the backup at both guard positions. But his seemingly unshakable confidence began to quiver. Soon he began talking about "hitting the wall," the NBA term for when young players reach a level of physical, mental, and emotional exhaustion. In one stretch he made just 30 of 100 shots, setting in motion what *Sports Illustrated* described as "the first rumblings of an anti-Kobe backlash."

The end of that February brought the Lakers an East Coast road trip in which he shot terribly, shooting 3 for 12, 1 for 8, 4 for 12, and 4 for 15 from the field through one four-game run. "This is the toughest stretch I've ever gone through," he said at the time. "I'm hating it, but I'm loving it. It's part of the challenge; it's part of the fun. Am I pressing? Maybe. That's something I'll have to think about. I want to go through periods when I'm struggling, because that's when you learn, and the more you learn, the better you get."

Yet even his optimism irritated teammates. O'Neal, in particular, continued to point out that he wanted to win a championship immediately and didn't have time to wait on Kobe to grow up. In a dozen different small ways, the Lakers season quickly fell into a finger-pointing session. Soon the L.A. papers were running stories that the players had met and voted 12–0 to ask that Harris be fired. The team downplayed those reports, but on its East Coast trip it had the look of a group about to come apart at the seams.

"I think he's a good coach," Robert Horry told reporters. "I think he knows what he's doing."

Few others spoke out in his support, and the team trudged through their eastern trip obviously frayed by the controversy. Especially rude was Kobe's return to Madison Square Garden, the scene of his All-Star spectacle. This time, the Garden fans rode him mercilessly and cheered rowdily with each of his misses on the way to 4-of-15 shooting. One young fan, however, did sport a sign asking, "Kobe, will U marry me after you move out of your mom's house?"

Once again Kobe had played poorly, and once again Harris cited the All-Star experience as the cause. "I felt like the NBA and NBC used him to his detriment," the coach said. "He was a willing participant, but when he came back he was more one-on-one oriented."

His shooting percentage alone had dropped to 34 percent, down from 45 percent before the outpouring of hype. With his decline in effectiveness, his playing time also fell. And his scoring average dropped to 14 per game. Even so, Jordan's words remained strong in Kobe's mind, and he was determined to find a way to meet the demands of his coaches while pursuing his offensive ideal. "It's important to tone it down somewhat and stay within the team concept," he said. "But I'm aggressive. It's also important not to lose the aggressiveness."

Even he acknowledged that the All-Star experience was proving problematic. "I wanted eventually to be one of the best players in the league," he said. "I just didn't know that other people would urge me to be that right now. Everybody's expecting me to be the next Michael. I thought I was going to sneak through the back door. Now I'll have to go about it a different way."

Kobe was bothered by an ear/throat infection, so the team sent him to a doctor, then allowed him to ride a train to Washington for the last game of the road trip.

Washington's Rod Strickland and Chris Webber took advantage of the Lakers defensive confusion to hurt them with the pick and roll, and even though Kobe and his teammates were able to attack in transition they fumbled away opportunity after opportunity and lost yet again.

Harris had decided Bryant was trying to revert back to his

flashy All-Star play and pulled him. On that night he played 12 minutes and scored four points.

Afterward Harris was ready with a prescription for how to end his misery. "What I think Kobe has to do if he wishes to be considered one of the outstanding players in the league is to use his skills to help make other players better—that's to draw the defense and then give the ball up," the coach said. "And he hasn't quite caught on as to how to do that all that well yet. I thought he was making really good progress before the All-Star break. For a time he was going two assists to one turnover. Now that he has to play some point guard, it's even more important that he use his passing skills more. He's very intelligent, and he has immense ball-handling skills. That's all that it requires."

What was even more impressive, Harris said, was that while most players struggle to learn their one position, Kobe knew the plays for all five positions on the floor. Considering the myriad number of plays Harris had for his team, that was quite an accomplishment. "He's one of the brightest," the coach added. "I'm not surprised at anything I see from him. I am concerned that it has taken him a little bit of time here to see that he can make people better. He hasn't quite caught on to that concept. It took Michael probably two or three years. But Kobe's so bright. I know he can see it. If he would just accept it. That's what it takes to be an outstanding player. Right now the defense falls right to him when he starts to make his move, because they think he's gonna shoot it every time. It's a great opportunity to give the ball up and make other players better. Then that makes the next possession down the road easier for himself."

Kobe was only making life hard for himself by pushing so hard for greatness, Harris said. "You can't be great at anything, whether it's writing or singing or sculpting or playing basketball, in a year or two. It takes a long time."

Normally Kobe loved the idea of having the ball in his hands and dictating the Lakers attack, but Harris's insistence left him approaching the task of playing point guard with a measure of dread. "You just have to go up there and make sure we get into a set offense every play," he said. "You think for five people instead of one. When I check into a game, the first thing I try to do is get Eddie going. Because when Eddie gets going and starts getting his rhythm, then everything for the team gets going. So that's my main objective."

He thought the team lacked a fundamental system in its approach to offense, and he had asked Harris to consider some changes. But he was resigned to the fact that even if Harris did agree to make changes they couldn't be done in the middle of the season. Rather, any real restructuring of the Lakers attack would have to begin with the next season. Which meant that he realized more turbulence lay ahead. "I'm in this for the long run," he told me. "I'm patient, but I'm not patient. I'm willing to make mistakes. I'm willing to go through stretches like this. You go through stretches like this on every level you play the game, whether it's middle school or high school or whatever. There's certain times where you're struggling while teams are adjusting to you. Now it's time for you to make a response, to adjust to them. It's the same thing that happened to me in high school. I'm going to fight through it. I'm not going to break."

The Letter

Probably the most accurate assessment of Kobe Bryant's second NBA season could have been measured in Jerry West's stomach acid. Earlier in the campaign the team's guardian had negotiated to trade Eddie Jones to the Sacramento Kings for Mitch Richmond, a powerful two guard with a polished veteran game, the idea being that Richmond provided just the type of tough leadership and scoring that the young club needed. But Jerry Buss nixed the deal, pointing out that Richmond would soon be 34 and needing an expensive new contract.

Buss's decision was a bitter defeat for West, and as the season wore on and began to unravel he spent late nights agonizing at his Pacific Palisades floor, eating his heart out over every detail of the season. He even went so far as announcing that he would step down as executive vice president by the end of the 1999 season. Sensing a coming transition, Buss began sending his son, Jim, on scouting missions with West and GM Mitch Kupchak.

Like many sports executives and their owners, West and Buss had always managed to survive the thorny aspects of their relationship. But as time wore on, it was clear that they shared many thorns and few roses. West thought he had Kupchak, a solid basketball mind, in place to groom as his successor, but the increasing presence of Jim Buss left him with the fear that a nonbasketball executive could be poised to take over. West loved the game and loved the Lakers too much to see that happen.

As the playoffs approached, reporters speculated about his future, and West put them off by saying he wouldn't make a decision until August. "I want to get myself calmed down," he told them, "where I don't have to worry about wins and losses, where I don't have to worry about injuries. Let somebody else worry about that."

If the timing didn't seem right, the circumstances certainly did. The Lakers talented but temperamental young roster was clearly high maintenance, so high that he had wearied from untangling their complaints about Harris and about each other. The game was simple enough, but they were all making it so complicated. He wanted to tell them "to not make the super play but the smart play. Not make the home run but hit a single. Make one pass that will lead to another pass that will lead to a basket instead of making one pass and a shot. Simple little things."

"I've had a number of players—and they were all young— say 'I want to win an NBA championship,'" West confided to a reporter, "and I asked them, 'Do you know how difficult it is to win an NBA championship?'"

Clearly, as February became a chamber of horrors, these young players hadn't the slightest clue how to win. And West began to suspect that neither did Harris, at least not with this group.

"Talent and character win in this league; effort doesn't always win," he confided to *Los Angeles* magazine. "We win games sometimes when we're simply more talented. What I would like to see is for us to grow up more, become more professional in our approach to the game. And if there's some way you could give someone a pill to give them six or seven years of experience in the league . . ."

Wanting to tell them these things, he composed a letter to his young Lakers and delivered it to them soon after they returned in the early days of March from their trip East.

"Each of you is on the verge of letting this season slip right through your fingers," he wrote. "You need to be thinking 'winning' 24 hours a day. You need to be consumed with Lakers pride. . . . You need to have personal pride in knowing that you are the best team players that you can be. . . . Only one team will be champion. . . . That team will be a machine that's fueled with compassion, desire, determination, drive, devotion, and pride. . . . That team could and should be the Lakers."

"I thought it was important for someone to make a statement to our players," he later explained. "I don't want them ever to be accused of not giving their best, and my best guess, from watching the games and being objective, which is my job, was we weren't giving that."

He had thought he had assembled a team that could win 60 games, but now he was tortured by the idea that this club would be known for underachievement. He said he couldn't even describe his misery at the thought of that.

Perhaps it was because he had never been a rah-rah guy that the note struck a chord. Perhaps they were just talented, and anything, any comment from anyone, would have set them off. Whatever it was, the numbers suggest that West's anguish was tangible and the letter expressed it.

After their loss in Washington on March 2, the Lakers came home, read West's letter, and began winning. They started with six straight victories, then suffered a loss to Seattle, then healed it with another five straight wins. A loss to Utah punctured their euphoria at this turnaround, but they quickly jump-started another six-game winning streak, the bulk of which came on yet another trip to the Eastern Conference. On April 10 they lost a home game to the Phoenix Suns when Antonio McDyess powered in 37 points. But the Lakers again responded by winning the final five games of the regular season.

When it was over, they could look back on an amazing run of 22 wins against 3 losses. Better yet, they had surpassed West's hopes of a 60-win season with a 61–21 finish. Even so, their record left them third best behind the 62 wins of the Utah Jazz and Chicago Bulls. But across the NBA there was an increasing chorus that the Lakers were poised to claim the league championship. They had been only the third team since the deployment of a shot clock in 1954 to lead the league in scoring while holding their opponents under 100 points.

All of this was accomplished with Kobe taking a remarkably low profile. Harris kept him on a short rope, using him as a defensive pressure point off the bench with Van Exel but always watching to yank him back if his offensive efforts displayed a hint of the Jordanesque. There were nights when he played a dozen minutes or less. His performances were dotted with games where he scored a mere four points, and on March 28 he registered just two in a blowout loss to the Jazz.

Even on a tether, he managed to finish the season with an impressive 15.2-points-per-game scoring average, mainly because he rose out of the doldrums in April despite suffering a bruised pelvis. He scored 20 against the Nets on April 2, although few noticed because O'Neal threw down 50 in the same game. In a home win over the Jazz the last game of the regular season, he hit for 25, including one key bucket after another as the Lakers put their key rival away.

During the game Utah's Karl Malone apologized for making such a big deal out of his waving off the screen in the All-Star game. "He told me, 'The media kind of took my comments out of context; it was something I really didn't say. They asked me a specific question, I answered a specific question, but everybody kind of blew it out of proportion,'" Kobe explained. "I accepted his apology."

As Shawn Kemp had predicted during the All-Star break, the public would be quick to turn on any young man who would be Jordan. During the playoffs an L.A. TV station would come up with the nifty idea of running a poll to see if fans thought the Lakers were better with or without Kobe. Fifty-five percent of the respondents said they were better off without him. Soon the subject was humming on talk radio and in newspaper columns. Sensing a crease of opportunity, playoff opponents would seize on that notion and begin talking it up.

The idea, though, had crossed Del Harris's mind long before.

Sudden Death

A plague of back spasms had visited Kobe during the days of practice leading into the first round series with Portland. Still, he was ready and able to deliver the Lakers from a tight finish to Game 1 in the Forum. Over the final nine minutes of the fourth quarter he scored 11 points (and would finish with 15) to close out a 104–102 win. The Lakers also claimed Game 2, but he was hardly a factor with 4 points. The same was true in Portland for Game 3, won easily by the Blazers. Harris finally turned him loose in Game 4, giving him 36 minutes of playing time, which he used to run up 22 points, 4 assists, and 3 rebounds in a blowout that allowed the Lakers to advance.

Next up was Seattle, also winners of 61 games, but the Sonics held home-court advantage by virtue of their regular-season series victory over the Lakers. Harris reverted to form in Game 1, using Kobe sparingly in a blowout loss.

Before Game 2 Kobe came down with the flu and was forced to sit. The Lakers won, and three days later the series resumed at the Forum. Although Kobe felt well enough to play, Harris again decided that he should sit.

"What people didn't realize is that I could have played in those games," Kobe would tell me a year later, the annoyance still strong in his voice. "Del just didn't want me to play. You never knew what he was going to do."

Game 3 brought yet another blowout victory, and afterward the Sonics' Sam Perkins opined that the Lakers didn't even miss Kobe. "It seems like they're more at ease without him," Perkins said.

Those comments and others from the Sonics stung Kobe. A year later, when Perkins had moved to the Indiana Pacers and the Lakers traveled to Indianapolis to play them, Kobe was eager to dunk in Perkins's face. He stared at him during warm-ups, but the big center would never look at him and never got in the game.

What made the situation worse was that Harris was essentially saying the same thing. Asked if the Lakers really needed Kobe during the series, the coach replied, "We've been trying for two years to bring Kobe Bryant along. To do that, we've had to have him play a backup position to an All-Star player, Eddie Jones. You can't take away too many minutes from that kind of a ballplayer. So we've got to play Kobe at small forward, or he's just a 10-minute guy, and that ain't gonna work too well for the ol' coach, is it?

"You've already got Rick Fox at small forward, so that means Robert Horry doesn't get to play small forward much. Which means he plays power forward, and he's backed up by Elden Campbell, who if he doesn't play power forward doesn't get to play much because he's backing up Shaquille O'Neal, which means, who's the odd guy out? The guy who the dumb coach never plays—Corie Blount. So, with Kobe out, it opens up the bigger lineup."

Asked if he feared Kobe would come out too aggressively, the coach replied, "It's possible. His tendency is to want to do. His normal responses are very aggressive, overt. But he's a very intelligent young man as well. I'm sure he'll try to be his aggressive self, but he has been working at becoming a player who fits more into the flow of our team."

For Game 4, Harris played Kobe three minutes in another Lakers win. For Game 5, with Los Angeles closing out the series in a rush, the coach kept him on the bench for all but 11 minutes.

"More than anything, it made me so anxious, made me so hungry just to play every aspect of the game," Bryant said afterward. "I'll be sitting on the bench, hearing the coaches say, 'Man, we've got to get some rebounds.' And it made me mad that I couldn't contribute. Besides seeing what the team was doing positively, it just made me hungry to go out there and help them any way I could."

Next up was the Western Conference finals and a rematch with the Utah Jazz. The Los Angeles media wanted to know Harris's plans for Bryant. "How much Kobe plays will depend on how he's going and our team is flowing," the coach said. "We have established a very good rhythm to our team, and it's important that when Kobe does play he helps keep the ball moving and distributes the ball, not stop the ball too much.

"We don't want him to stop going one-on-one—because he's an excellent one-on-one player—but we want it . . . in context of the offense as appropriate," Harris said. "If he gets it and holds it, that would break down our rhythm."

"Kobe is the most talented guy I've ever seen play the game," Robert Horry told reporters. "From him sitting on the bench and watching what we're doing, I think he understands more about rotating the ball, taking open shots, not holding it. He has a tendency when he catches to hold it and see what move he's going to make."

Some reporters wondered if Kobe might wreck the Lakers playing rhythm by seeking redemption for his 1997 air balls against the Jazz. "This is a whole new season," Kobe told them. "It would be kind of selfish for me to go in there and try to seek redemption.'"

Actually the Jazz managed to settle the issue of Lakers redemption rather quickly. There would be none. In Game 1 at the Delta Center, Karl Malone and his teammates jumped out to a 40–15 lead, an event so traumatic that it revived all the old Lakers demons. In the stress of the moment they again turned on each other, resorting to finger pointing. With each game their nightmare grew worse. The Jazz shoved their way to a sweep with wins of 112–77, 99–95, 109–98, and 96–92.

For Kobe the soundtrack to this horror was the wall of boos that rolled down from the Delta Center upper reaches and the crowd's derisive chants of "Ko-be! Ko-be!" In the first two losses he missed 17 of 24 from the field. "You are going to go through periods when your shots aren't falling," he said. "In the Seattle series, everything was in rhythm; our shots were falling. That hasn't been the case in this series. I'm just going to continue to be aggressive and more effective at the defensive end."

He was far from alone in his misery. Unlike Seattle, the Jazz spent little effort double-teaming O'Neal and chose instead to keep defenders on the Lakers shooters. The strategy strangled L.A.'s young guns. Van Exel shot 23.8 percent, Fisher 34.8 percent, Bryant 36.7 percent, Elden Campbell 21.4 percent, Horry 36.0, and Rick Fox 40.0.

"You can't lose confidence," Van Exel told reporters. "You have to keep taking your shots. We've never been told not to shoot, so nobody was looking at the bench and wondering if they should shoot the next time."

"Harris kept expecting the guards to warm up, but it never happened," observed veteran reporter Mitch Chortkoff.

At the other end the Jazz ran their pick and roll every time they needed it. "We could never stop their offense," Van Exel would say in the aftermath. "They ran it the way they wanted the whole series."

In the midst of this debacle, Jazz broadcaster Hot Rod Hundley weighed in on Kobe, calling him "all showbiz." This from Hundley, the onetime Lakers dribble king who used to shoot hook shot free throws as a joke and dribble up beside Doris Day sitting courtside during a game and wink at her. This from Hundley, a number-one pick in the draft whose career never panned out because he spent so much time partying that he decided to name his autobiography *Clown*.

Coming to Kobe's aid, O'Neal called him "Hot Rod Dumbley."

Asked about the matter, Kobe said, "That's his opinion. It doesn't bother me. As the years go by, comments like that evaporate."

The Lakers had bigger problems anyway. The *Los Angeles Times* would later reveal that during a practice leading up to Game 4, Van Exel committed an offense that finally erased what was left of any team chemistry. As the practice closed, the players moved in to clasp hands and break from their huddle. Instead of yelling the usual "Lakers" to break the huddle, Van Exel improvised and shouted "Cancun," the implication being that he was ready for vacation.

Furious, O'Neal reported the incident to West. "Guys have to find out what is important to them," said O'Neal. "If they don't want to play, then get off my team."

With a reputation for trouble, Van Exel had watched team after team pass him over in the 1993 draft until West took him with the 37th pick. The left-hander quickly showed tremendous quickness and a flair for rakishly deep three-point attempts, traits that would eventually make him an All-Star. But the toxic side of his persona persisted. There were frequent tiffs with Harris and a seven-game suspension he drew for bumping referee Ron Garretson.

"We had a few incidents that were blown up, but we worked together many days with no problems," Harris told reporters after Van Exel was traded to Denver.

In return, Van Exel would later call Harris the "cancer" who destroyed the Lakers chances of winning. As for Kobe, he wasn't sad to see Van Exel go. Not because of anything personal. Van Exel simply didn't have a strong work ethic, and in Kobe's eyes that was the ultimate sin.

Kobe goes for style points.
© NBA *Photos/Andrew D. Bernstein*

The camera is a definite
friend.
© NBA *Photos/Nathaniel S.
Butler*

The Kobe-Shaq relationship is a work in progress.
© NBA *Photos/Andrew D. Bernstein*

As a rookie, Kobe wowed the crowd for the NBA's final Slam Dunk contest.

© NBA *Photos/Fernando Medina*

A breakaway finish is never routine for Kobe.

© NBA Photos/Andrew D. Bernstein

Tiger Woods said he was glad to finally meet a superstar younger than he.
© NBA *Photos/Andrew D. Bernstein*

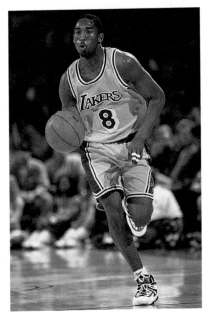

The ball-handling skills are impressive.
© NBA *Photos/Andy Hayt*

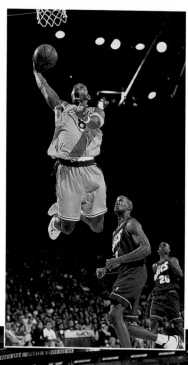

Having endured criticism from the Sonics in the 1998 playoffs, Kobe always likes to shine against Seattle.
© NBA *Photos/Andy Hayt*

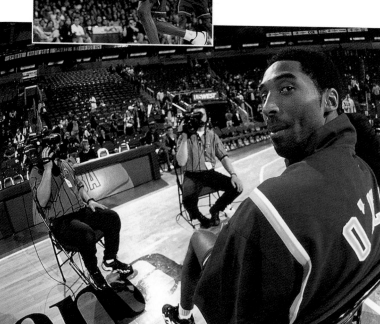

The media have become a companion.
© NBA *Photos/Andrew D. Bernstein*

Kobe has the length to get to the basket.
© NBA *Photos/Andrew D. Bernstein*

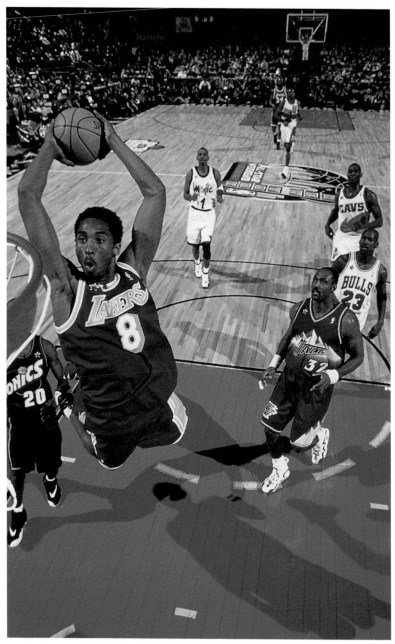

Kobe became the youngest starter in the history of the All-Star
Game in 1998.
© NBA *Photos/Andrew D. Bernstein*

Sometimes Kobe's sorties to the basket encounter turbulence.
© NBA *Photos/Nathaniel S. Butler*

Both Shaq and Kobe know that learning to work together is the key to their future.
© NBA *Photos/D. Clarke Evans*

Slam time in Seattle.
© NBA *Photos/Garrett Ellwood*

His sheer joy on the court is readily obvious.
© NBA *Photos/Glenn James*

Jordan provided a unique role model.
© NBA *Photos/Andrew D. Bernstein*

Kobe finishes in Sacramento traffic.
© NBA *Photos/Rocky Widner*

Kobe's rousing dunk over
Utah's Greg Ostertag helped
seal a 1999 Lakers win over
the Jazz.
© *NBA Photos/Glenn James*

Kobe dazzled Houston in the 1999
playoffs.
© *AllSport/Harry How*

Phil Jackson offers much promise as coach of the Lakers.

© NBA *Photos/Robert Mora*

The Spurs corralled the Lakers in 1999.

© NBA *Photos/Andrew D. Bernstein*

For the briefest time, Kobe, Shaq, and Dennis Rodman seemed to click.
© NBA *Photos/Glenn James*

"I will not be broken," Kobe vows.

As unsavory as Van Exel's final days as a Laker were, they did little to obscure the entire team's difficulties. The situation prompted Magic Johnson to complain publicly about Harris's failure to make adjustments to counter the Utah offense and about the Lakers whining and backbiting.

"We never did anything different," Johnson told reporters. "We never changed. And our players did too much whining. We complained about the Jazz players holding. Well, in this league you hold to get an advantage. Everyone does it. I did it. Really, our focus was all wrong."

In the wake of the Lakers very sudden collapse there was speculation that Harris would be fired. But he had one more year on his contract for $1.1 million, and Lakers owner Jerry Buss was too strapped at the time to waste that kind of money and then turn around and pay a higher-profile coach four times as much.

Asked his take on the season, Harris observed, "We still won 61 regular-season games and gave people a lot of enjoyment."

It had been a strange ride for Kobe Bryant, from the sheer heights of the All-Star weekend to those long, low moments on Del Harris's bench. Now that it was over, he hardly spoke to his teammates. As he saw it, they had been out to show him, from the very minute he returned from New York. It was a group thing, each of them deriving some satisfaction from the showing. The whole process had been tough for Joe Bryant, too, bringing to mind those days of frustration in Philadelphia early in his NBA career.

The family, of course, had been supportive of him. But his was the kind of anger that didn't want support.

"I've been humbled," he said as the year was drawing to a close.

But not broken. Never broken.

The rush of the whole experience had brought him face to face with Michael Jordan. His prize had been those earnest words of advice, provided in the briefest moment of common understanding. It was as if Jordan knew him better than anybody else. As if he and no one else understood what he was going through.

Stay aggressive, he said. You gotta stay aggressive.

Kobe took those words and wrote them on his heart.

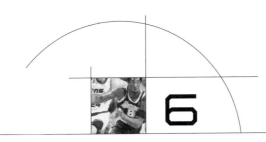

6

LOST WEEKENDS

"Nobody ever really came out and said that they felt Kobe's selfish play was our problem. But that's what everybody felt." —DEREK FISHER

The NBA lockout, a financial struggle between the league's owners and players, wasn't resolved until January 1999, meaning that even as negotiators ironed out the final details of a new labor agreement, players from each team got together for informal sessions to help prepare for when their teams could officially begin practice.

In that spirit, Shaquille O'Neal, Derek Fisher, Corie Blount, and Kobe found themselves playing a little two-on-two in mid-January. Months after their problems it remained obvious that Kobe's struggles with his teammates the previous season had cut deep into their relationships. His basic strategy in dealing with the other Lakers was to talk as little as possible. "There are times you'll ask him a question, and he'll say yes or no. And that'll be it," Derek Fisher explained in a 1999 interview. "Other times he'll be a little more expressive. But Kobe does such a good job of never allowing people to know what's going on with him, how he's feeling or what he's thinking."

Fearing that continuing the cold relations would damage the team, Fisher had begun approaching Bryant during the 1998 off-season, using small talk as a way to get to know him better, because, after two years, Fisher knew very little about him. "I tried to find ways that we could just talk," the Lakers point guard recalled. "Talk about things not even related to basketball, how his family was doing, things like that. I knew one of his sisters had gotten married and was pregnant. I'd ask how she was doing. He was fairly responsive."

Kobe was also cautious. He viewed Fisher as part of O'Neal's clique on the Lakers, the group Kobe felt was responsible for "showing" him after the All-Star game. There had been too many times when he was open on the wing in transition, the perfect situation for him to attack the basket, where he felt Fisher had failed to get him the ball. So he viewed Fisher's efforts with a raised eyebrow.

But in the off-season the two players sometimes trained at the same times and places. Kobe saw how hard Fisher was working on his shooting and his conditioning. The one standard by which Bryant measured other players was how hard they worked. He had little regard for the people, no matter how talented, who refused to make the effort to get better. His first year in the league he had something of a phone relationship with Portland's Jermaine O'Neal, another teenage rookie, but Bryant soon cooled that friendship when he concluded that Jermaine O'Neal lacked work ethic as a player. Bryant himself liked to shoot 1,500 or more shots each day. When he saw Fisher working hard, he was quick to encourage his effort and to compliment his improved shooting.

And that in turn led him to feel more comfortable in January 1999 when the opportunity arose to play two-on-two with Fisher and Shaquille O'Neal and Blount. Since his days as a youngster battling his father in one-on-one battles, Kobe had always been an extremely physical practice player, the kind of guy to use elbows, hip checks, hard box-outs, or any other advantage to challenge opponents. After all, he and his father, who loved each other very much, could battle furiously yet remain emotionally detached after the conflict and even laugh about it.

Kobe's Lakers teammates didn't approach the game the same way. The only one capable of battling Kobe and not getting upset was Eddie Jones, which meant that he and Kobe would have furious battles in practice yet never feel the need to carry it beyond that. "I'm gonna bust your ass," Kobe would tell Jones during their battles, which only drove the intensity higher. Other Lakers, however, harbored an intense dislike for Kobe because of the way he attacked practices.

Ideally, every Laker should have had Kobe's attitude toward competing and being physical in practice, Fisher said. "That really was the way we all should have been competing. With Kobe's spirit."

It didn't work out that way, though. And the Lakers troubles in 1999 would begin with that January pickup session. More than five weeks later word would leak into the L.A. newspapers that Shaq had slapped Kobe during practice. The reports didn't detail when the incident happened or what was involved, but it would be cited as a sign of their growing dislike for each other. Fisher remembered being amazed at those newspaper reports, because they came so long after the incident and because there had been only four people in the gym at the time. Who had leaked news of the incident, he wondered.

"It had just been physical," Fisher recalled. "Both guys had gotten tired. Neither guy really started it. It started just from them both being physical."

And the altercation itself didn't last long, but the repercussions did. "Some true feelings came out," Fisher said. "They didn't really say all that much, but it was done in an extremely negative way. You could tell the guys had negative thoughts for each other."

Worse yet, it was clear those feelings weren't going away any time soon, Fisher said. "It would always be remembered."

One member of the Lakers staff said the situation happened

because O'Neal wanted to make a point. "It sent a message, but Kobe didn't receive it," the staffer said.

Although the lockout meant that the 1999 NBA regular season would be shortened to 50 games, the Lakers suffered through a crazy mishmash of a campaign that in effect was four different seasons crammed into one. First, there was the preseason and opening 12 games that Del Harris coached the team. The second season began when Harris was fired and assistant Kurt Rambis promoted to the job on the same day that the team added strange agent Dennis Rodman to the roster. That second season, in effect, lasted another 11 blissful games until the team decided to work a major trade, sending Jones and Elden Campbell to the Charlotte Hornets for what would essentially be Glen Rice and J. R. Reid. After a month of turmoil adjusting to the trade, the fourth season would begin with the abrupt release of Rodman, after which the team would settle into a new and different round of internal conflict.

"It's been a season of many changes. Many changes," Kobe said wearily in April.

During each of these seasons within the season the Lakers would suffer through a blur of frustration, but there would always be one constant—the team's dislike of Kobe. The tension within the team would require a series of meetings intended to deal with chemistry problems, yet the malignancy was never addressed frankly.

"It was all sort of beating around the bush," explained a longtime Lakers staff member. "The whole thing is about Kobe. The whole failure of the team is about him."

Asked about the staff member's opinion, Derek Fisher said, "That's the way I perceived it. That was the way that it was. There were a lot of people who felt that way. Nobody ever really came out and said that they felt Kobe's selfish play was our problem. But that's what everybody felt."

Kobe's friends and family would see the response as an

intense case of envy, for his status and for the $71 million contract he would sign before the season opened. The situation would grow so bad that some in Kobe's camp wondered if his teammates were intentionally failing to let him know when opponents were setting screens on his blind side.

In part Kobe's defense mechanism for dealing with the matter was his increasing alienation. The worse his relationship with his teammates, the further he withdrew into his shell. This, in turn, led the team to struggle because it lacked unity.

Essentially, the team was first fractured along the lines of Kobe versus O'Neal and the rest of the roster. When Glen Rice came to the team in March, he added a third clique to the equation.

Asked about the situation, Kobe acknowledged that he had no real relationship with any teammate. "All that matters is what we do on the court," he said.

Yet the Lakers on-court performance disintegrated so badly at points during the season that it led reporters to speculate on the nature of Bryant and O'Neal's relationship. Some would figure the relationship bordered on hatred, which wasn't true. Others would cast the struggles of Shaq and Kobe to come to terms with each other as more evidence of the spoiled nature of Generation X players. That also wasn't the case. Basketball history is replete with stories of teammates who struggled to mesh their games and their personalities.

Forty years after George Mikan and Jim Pollard led the Minneapolis Lakers to six pro championships, I had the pleasure of spending a day with Hall of Famer Pollard, a slasher who loved to get to the hoop. He talked of the conflict he had had with Mikan, an immovable force at center who always seemed to clog the lane when Pollard wanted to drive.

Larry Bird and Kevin McHale faced their own cool off-court relations even as their Boston Celtics teams won three championships.

As did Magic Johnson and Kareem Abdul-Jabbar, who won five NBA titles together. Kareem always felt that Magic got the credit for their work together. "Because of Earvin's special charisma, the story was always written a different way," Abdul-Jabbar told me in 1993.

It is the challenge of great basketball teams to sort out and untangle the relationships, to divide the credit and the shots, not to mention the endorsement contracts.

In that regard it was understandable that Bryant and O'Neal struggled mightily during the 1999 season. There were times when their relationship could have boiled over into out-and-out hatred, but the Lakers organization somehow managed to get them through five difficult months of growing pains. That left the future looking reasonably bright but meant that 1999 would be remembered as the pits by all involved.

"It's been a tough year," Kobe said as it neared an end.

Did that mean it had been the toughest of his young life?

"Yeah," he said softly. "It is."

At the same time it was a year in which he had started every game that the Lakers played, a year in which he had pushed his scoring average to 19.9 points per game and set career highs for assists and rebounds in a game.

But it was also a year of many, many changes, far too many for a young roster still struggling to mesh.

Time had revealed that the most tenuous and most critical facet of Jerry West's plans for building a championship contender was the relationship between Shaq and Kobe. West knew that if only they could figure out how to work together, the rewards would be vast.

But both Kobe's and Shaq's view of the situation was obscured, West said. "I think sometimes people read their press clippings too much in this league."

O'Neal was a huge, fun-loving man yet surprisingly sensitive to any criticism. After Del Harris was fired, the coach would tell associates that the center was perhaps too fun-loving, too much of a comedian, to be an effective team leader. He had a great sense of humor and loved to amuse himself and others with it. In his first season in Los Angeles, O'Neal used that humor to nudge Kobe toward being more of a team player. The center even composed a ditty, set to the tune of "Greatest Love of All," aimed at Bryant.

In the locker room, Shaq would croon: "I believe that Showboat is the future/Call the play and let that m——f——er shoot. . . ."

He'd sing a verse, then come back with the next a little louder: "I believe that Showboat is the future. . . ."

Kobe wouldn't exactly fall in stitches at the derisive perfor-mance, but he wasn't thin-skinned about it either. They were simply different in their approach to life. O'Neal enjoyed nighttime, the clubs, the L.A. music scene. Kobe had a differ-ent agenda, namely his ambition. "I feel weird going out, on the road, knowing that you have a game the next night," he explained when asked about the matter. "That's not handling your business."

"In Kobe's defense, he's a young guy, much younger than all these other guys," photographer Andrew Bernstein pointed out. "When he came in that first year, the Lakers had all these guys like Byron Scott and Jerome Kersey, guys who could have been his father. Kobe seemed to feel that he had to create an image of himself that he was older than he was, more mature, grown up and above his years."

Usually when you see young players attempting to act older than they are, they wind up doing something stupid, Bernstein said, but not Kobe. "You haven't heard a thing about Kobe Bryant doing something like that from the day he entered the league. Heck, there aren't even any stories about him like that from high school. No carousing. No drug problems. No missed curfews. No missed practices. The whole thing. The kid is always practicing, shooting free throws, whatever it takes. He's building a basketball court in his house just so he can practice even more. He's got the same love for the game that Michael and Magic and Larry had."

For the most part Kobe and Shaq had enjoyed a good relationship for their first season and a half. When Kobe heaved up air balls in the 1997 playoffs, O'Neal was the first person to his side, telling him not to worry, that redemption would soon be his. The good feelings lasted until Kobe's 1998 All-Star experience. From that point on they seemed caught in a growing misunderstanding fueled by their different natures.

"Kobe tends to keep to himself a lot," explained Bernstein, who sometimes traveled with the Lakers on their team charter airplane. "A lot of people might interpret that as being aloof or arrogant or whatever. He's just a private guy. On the bus he kind of is by himself. And on the plane, too. He's friendly, he's approachable. But sometimes he's studying or listening to music or he's asleep or whatever. A lot of guys play cards, and Shaq tends to be the ringleader on the plane, going up and down the aisles and having fun. Kobe tends to be kind of private.

"You can't say one is better than the other," Bernstein said. "They're just two different guys."

But as the 1999 season wore on, Kobe's small circle of supporters would come to see O'Neal as envious. For years rumors had persisted that the reason O'Neal left Orlando was his envy of Penny Hardaway, who had enjoyed tremendous success with the creation of his L'il Penny marketing alter ego. Kobe's presence in Los Angeles posed a similar threat. His number 8 Lakers jersey outsold O'Neal's in sporting goods stores around southern California, just one of many points of marketing competition between the two in which Kobe had taken the upper hand.

As the 1999 season wore on and the tension between Shaq and Kobe built, O'Neal's supporters denied that envy had anything to do with the situation. "People say Shaq is jealous. That's way far from the truth," Derek Fisher said. "All Shaq wants to do is win."

"I want him to get all those commercials and do all that stuff," O'Neal volunteered during an interview when asked about Bryant. "Because with marketing, when they see Kobe, they see me. And when they see me, they see Kobe."

"Shaq really wanted to have this great relationship with this kid and the two of them lead this team to a championship," said one veteran Lakers employee. "He wasn't jealous of Kobe or anything like that. He still isn't. Shaq has tried to get him under control. The kid has this attitude: 'You may be Shaquille O'Neal, but I'm Kobe Bryant. I'm every bit the player you are plus some.' "

At one point during the 1999 season, O'Neal would point at Bryant across the Lakers locker room and tell reporters, "There's the problem."

Beyond that first slap, though, the season held little direct confrontation, due in large part to the efforts of Rambis and the Lakers coaches to keep the rumblings from flaring into the kind of trouble that could never be repaired. "Shaq and I have never even talked about it," Kobe said when asked about their difficulties. "We communicate about it through the media mostly."

Which meant that if it was discussed at all the subject was raised as innuendo.

Asked if he had tried to help Kobe through his growing pains, O'Neal replied, "I try not to help guys out too much. Experience is the best teacher. Kobe really didn't go to college. He went to high school, and he's different. Kobe's a great player, and he's gonna get a lot of press. He's a new, up-and-coming kid. Certain people understand that. Certain people don't. I understand that. I just try to stay out of his way and encourage him."

One person who didn't understand Bryant was Ruben Patterson, the Lakers 23-year-old rookie from the University of Cincinnati. A six-foot-six forward, Patterson possessed a strong defensive ability that stemmed from his emotional approach to the game and to life. Never one to back down, he had played overseas briefly during the NBA lockout and soon found himself challenging coaches and teammates alike in face-to-face confrontations. An older American on his team had tried to take Patterson under his wing and help him calm his raw emotion. Patterson, though, only seemed to know one speed.

Beyond that, his first year as a pro had been marked by the death of his mother, Charlene Patterson, who had been the strong figure in his life, fending for him as Patterson grew up in inner-city Cleveland. When the lockout ended, he returned to the States to join the Lakers. Their second-round pick, he faced a battle to earn the NBA's minimum salary.

Patterson's circumstances and fiery personality clashed immediately with Kobe, resulting in furious practice battles throughout the season between the two. Kobe, again, approached these battles the way he had the meetings with his own father.

"Between Ruben and Kobe something was always going on and escalating," Derek Fisher said. "Ruben wouldn't back down. It got out of line a couple of times, because of Ruben's nature. Kobe can get into a tussle and still not take it across the boundary. He can push and shove and fight for position and not react emotionally. On the other hand, Ruben is a rookie, a guy always trying to establish himself, and he wasn't gonna back down."

Somehow even these confrontations factored into the players' sense that there was a double standard for Kobe, a Lakers staff member said. "They would get competitive in practice. Kobe would 'bow him up, but Ruben couldn't do to Kobe what he wanted to do to him, because management would come down on him. Kobe was untouchable. Kobe could do what he wanted."

In the old NBA somebody would have decked Kobe Bryant a long time ago, the staff member said.

Beyond practice tussles, though, the real issue was Kobe's approach to the game. His teammates saw his slashing style, his efforts to domineer and control the ball, as the height of selfishness. Part of the problem even involved West's insistence that the coaching staff had to play Kobe because he was an exceptional talent who needed to play to develop.

"As players we had to deal with Kobe's success and the way the organization viewed Kobe," Fisher explained. "It was clear the organization was satisfied with how Kobe played, as was the coaching staff. It was clear they were not gonna hold him back or slow him down from the player that he wanted to be."

That meant that others on the team would have to sacrifice their development for Kobe, Fisher added. "Shaq also benefited from the star system. That's the way the NBA works. But it can be demoralizing to a team, demoralizing to the players making the sacrifice."

Kobe clearly was isolated by his status. Perhaps his consolation in that was that the isolation itself was another trait he shared with Jordan. Phil Jackson had once explained to me that one of his first major tasks upon taking over as head coach of the Chicago Bulls was deconstructing the walls that had been built up between Jordan and his teammates.

"That attitude, that tremendous competitiveness, sometimes makes it tough to be a teammate, because you see that tremendous competitiveness is gonna eat you up everywhere," Jackson explained. "It's gonna eat you up playing golf with him next week, playing cards with him next month. That attitude of arrogance is gonna be there. It's not always the best for personal connections and friendship. But it certainly makes for greatness."

The result of his competitiveness and his status was Jordan's self-imposed isolation. "He lives in his own world a great deal," Bulls assistant coach Tex Winter had once explained to me, speaking of Jordan. "I don't think he wants people to figure out what Michael Jordan's thinking. It's one of his strengths."

If anything, Kobe's age only made those walls of isolation higher, harder for both sides to see over.

Confronted with the schism, veteran Lakers point guard Derek Harper, who had been brought to the team at the start of the season, tried to play a healing role. He spent much of the season talking to his younger teammates about establishing unity and togetherness. His approach helped calm the passions to some degree. But as time went on, it became increasingly clear that it wasn't so much that his teammates didn't want to heal their differences. They just didn't seem to know how.

Money

The 1999 season opened with a major blow for Kobe. In one fell swoop he lost better than $30 million.

For a time it appeared that there would not be a 1999 NBA season, but after months of the owner-imposed lockout, the players' association and the owners reached an agreement. Kobe Bryant was one of only five players to vote against it. In short, the new collective bargaining agreement would cost him more than $30 million because it put a cap on the size of the contract he could sign, trimming a deal that could have run well in excess of $100 million down to $71 million.

"I felt good about what I did," Bryant said of his vote. "I can live with my decision. I hope everybody else can."

Yes, he was a player who had always claimed to play for the love of the game. But as his agent and father pointed out, $30 million was a lot of money to lose. There were others, though, who scoffed at the circumstances. Even $71 million seemed a huge sum for a player who had started in fewer than a dozen games in two NBA seasons. In their search to find Michael Jordan's kind of star power, however, the league's owners found themselves paying not for what a young player had accomplished but for his potential to be a star.

Kobe Bryant was potential personified, Jerry West told reporters. "To some degree, he has to be looking over his shoulder. He's a 20-year-old kid who has more energy than the whole team put together. When he looks at his game, all he needs to do is slow down, read situations, and not take the whole thing on himself. He's a big draw, and he's one of those guys you just sit back and say, 'Hmmm, I wonder what he's going to be like when he's 25.' He's one of those players who is going to be truly exceptional if he keeps going forward."

Paying steeply for potential had become commonplace in American professional sports, but that didn't stop the circumstances from having a dampening effect on the Lakers team psychology as the 1999 season opened.

Despite his opposition to the new league guidelines, Kobe quickly reached an agreement with the team on a new six-year contract that was announced on the cusp of training camp. Under league guidelines Bryant's contract had a maximum starting point of $9 million a season with annual raises of no more than 12.5 percent. "We all knew it was coming up pretty soon," Kobe told reporters when asked about the deal. "But I don't think people expected it to happen this quick. It's quite a relief. So, we don't have to go through the whole season with people asking, 'Well, when is the deal? What's happening?'"

Bryant's contract fell in line with similar deals signed by Philadelphia 76ers guard Allen Iverson, Vancouver Grizzlies forward Shareef Abdur-Rahim, and Boston Celtics forward Antoine Walker, all of whom had been drafted in 1996 with Kobe and were nearing the end of their initial three-year contracts.

In his last season of the old contract, Bryant was scheduled to earn $1.3 million for 1999. "He's a remarkable young kid, and he's certainly ahead of himself in a lot of ways," West said. "His future is enormous, and on top of that he's managed to keep his perspective and his focus about what type of person he wants to be and what kind of player he wants to be."

That focus included having a sense of obligation to the fans, which coincidentally had become one of the league's strategies for winning back the hearts of a public turned off by the squabbling of the lockout. The season started with a public relations show of having players hang around after games to meet and greet fans. An initial hit, the practice soon died out once the NBA got into the frenetic pace of its shortened schedule. Andrew Bernstein said he admired Kobe's persistence in connecting with fans. "These days players are not going out of their way for fans per se," the photographer said. "They get on the bus at the airport. They get off the bus at their hotel. The bus pulls right up to the entrance. There's no interaction with fans at the airport because the bus goes right to the tarmac. At the arena the bus goes right down a tunnel right next to the locker room exit door.

"On a trip I made with the Lakers to Phoenix, there was a whole group of fans waiting for the players at the Ritz-Carlton before they went to practice. They kept screaming, 'Kobe! Kobe! Sign this.' But the team was trying to get to practice. So Kobe said, 'I'll get you later.' Which is what everybody says. They always promise that after practice they'll get them later, and they rarely do. So I rode back with them about two hours later, and the same group of kids was still waiting at the hotel, with all the stuff to sign—the basketballs and the cards and the T-shirts, all that stuff. Every guy got off that bus and went up to their rooms. Kobe was the only guy who made a left and went over to a group of about 25 kids and spent about 20 minutes signing autographs."

There certainly were instances when he was less accommodating, but beginning in his rookie year Kobe had made a practice of attempting to hang out with other teens in mall food courts. As his celebrity grew, that unfettered time seemed to slip away from him. But he would find that connection at odd times, jumping out of a limo to sign for young fans waiting for him in the rain or chatting on-line wherever possible.

Having missed college, he lacked the social network that boosted others his age, which meant that a substantial amount of his time was passed alone. Even when he slipped into the Lakers coaches' offices after hours to view still more videotape, he did it alone.

Although he professed not to be overly concerned about money, there was little way to inhabit the strange and rare atmosphere of the NBA and not be affected by it. Jordan himself viewed money as just another means of keeping score on his vast personal competitive landscape. Many players viewed the acquisition of wealth the same way.

Even West was caught in the throes of a financial standoff with Jerry Buss. Supposedly the owner had promised the team's executive VP a $2 million bonus, then held off in delivering it. Faced with Buss's reneging, West began hinting to reporters that he was thinking about leaving the Lakers to work for another team, which had O'Neal himself offering veiled threats to leave the team via free agency.

"If Jerry West would leave for health reasons, that would be understandable," O'Neal told reporters. "If he would leave for any other reason, I would be very, very upset. Jerry West is the reason I came to the Lakers."

"Had I left, I would have been careful to say I was resigning rather than retiring," West told them. "I don't know any other work."

Eventually the bonus was paid, and West was given a fat new contract, set to kick in with the 1999–2000 season. At least part of Buss's reluctance to pay out monies stemmed from the reshuffling of the team ownership structure to include Rupert Murdoch's Fox entertainment conglomerate as a minority partner and plans to move the Lakers into the Staples Center, a $300 million building under construction in downtown Los Angeles, for the 1999–2000 season.

Besides West's contract, the clearest sign of Buss's financial maneuverings to the players was the team's decision not to renew Del Harris's contract before the 1999 season, despite the fact that he had driven the team to 61 wins and the conference finals the season before, that coming after he had bettered the team's win totals each season he had been on the job. The coach went into the schedule as a lame duck, and everyone involved sensed that situation wouldn't fly very long.

Riding the Whirlwind

Kobe's big new contract was the first sign that he would soon move into the Lakers starting lineup. "We're hoping this is the year it all falls into place for Kobe," Del Harris, acknowledging the inevitable, told reporters. The only question was, where would Kobe start? At two guard Eddie Jones was an All-Star, so the two of them presented management with something of a traffic jam. It was Rick Fox's foot injury that wound up solving the problem in the short term. That cleared playing time for Kobe at small forward, a move he solidified with his early-season performances. The team had an obvious void at power forward and badly needed someone to help O'Neal with the rebounding and defensive chores.

West had tried unsuccessfully to trade for Tom Gugliotta or Charles Oakley, leaving both O'Neal and Jerry Buss pushing for the team to sign free agent Dennis Rodman. O'Neal told reporters that he needed a "thug" to play alongside him in the Lakers frontcourt. West, though, was wary of Rodman's age and unbridled nature.

What's worse, every deliberation was rushed. Because the labor lockout had cut more than three months out of the 1999 schedule, the NBA was forced to cram 50 games into 89 days—and three games into three nights on some occasions.

Usually training camp and eight or nine preseason games are scheduled across the month of October for each team, but the 1999 season didn't start until February, meaning that teams had just two weeks to prepare.

What's worse, once the games did resume, fans seemed reluctant to support the NBA the way they once had. Another factor that hurt was the retirement of Jordan, the most popular player in the history of the game. In the face of all these troubles, the league was just trying to get back to business as usual—and to survive.

From the start it was an uphill battle. Attendance and television ratings drooped. So did scoring and shooting percentages. And injuries were up. Across the league fans, players, and coaches found themselves trying to cope with a strange season. "Our attendance is flat; maybe it's down a percent.

Our television rating—I'll call it flat," NBA commissioner David Stern told reporters. "To me it doesn't matter. If we can somehow stay about average for the rest of the season, we will have achieved a great success, especially with cynics saying we were dead and buried."

Injuries sidelined a number of key players, including Charles Barkley, Latrell Sprewell, and Jamal Mashburn, leaving players and coaches clearly feeling the ill effects of the crammed and rushed schedule. "Man, this is a dog year," the New York Knicks' Larry Johnson said. "A lot of guys are going to be out on the floor with some kind of hurt, but you just deal with it."

One of the obvious results of the hastily assembled competition was that teams and players weren't playing as well. Shots were missed. Scores were low. Turnovers were high. Vin Baker, the Seattle Super Sonics' All-Star forward and a 62 percent free-throw shooter, missed his first 18 foul shot attempts.

However, Kobe's extensive off-season conditioning work, his study of Scottie Pippen's defensive techniques, and his focus on offensive footwork sent him charging out of the gate with a burst of energy that revealed just why the Lakers had committed so much money to a mere 20-year-old. He did that by providing just what the team needed: rebounding. Plus he presented nightmares for opponents to guard. "There's not a small forward in the league who can guard Kobe," Derek Harper pointed out, adding that the only person stopping Bryant would be Bryant himself. "That's Kobe's biggest challenge," Harper said, "knowing when to go and knowing when to slow."

In the Lakers season-opening win over the Houston Rockets, he used his added strength to wrap his long arms around a career-high 10 rebounds to the Lakers totals, used his defense to frustrate the Rockets, and relied on his new offensive work to slash his way to 25 points.

The rebounding was immediately seized on as a sign of his maturity. It was dirty work, but it was what his team needed. To prove that he was determined about it, he added another dozen boards in the Lakers second game, a home loss to Utah. The very next night they traveled to San Antonio for a key road win, and Kobe fought his way to another 10 rebounds against the Spurs' large front line. Then over the next two games he did it again, going for 10 rebounds a game, a three-fold jump over the 3.1 boards he had averaged for 1998.

"I've added a lot of dimensions to my game," he said. "My mind-set coming into this season was to try to be a better rebounder and be better defensively, try to cause some havoc on the defensive side. . . . Obviously I didn't know I was going to be a starter—so that gives me more chances to get rebounds."

After begging so long for Kobe to shift his focus to the team, Harris was dutifully impressed. "I'll tell you what," the coach said, "he really is showing that he really may not be just an accidental rebounder. He's such a smart guy, he knows where the ball is. And he knows that rebounding is important to us at that particular position."

Through the Lakers first 10 games he posted averages of 20.6 points, 9.3 rebounds, 1.4 steals, and 1.3 blocked shots and shot 46.4 percent from the field, up from 42.8 percent the previous season. Because of the off-season effort, he was clearly bucking the trend of the vast majority of players who were struggling to regain their form after the long layoff.

The situation prompted USA Today's David DuPree to ask West what if Kobe had gone to a team that used his offensive skills constantly, much as the Chicago Bulls had done with Michael Jordan in 1984. "If he had played in a situation like that, it might be really remarkable where he might be today," West admitted. "But I think that the patience, the setbacks, the good nights and the bad nights, and the criticism that he's faced in this situation will help him. He's faced an awful lot of criticism at an early age. And how he handles that, along with his quest to be the best player, will determine just how good he'll be. I'm just glad he's on our side."

At best, though, Kobe's rebounding effort was viewed as a stopgap measure. Through the first games of the season O'Neal continued to call publicly for management to upgrade the roster. This in itself indicated just how great the pressure was on the 26-year-old center. He had played six years in the league without winning a championship, a factor that his critics pointed to whenever discussions of his game, his leadership, and his free-throw percentage arose on talk radio. "Ultimately he will be judged by how many championships he wins," Harris told reporters. "That's how all the big guys are judged."

After the Lakers lost to Utah in the second game of the season, O'Neal told reporters not only that he needed Dennis Rodman at power forward but that the team needed better perimeter scoring. Jones, the starting two guard, had struggled to open the season in the wake of several reports that he would soon be traded. The tension in the locker room thickened once O'Neal began campaigning openly for a new scorer to replace Jones. "We need a great shooter," O'Neal said. "We have good shooters; we need someone who's known as a shooter."

Speaking of Utah's Stockton and Malone, the Lakers center said, "They have a great one-two punch. We have a one-and-sometimes-two punch."

Nick Van Exel, who had been traded to Denver in the off-season after O'Neal's complaint, smiled at the situation when the Lakers visited Denver for the fourth game of the season. "If they don't win a championship this year, I wonder who they're going to blame it on," he mused.

the edge, right there in plain view for everyone to see. As open books went, his was a fascinating mix, one part mystery thriller, one part comic book, one part experimental poetry. That's why fans in Chicago swooned over him after he joined the Bulls in October 1995.

Throughout his career, Phil Jackson and Rodman's other coaches and teammates hadn't quite known what to expect from him on any given night. The scary part, said Bulls assistant coach Tex Winter, a grandfather figure to Rodman, was that even Dennis himself had no idea where his raw, exposed nerve and boundless energy would take him next. Make a wild, full-stretch dive for a loose ball? Kick a cameraman in the groin? Declare he's ready to quit the game? Produce an unexpected play of pure unbridled heart, one that turns an entire arena on its ear? Each and every one of these items, plus countless others, is on the Rodman menu.

Thus the people who know Rodman weren't surprised when he announced his retirement in January 1999. Just as they wouldn't be surprised days later when he "unretired." Just as they hadn't been surprised in the final weeks of 1998 when he had married actress Carmen Electra in Las Vegas, then announced an annulment, then announced that he was blissful in the union.

But of all his zany moves, that briefly announced retirement would prove to erase any hopes of Rodman's making a serious effort for 1999. It would also cost him somewhere between $5 and $20 million and zap the Lakers in the process.

By announcing the retirement, Rodman abruptly surrendered his "Larry Bird rights" under NBA guidelines, which would have allowed the Bulls to sign him for a fat salary and trade him to another team. In the wake of dismantling their championship team, the Bulls were perfectly willing to give Rodman a sign-and-trade deal that would have given him a salary somewhere between $5 million and the $10 million he earned in 1998. In fact Chicago's management had done the same for former Bulls Scottie Pippen, Steve Kerr, and Luc Longley, and all had gotten fat raises from their new teams in the process.

"It's easily the dumbest move of his career," confided a furious Dwight Manley, Rodman's friend and agent. "The Larry Bird rights are something that can never be retrieved."

In 1995, when Rodman had come to Chicago in severe financial difficulty and on the verge of bankruptcy, it was Manley who turned his financial status around and began generating tens of millions in new income. Instead of throwing his money away on the craps tables in Vegas, Rodman began raking in substantial sums from a variety of entertainment endeavors, including pro wrestling stints, parts in movies and television shows, and a bestselling book.

Sensing that Rodman was about to do something very stupid and announce his retirement in January, Manley tried mightily to get him to understand the seriousness of the circumstances, but sources close to the situation say that Rodman was apparently too busy trying to plan a Super Bowl party to be bothered with the details. Then, impulsively, he announced his retirement, which forced the Bulls to renounce his rights, meaning that he lost his precious Larry Bird exception as a veteran free agent.

"It was his indecisiveness and lack of focus that cost him his Bird rights and caused him to be renounced," Manley confided angrily. Rodman had always seemed willing to pay a high price for the luxury and freedom of being a goofball. But this time the cost was very high. It meant that he would be able to sign a contract for only a minimal salary of a million or less.

Even worse, the minimal contract would mean that no NBA team could possibly hope to control Rodman's behavior. In fact Rodman was welcomed back to the Bulls for the 1997–98 season only after he signed an incentive-laden contract that kept him focused. If he behaved, he got paid. For the most part that contract worked, as Rodman again won the rebounding title (his seventh) and even hit key free throws in Game 5 of the NBA Finals to help the Bulls win a sixth championship. But his loss of the Larry Bird rights meant that no NBA team could pay him enough to offer reasonable incentives. Realizing this and being thoroughly frustrated, Manley severed his relationship with Rodman, which alarmed Rodman's friends because Manley was the one keeping the whole act together. "Dennis and Dwight got in an argument when Dennis got married to Carmen Electra [in late 1998]," explained one Rodman friend. "Then Dwight was pushing him to play once the lockout ended and the season started, and Dennis just wanted to party. Dennis kind of wants to play but not enough to work and do the conditioning and the whole thing."

Unaware of all these problems, the Lakers and O'Neal had begun expressing interest in the zany power forward. Actually Rodman and Jerry Buss had gone out drinking together, where they had hatched the idea, perhaps drawn up on a cocktail napkin, that Rodman come to L.A. to play. West was highly skeptical of the scheme. He knew that the team was considering releasing Harris, and he didn't want the new coach to have to contend with Rodman from the first day. But the public demand, led by Buss and O'Neal, was growing.

Only when negotiations began did Rodman realize just what he had done. Aware that he would play for a prorated sum of about $600,000, he began asking the Lakers for ways to pay him under the table. West wasn't about to get into that. Eventually the team would agree to pay the costs of his security guards, but nothing beyond that. Which meant that for days Rodman stewed.

"It ain't about Dennis Rodman trying to be greedy. It's not about that," Rodman told ESPN. "They've put me in a bind where I can't do anything but make the minimum."

In the process Del Harris's fate got sealed, and West spent days and nights in absolute misery, contemplating the impact, not to mention the loss of dignity and respect.

Los Angeles braced for Rodman's joining the team, but just how crazy the whole episode was going to get became clear that third week of February when Rodman held a press conference at Planet Hollywood, during which he discussed sexual relations with his wife in graphic terms and eventually broke down sobbing.

"I'm never gonna win with you guys," he told the gathering of reporters. "No matter what I do in this league, I'm never gonna win."

When he left, reporters still weren't entirely sure if he had announced that he was joining the team.

Meanwhile, the Lakers were dashing back and forth from one loss to another in their hectic road trip. On that Monday night, February 22, Harris's team blew a 10-point fourth-quarter lead and lost in Denver in overtime. "He thought I was a problem? I want to see Dennis go over there personally," Nick Van Exel said afterward. The former Lakers guard went on to say of his days in Los Angeles, "I wasn't the cancer. The cancer is still there. He has white hair. And until they get rid of him, they're going to keep having lapses like this."

The Lakers rushed out of Denver to fly to Vancouver for their third loss in three nights, the franchise's first-ever loss to the Grizzlies, immediately after which Derek Harper called a players-only meeting. "We're bleeding as a team," he explained later. "Someone had to try to put a Band-Aid on it."

From there they returned home to be greeted by the official announcement of Rodman's signing. "Dennis Rodman is the greatest rebounding forward in the history of basketball," West told reporters at the press conference. "He is also an excellent defensive player and a proven winner with five championship rings. We hope that his addition to the team will take us another step closer to the championship level we hope to attain."

"What got me over the hump was the fact I'm bored," Rodman said. "I'm tired of not doing anything. I want to go back out and entertain the people."

"He'll be like fresh water," Kobe predicted. "He'll definitely give us a burst of energy."

A reporter pointed out that at least some of Rodman's early comments to the press had implied some criticism of Kobe himself. "I don't care," Bryant replied. "If somebody is going to say something negative toward my game, I'm going to evaluate it, and I'm going to see if there's truth to it, and I'm going to improve my basketball game. The way I look at it, whether it's negative or positive about my game or about any player, it doesn't matter. Because I'm going to get to where I need to go eventually."

Actually Kobe viewed Rodman as something of a Bill Russell figure, a brilliant competitor who through rebounding and defensive energy managed to lift his teams to championship-level performances.

There were other factors too. Rodman was certainly not part of O'Neal's clique. And like Bryant himself, Rodman rarely, if ever, spoke to teammates off the court. Some observers, such as Andrew Bernstein, worried that Rodman's antics might influence Kobe negatively. But Rodman had in his previous NBA stops shown an intense work ethic and expected much from his teammates in practice. In fact, during Rodman's tenure in San Antonio, he had refused to speak to David Robinson, or even acknowledge his presence, because Robinson, despite being very talented, showed a lax attitude toward practice.

"Dennis had a real problem in his respect for David Robinson as a player," explained former Spur Jack Haley. "He had problems with David's intensity and work ethic in practice.

Dave is probably the greatest athlete in the game. Dave can go out and get 30 points and 12 rebounds without putting forth a real effort. He's that good. Therefore, he's not a big practice guy. Not a big work ethic guy. Dave was always sitting out practices. It's tendinitis. It's, 'I'm sore today.' Whatever it was, Dennis is a practice guy, and it didn't sit well with Dennis. That caused a lot of their problems, just work ethic."

Kobe, on the other hand, possessed an iron will to practice. Which helps explain why, while he kept his conversations with teammates to an absolute minimum, Kobe quickly took to Rodman and was eager to ask him questions. Specifically, Kobe wanted to know how Rodman, a wise and crafty defender, would defend him when Kobe had the ball in the vicinity of the upper right side of the key. So he went up during one of their early practices and asked. "I knew what his answer would be even before he told me," Kobe confided. "But I just wanted to hear what he had to say."

Rodman told him players around the league were shepherding him to the right of the goal, where they hoped Kobe would put up one of his routine off-balance shots. Kobe had guessed that, but to hear Rodman confirm it was important.

"He has that knowledge," Kobe said appreciatively.

Whirlwind, Part Two

Del Harris had coached 14 seasons in the NBA, long enough to distinguish himself as one of just 20 people to win better than 500 games. He had come to the Lakers for the 1994–95 season to inherit an underachieving team that had won just 33 games the year before and missed the playoffs. Harris promptly coached them to a 15-win improvement and back into the postseason, an effort that earned him distinction as the 1995 NBA Coach of the Year.

The next season he pushed them to 51 wins, which made them respectable enough to attract O'Neal as a free agent. The first season with Shaq and Kobe had brought another elevation in win totals, to 56, and then to 61 the season after that. The totals were quite impressive for a scholarly ordained minister. But his young Lakers could not beat the Utah Jazz in the playoffs, meaning that Lakers management decided to fire him after those three straight February losses. At age 61 Harris saw his effort to mold Shaq and Kobe into a team come to an abrupt end.

West had noticed the Lakers quitting in their fourth-quarter loss at Denver, and he concluded that Harris had lost the ability to motivate them. When the team announced the decision, reporters asked O'Neal if he had asked management to drop the ax.

"The thing about this management here is we never have to go upstairs," O'Neal replied. "We have guys on this management team that played the game, that dominated the game, that were legends of the game. So they know what we feel, they know how we feel, so we really don't have to go upstairs and say certain things. It's unfortunate, because Del was a good guy. He was very knowledgeable, and it's unfortunate that a good guy like him takes the blame for our lack of cohesion."

Reporters then seized that to ask if problems between the center and Kobe had required finding a stronger coach. "I don't really think there's dissension in the team," O'Neal said. "I think you all want to see dissension between the team, but we all like each other, we all hang out. You all want to see it. You all want to see me and Kobe fight."

West and Mitch Kupchak announced the move at a news conference. "The thing that makes it so tough," said West, "Del Harris has been a friend of mine for years and someone who's done just an absolutely incredible job here. The nature of these jobs here, they're fragile. Our jobs are fragile. To say we're blaming Del Harris for our play now would not be the case. We simply need to move forward, to try to reenergize ourselves, to refocus on our goals. And our goal is to field the very best possible team we can have. And we have not witnessed that particularly here, lately. I just feel the last two games we played were something that has not been acceptable. . . . There just looked like there was a deterioration. I talked to Jerry Buss this morning. We had a long conversation. We just felt the time was now, even though it was an awkward period for us."

Making the issue difficult was the fact that Harris had lost both of his parents during the off-season and spoke openly of his grief in addressing the decision. "Sometimes," he said, "we have it in our mind, what is going to be the best way to honor our parents, our friends, our families, or ourselves. I thought that it would be winning all these games and being the guy. But there was a deep thing that happened to me, and I think that has visited me. Since all this happened, I've been a different person. I've had a void in my personal life in these last few months, and I need help every day because it's a consistent day-to-day battle. So I don't feel like a loser today. I feel like I'm winning in the bigger battle, the more important game of life.

"I appreciate the opportunity to coach the Los Angeles Lakers," he added. "That's as high as you can get in what I do. . . . You know, if I owned the team, I might make the same decision, in all honesty."

Kobe, for one, wasn't sorry to see the change. He confided that he felt he had learned little under Harris. His appeals to add more sophistication to the offense had gone unheeded for yet another season. And now that the 1999 season had begun, it would be virtually impossible to make changes with the difficult schedule. Absent of that change with the team, the climate was already growing to make him the scapegoat for the breakdown in the offense. Kobe would complain privately about the situation, but one longtime Lakers staffer rejected Kobe's take on the situation.

"That's a typical Kobe thing where all of a sudden he's projecting it onto others," the staff member said, "instead of looking within himself and asking, 'What did I do to cause this?' That's one of the reasons that everybody else has such a difficult time with Kobe."

Still, Harris's dismissal left both Kobe and his teammates stunned. Asked about it, Kobe told reporters, "It was kind of a touchy situation. Everything just kind of collapsed all at once. And the burdens fell on Del. I think from Day 1, some players were tuning Del out. That just happens. That happens with Larry Bird, happens to Larry Brown, whoever it may be. I tuned him out a couple times. I mean, it just happens. I like to think we paid attention more often than tuned him out. . . . Del's the old school. A lot of us young players nowadays have a different style we respond to. Modern coaches are more personality, more people-oriented."

To coach the team on short notice, the Lakers turned for one game to 71-year-old assistant coach Bill Bertka while they decided on an interim replacement. That night the Lakers beat the Clippers by 15 points. Afterward Buss met with reporters and said he was in no hurry to name a replacement and that even former Bulls coach Phil Jackson might be in the mix.

"We're not under any time pressure," Buss told reporters. "We're playing pretty well right now."

Asked about Jackson, the owner replied, "All possibilities are open. I would talk to everybody. I want to win. And we'll have a lot of talks, and whoever seems to be the candidate that has the best chance to lead us to glory will be the coach, period. Over the summer we will decide who has the best chance to lead us to the promised land, and that's who we will choose. All things are open during the summer."

Asked about trying to win with an interim coach, he said, "We're obviously a contender. If everybody stays healthy, we've got a very, very good chance to win."

Reporters then pushed to know how he felt about the Rodman turmoil having a negative effect on the team. "*Turmoil's* a word that the media uses," Buss said. "My word is love. I love this team. You guys see it maybe as turmoil. I see it as a lot of love."

West and Kupchak seemed caught off guard by Buss's holding off on a decision. Their choice of a replacement rested between Kurt Rambis and Larry Drew. Drew, who is African-American, had been with the Lakers a year longer and had bench experience from coaching the team's entry in the L.A. summer league each off-season. Veteran Lakers reporter Mitch Chortkoff said that Harris had almost been fired in March 1998, and if that had happened, Drew would have been the obvious choice. But Rambis had become a hot coaching commodity over the 1998 off-season and apparently had offers to coach both the L.A. Clippers and the Sacramento Kings. He turned down both to remain a Laker assistant, leading some observers to speculate that the team had encouraged him to stay to take over for Harris.

Later, after the debacle had fully unfolded, Chortkoff and other reporters would offer that Drew was the better choice. A former pro point guard, he had the respect of the players, not to mention a solid command of Xs and Os. Plus, he had outstanding communication skills and was very patient in explaining matters to the media.

Rambis, on the other hand, seemed to detest dealing with the media and often chose to needle reporters sarcastically. Obviously, media relations was not the most important aspect of coaching, but it was an important one, particularly in Los Angeles. Rambis, though, was management's choice to take over the team on an interim basis while Drew was given a raise and kept on as an assistant. A former Lakers power forward who had played a rebounding role on several of the franchise's Showtime championship teams, Rambis immediately showed that he could command the respect of the players as a person. But establishing himself as a head coach was another question, especially during the blur of changes the team made in a very short time. One of his roles as an assistant had been to work with the little-used rookies before games. Dressed in shorts and T-shirt, Rambis would run them through the range of cuts and shooting drills, a practice he decided to keep once he ascended to the head coaching job. It was not the kind of chore that other head coaches around the league would do. "He was more like another player," said one longtime Lakers employee who was fond of Rambis. "He had a hard time being an authority figure."

And an authority figure is just what the players were looking for. Asked if the new coach should plan on immediately confronting O'Neal and Kobe about their getting along, forward Robert Horry replied, "You have to talk to Shaq and Kobe about that. It wouldn't bother me at all. . . ."

Later, as the season unraveled, talk would begin to circulate among players and Lakers staff members that Rambis was "in over his head." In fact, said one longtime staff member, "I've never seen a coach more in over his head."

Yet the argument could be made that any coach who assumed the reins at midseason during the Lakers rush of chaos would have quickly found himself in deep trouble. The waters were turbulent and swirling. Many of the factors were way beyond Rambis's control. "I'm just a pawn in this situation," he would jokingly tell reporters before the matter turned truly ugly.

The main battle Rambis faced was that of holding together the tenuous relationship between Kobe and the rest of the team. He would ultimately accomplish that but at great sacrifice. Derek Fisher later confided that as the team struggled with its many changes and the frustrations mounted, O'Neal seemed determined to confront Kobe about what many others on the roster saw as selfish play. That, they decided, had become the reason for their failure.

But O'Neal never went so far as to confront Bryant, Fisher said. "He was told to back off of that. Kurt let him basically know that it was his job to coach the team. Kurt was frustrated with Kobe's selfish playing," the point guard explained. "But Kurt was also tired of seeing the rest of the team react negatively to everything Kobe did."

From that critical standpoint, Rambis did the best that any interim coach could hope to do. He prevented his frustrated young players from self-destructing. Their short-term relationships were obviously tense, but because Rambis stepped in, their bright future remained intact, even if it meant someone else would be coaching them.

Besides, his first task as head coach of the Lakers was not to focus on Kobe and Shaq. Rather, he had to decide how to contend with Mr. Rodman.

At the very least, other teams around the Western Conference seemed gleeful about the Lakers chances of falling apart. "If he can disrupt them in any way, that's great for us," Houston's Scottie Pippen, a former Rodman teammate, said of the situation. "You know Dennis will bring a lot of rebounds and defense, but from a chemistry standpoint, if they're disrupted already, I don't know if Dennis is the guy to come in and bring them together."

For his part, Rambis had obvious reason for concern, but he tried to make light of the matter by hinting at Rodman's cross-dressing ways. Asked about disciplining Dennis, Rambis smiled and replied, "I don't see myself as an authority figure. It's a working cross-sectional relationship. And I did say *cross-sectional*, not *cross-dressing*."

In Chicago, Phil Jackson had explained to me that he, Jordan, and Pippen would discipline Rodman the way a principal at a school disciplines a misbehaving child. They would call him into the office and fuss at him, reminding him of his leadership role on the team.

Rodman craved to be a leader, despite his image, Jackson observed. Rodman would confirm that as a Laker. Still, it was just a matter of days before he came into conflict with Rambis over practice. As Rodman told his Chicago friends, practices in Los Angeles weren't that important because everybody just kind of did his own thing, as opposed to Chicago, where practices were highly structured.

"It doesn't matter out here," Rodman told a friend.

Kobe confided that indeed Lakers practices were loose. Although Rambis had come up through the Pat Riley system of tightly controlled practices as a player, he had inherited the climate set by Del Harris.

"Kurt made it a little better," Kobe said. "Some days guys knew exactly what they had to do. Coaches, too. But a lot of days people just did what they wanted."

From the start, Rodman had no respect for the arrangement, which meant that the Lakers coaches had little chance of pulling him in line. "What happened here was not Dennis's fault, although everybody tried to blame it on him," said one longtime Lakers staffer. "Once he saw how screwed up things were here, he said, 'I'm not gonna be a part of this.' And you couldn't blame him."

After two quick wins over the Clippers during their transition period, the Lakers faced yet another Sunday game on NBC, this time against the Rockets, a contest highlighted by Michael Jordan's appearance in a courtside seat next to Jack Nicholson.

Rodman highlighted the Saturday before the event by arriving late to practice, giving the new coach his first test. "The players know the rules, no matter who they are. But he's definitely going to have a leeway," Rambis told reporters. "He's a free thinker. And if he wants to do things differently, I do not have a problem with that, as long it's within the structure of the guidelines and the rules that we have set for the team."

Perhaps even more than the coaches, Rodman was feeling out O'Neal. After all, the Lakers were the center's team. Was he worthy of respect? As opponents, the two had often clashed, with Rodman making it clear that he thought little of O'Neal's understanding of what it took to win a championship. As Rodman was poised to join the team, reporters had asked O'Neal about the words they had exchanged in the past. "Now he's my teammate, so it's all been erased," O'Neal said. "I welcome him from the bottom of my heart."

In a short time it would become clear to Rodman's friends in Chicago that he had no real respect for Shaquille O'Neal. And it didn't take him longer than those first few practices to discover it. When Rodman was with the Pistons, Isiah Thomas had been fierce in policing the roster, keeping everyone's eyes on the prize. And with the Bulls, Jordan sliced up any teammate not prepared to meet the challenge. Rodman would have rather crossed God Almighty than either of them.

O'Neal, though, made no step to confront the Worm in those first days with the team. I later asked O'Neal about the circumstances, and he indicated that he didn't see such policing as his role. "They should have nipped it in the bud in the beginning," he said of the coaches. "I told them when he came, 'I'm not gonna be baby-sitting. I'm not gonna be arguing.' I'm a man of few words."

His lobbying, however, had been the main reason for Rodman's becoming a Laker. And O'Neal was obviously pleased to have Rodman's rebounding and frontcourt toughness as part of the Lakers mix. "I've always wanted a thug forward in my life," O'Neal told reporters. "You really don't know how good people are until you get a chance to play with them. He's going to get the rebounds and protect me. I've listened to him talk, and we've had conversations. He has a lot of knowledge of basketball."

Plus, Rodman seemed to agree with O'Neal's view of what the lineup lacked. "They definitely need a shooter bad," Rodman pronounced in his first days with the team. "And if they get another person that is a role player, they have a shot. If they don't get those pieces, it'll just be like Seattle. So many years they have had the best team, best team, best team, coulda, coulda, coulda . . . but they don't win."

Even with the early complications, it became immediately clear what the eccentric forward could do for the Lakers, for O'Neal, and for Kobe. Playing at small forward, Kobe suddenly no longer had to concentrate on the defensive boards. Instead the coaches told him they wanted him releasing upcourt, because they wanted him on the wing where he could score in transition after Rodman had controlled the defensive board and fired an outlet pass upcourt.

"I'll get those easy baskets," Kobe said with a smile.

It worked beautifully beginning with their very first game together. Then it worked again that Sunday on national TV against the Rockets. It was just the kind of game both the Lakers and the NBA needed. In addition to Jordan, the event attracted Randy Moss, Lisa Leslie, even a blast from the funky past in Rick James. At the last minute, Tiger Woods realized that he should be there, but it was too late. Even the Rockets' Charles Barkley couldn't find him a seat.

In the locker room before the game, Barkley fussed at the media. "I'm so disgusted by NBC and the L.A. press," he told reporters. "You guys make me sick. I'm sick of NBC showing the Lakers every week and saying how good they are. You guys all picked the Lakers to win the championship a month ago, and now all of a sudden they're struggling and they bring in Dennis Rodman and he's the savior. It shows how stupid you all are. I always tell you guys, you don't know anything about basketball. Dennis Rodman is the savior? That's why you all need to shut up and write down what we tell you and don't voice your own opinion.

"NBC thinks because they show the Lakers every weekend they're a championship team, and you all think Kobe is the next Michael. They're not and he's not. I'm sick of NBC showing the Lakers and saying how good they are. They're a glamour team."

As usual, Jordan took a more gracious route than his good friend Barkley. The Forum, in its last season as the Lakers' home court, had been the scene of several of his greatest moments, from the 1984 Olympics, where he had led the U.S. to the gold medal, to the first NBA title for his Bulls in 1991. Jordan didn't feel comfortable going back to Chicago after closing out his career in a feud with management. Still, he wanted to attend a game, and the Forum represented friendly confines. The building's game operations crew punched his face up on the giant scoreboard screen, prompting the sell-out crowd into an outburst of appreciation.

He sat uneasily at first, then rose and acknowledged the applause. "I didn't want to take away from the game," he explained to reporters later. "The game is important."

He again took his seat, but the crowd kept pounding out their appreciation, pushing him almost to tears, he admitted later. "I was touched by it. But I held steady. It was great because I never had a chance to say good-bye to a lot of fans on the road. The Lakers fans, even though we had a heated rivalry with their team over the years, have been really great to me. I appreciate it.' "

His abrupt retirement after the lockout was at least part of the motivation for his appearance, his first at an NBA game since his decision. He explained, "I just never had a chance to say good-bye to a lot of the fans on the road, all the people who came out to support us. It was a very fortunate thing that I was able to come to a game here.

"I've missed the game, but I know I've made the right choice," Jordan went on. "I'm still a fan. I'll always be a fan of the game. But there's other things I want to do with my life. I'm very happy. My life is going in whatever direction I choose, and I'm doing different things, the things I choose."

Kobe admitted to being thrilled by his presence and did his best to present Jordan with a dunk or some other aerial display whenever the circumstances allowed. More than a bit tight, Kobe wound up scoring 18 after making just 8 of his 20 field goal attempts and turning the ball over four times. Regardless, the Lakers won in a blaze, with Rodman getting 10 rebounds.

"We'll just have to wait and see what Dennis brings to this team," Houston's Scottie Pippen said afterward. "They're going to enjoy and like him for the first few weeks, but as things start to fall apart, you're going to be able to tell, really, where they are as a team. They're not always going to get on a string and start winning games. There's always something bad in an NBA season. Let's see how they face some adversity."

Thoughts of bad things, however, had seemingly receded in the L.A. haze. The next night the Lakers won in Phoenix, then returned home and beat the Suns in the Forum behind Kobe's 32 artistic points, 23 of which came in the second half. Over time a pattern had been emerging. Once he slipped into scoring mode, his effort could overwhelm opponents, who usually laid off him, guarding against his drive and daring him to shoot the jumper. When his outside shot started falling, he showed that he could rather easily take over games, something he did in the third quarter against the Suns. Once the shot fell, defenders had to step up and guard him, which opened the way for his drives.

"I knew there were going to be openings for me, and I just had to be aggressive," he said. "I saw them again and took them."

He admitted to being motivated in part by the Suns' taunting him about his defensive struggles. "They were smiling at me, and I saw them giggling on the bench—yeah, I don't like that, man," he told reporters. "I don't appreciate things like that.

"Sometimes I might get a little too hyped up. I think I did tonight, but I liked it."

Rodman's night included 17 rebounds and an air-ball free throw so horribly misjudged that he smiled afterward, licked his finger, and held it up as if testing the wind.

He wasn't the only person checking directions. With their record at 5–0 since Rodman's arrival, fans and players alike were caught in an ebullient shimmy. Two nights later they added a home win over Seattle, and the Forum again shook with delight.

In fact the whole franchise might have floated away on a tide of joy if not for the persistent worry that the trade deadline loomed less than a week away. Everyone involved felt the sense of foreboding over the rumors. According to insiders, a deal had been drawn up and awaited only the final details that would send Eddie Jones and Elden Campbell to Charlotte for Glen Rice, B. J. Armstrong, and J. R. Reid. Rice, the key player in the deal from the Lakers perspective, had been out of action for more than a year after arthroscopic surgery to remove bone spurs from his right elbow.

Surely the Lakers front office wouldn't dampen this winning streak, observers said. But Buss in particular wanted to trade Campbell because the big center was paid $7.5 million as the reserve behind O'Neal. "Our owner didn't want to pay that much money for somebody coming off the bench," West later explained. "I don't own this team. I take directions from the owner."

Campbell was clearly talented enough to be a starter, but O'Neal demanded substantial minutes. Del Harris had attempted to use Campbell at power forward with O'Neal but soon discovered that two big lumbering players in the frontcourt meant the Lakers were terrible getting back on defense. "It's just very difficult to play them both at the same time," Harris had explained.

While West was worried more about losing Campbell, the Lakers fans let it be known how much they cared for Jones, frequently chanting "Ed-die! Ed-die! Ed-die!" whenever he made something happen defensively. Jones would supposedly be thrown into the Charlotte deal to make it work from a salary cap standpoint, but some in the media doubted that was a necessity. Instead West himself implied that he had come to believe that Jones would want a huge pay increase when his contract ended in a year. So Jones's defense became expendable, and he was factored into the deal. But would the Lakers agree to it? That debate had rolled on since the opening days of the season.

The constant rumors and media speculation about the trade had worn on Jones for weeks. "I mean there have been days where I could have sat around and just cried my eyes out," he told me later. "Once I started feeling like that, I just wanted to work on something, do something, that would totally take my mind off what was happening."

"I've known Eddie a long time," Kobe said. "I could tell it was bothering him. It can't help but bother him. You hear it so many times, it has to affect you. But he kept his head. He never talked about it here in the locker room. He never moped about it. He just went out there and played."

"It became a total distraction to me," Jones said of the trade talk. "It came in abundance. The first few times I heard it, I was like, 'Well, I'm not gonna worry about it. Maybe my play will show these people how good I am.' Then you hear it again and again, and it was like, 'Well, I gotta go out and show them again.' Then you show 'em, and then you start hearing it again."

"It's unfortunate," Rambis said, "that our business has to treat people like pieces of meat, it really is. . . ."

Beyond his defense, Jones made another unrecognized contribution to the team with his ability to smooth out the relationship between O'Neal and Kobe. Once he was gone, just how important that was would become clear. "When you're in a situation with two great players, there has to be somebody who's the mediator," he would later explain. "I used to always be the guy who would say, 'Hey, man, we're gonna get this guy the ball.' I would say it. I could take somebody looking at me strange."

Although Jones and Kobe were clearly not as close as they had once been, theirs was the kind of relationship that worked smoothly on the court. "Kobe understood," Jones explained. "He knew I knew the game. He knew I wouldn't do anything that would do him wrong. He knew I would do all the right things to make our team work."

Indeed more than any other Laker, Jones had no hesitations about nudging O'Neal away from his defensive laziness. "I would tell him anything," Jones said. "To challenge shots. We needed to challenge shots. 'Do it. Let's get it going.' "

Kobe's associates said that his large contract seemed to bother Jones immensely. And then there was the obvious factor that while he could play small forward, Kobe's best position was the one that Jones played, the two guard. Still, that potential conflict mattered little to the two of them, Jones said. "It was never hard to get along. I knew I was the two guard there. He said nothing. We were playing against each other in practice each day. We competed hard. We enjoyed each other's talent. We made each other better. He loved the way I competed defensively. And offensively, I loved the way he competed. I told one guy recently, I said, 'Let me tell you something about that kid. He might be the most talented player I've ever seen in my life.' I mean he can do wonders with a basketball that people haven't seen yet. I'm serious. The things he used to do in practice, things that he would spend hours before practice started and practiced on, those things were incredible. I was in awe, man. I really enjoyed watching this kid play."

Once the Lakers began winning, many observers thought there was no way the trade would go through. Jones and Rodman on the floor together gave the lineup a decidedly defensive mind-set. With each passing victory Rodman's rebounding and hustle drew louder, more raucous responses from the

Forum crowd. Although he hardly spoke to his teammates off the court, they said it didn't matter. On the court he had brought them together by sitting at the back of the defense, talking them through situations. The entire team's enthusiasm could suddenly be measured in their new intensity. Solid proof of that came with their seventh straight win, in Utah's Delta Center of all places, where the Jazz had a 20-game home winning streak. Not surprisingly, it was another Sunday afternoon NBC game.

"I love playing here, I really do—because it's such a challenge," Kobe would say afterward. "As soon as you step into the arena, people expect you to lose."

Because of the Lakers hang-up about the Jazz (Utah had won 5 straight over Los Angeles and taken 13 of the previous 16 games), the coaching staff decided to dispense with any technical preparations, telling the players that it wasn't about Xs and Os; it was about heart.

Early in the game a young fan sitting near the Lakers bench began daring Kobe to try to dunk. At the end of the first quarter Kobe turned to him and promised that he was going to slam over Utah center Greg Ostertag before the game was over.

On his way to scoring 24 on the afternoon, Kobe made sure he kept his promise with just under five minutes to go by driving hard into the lane, rising up over Ostertag, and dunking ferociously, an emotional play that helped the Lakers keep the upper hand. As he skidded to a landing and turned to run back upcourt, the NBC cameras caught him jutting his chin and directing a knowing smirk toward the sideline. He was staring down his young heckler, who grinned good-naturedly.

"I generally don't let people get me going," Kobe later confided. "I just felt like having a challenge."

For the time being at least, the Lakers had broken the Utah spell with a 97–89 win. Afterward Kobe had a friendly word for his heckler. "I told him, 'I dunked on him, and we beat you all, too.' He was like 'OK, OK, all right, all right. I'll see you the next time you come to town.'"

The good feelings from the winning streak were so great that even another bout of Rodman tardiness the day before the game couldn't bring them down. Rambis had simply fined him again and told reporters, "You guys are making a big deal out of nothing."

The grand parade, however, was about to encounter a road full of nails. The Lakers claimed a win over the Clippers that Tuesday, March 9. The next morning Pam Bryant informed Kobe that news reports said Jones and Campbell had been traded. Later reporters wondered if he was glad that Jones had been traded to create room for himself at two guard, but Kobe denied it. "We always felt we could play together," he said. "We always felt that way. Even in practice, when they put Eddie and me together, whether it was in the backcourt or whatever, we played so well. We never viewed it that way. Never.

"Now I told him I was gonna bust his you-know-what on certain days in practice, but that was just being competitive. It was nothing more."

"Actually I was hoping it would happen," Jones explained later. "I never told anybody that I wanted out, but I did. I didn't want any of the fans to feel like I wanted to leave L.A., to leave them. But the situation that I was in, I wanted out."

As for Kobe, Jones said, "Whether I was at the two guard, or he was at the two guard or the three, I knew that we could be together on the court. I know how to play the game. I know to step off my game when I see someone else doing well. He understood that. He understood where I was gonna be on the court. I understood where he was gonna be on the court, so I think we could have lived together. I don't think the trade was made because of that.

"I knew they couldn't get rid of Elden without me. I knew that. If they wanted to get something, they were gonna have to throw me in with the deal. I was like 'Let it happen.' I didn't care where I was going. I just wanted to get out, because I felt mistreated. I felt disrespected."

The night after the deal, Forum fans again struck up their chants of "Ed-die!" and they would add a lamenting chorus weeks later on the last afternoon of the season, as the Lakers were again facing humiliation in the playoffs.

At first Glen Rice appeared hesitant to come to Los Angeles. He had been in a contract dispute with the Hornets and was worried that the troubled Lakers would prove to be a bad career move. Then there was the matter of his elbow surgery. There was no question he was one of the premier shooters in the game, but he was the kind of player used to being a team's first offensive option, not its second or third.

The day of the trade reporters asked Kobe if one basketball would be enough for the three of them, which prompted a smile. "Sure it will," he said. "This just gives you guys something to talk about."

West had his doubts, although he would wait weeks to express them. In exchange for Campbell and Jones, "we took a player who had not played in nine months," West said of Rice and his elbow surgery. Rodman's appearance with the team had prompted West to spend less and less time around the Forum, which allowed him to avoid commenting publicly on the team's myriad moves. It did not, however, keep him from pacing the floors at home late at night. Rice would struggle at times to fit in with the team, as would have any player coming to a new situation in the middle of a high-pressure season. On the other hand, on many nights the fans could clearly see the value that a great shooter like Rice could have in complementing an inside attack that featured a force like O'Neal.

West's main concern, though, had little to do with Rice. He knew the real effect of the trade would be tons of added pressure for Kobe. After having opened the season in fine fashion at small forward, he would shift to two guard with the deal. What's worse, there was no real backup on the roster who could give the team solid perimeter defense on the nights Kobe struggled. In fact West was so concerned about Bryant's defensive shift to shooting guard that the executive showed up at the Lakers practice in a business suit the day the Rice trade was announced to give Bryant a personal coaching lesson in the intricacies of off-guard defense.

It was a huge defensive transition to make in midseason. "I felt he was doing great at small forward," West said of Kobe. "At the small forward position he was defending incredibly well."

In his suit and tie West danced around with Kobe for more than an hour, offering tips on the high screen and roll and showing him how to take shortcuts to beat your man to the key spots on the floor.

West also knew that showing him would be only a tiny portion of the lesson. Most of the hard stuff Kobe would have to learn on his own, during games.

"He knows what he's talking about," Kobe said, sliding into a courtside seat after West departed. "He knows the game, period. Anytime he comes down here I get it. All kinds of things—defensively, offensively, the mental parts of the game. He's very deep. That's like golden knowledge, when you get knowledge from one of the top 50, one of the top 5 players of all time, man. You gotta relish that."

Told that West had averaged 16.5 rebounds a game as a six-foot-two senior forward in college, Kobe shook his head. "That's incredible. He loves to play, and he loves to win."

At two guard Kobe would also have more ball-handling chores. Again, this was one of his strengths, or it would be in the future, after he gained a solid understanding of the terrain. At small forward he had averaged a whopping 3.5 turnovers per game over the first five weeks of the season. "It is high," Rambis admitted. "It's not what we want. It's not acceptable, and he knows that. But he has to learn. It happens in a split second when the avenue is there to take and when it shuts down. He's doing a better job of it. Is he perfect? No, but he's doing a better job than he has in the past.

"Some of his turnovers, too, are trying to do the right thing," the new coach added. "It just didn't work out. He was trying to make the pass, and it was too hard. Or he was trying to thread the needle."

Rambis's attitude marked something of a departure from Del Harris's approach. Both West and Rambis knew that the only way to learn the tough lessons about ball handling was to play. This, of course, presented a conflict for any coach, because too many turnovers meant losses, and losses meant the coach getting fired. Although he was an interim coach, with no guarantee of a future, Rambis and his staff set aside those concerns to let Kobe learn. It could be pointed out that they had little choice, but they did so willingly, with an eye for protecting Kobe as the pressure rose.

And it would rise. O'Neal was full of anxiety about winning and immensely frustrated. He and the other players had constructed a code for expressing their dismay each time Kobe erred, making each effort a contest within the game itself. As the turmoil unfolded in the weeks after the trade as the Lakers struggled to adjust, Kobe served as the lightning rod for the rising anguish.

"I'm a very impatient person," O'Neal said frankly when I later inquired about the situation. "On paper, since we've made the changes, it's a deadly team. On paper. But we haven't played together at all."

Asked to evaluate Kobe's progress, the center said, "He's coming along pretty good. But when you get to this league, people expect you to grow up right away. Some people can grow up right away. Some people can't. I guess we just have to be patient with him."

"When Kobe makes a turnover, it's different than when Derek Fisher makes a turnover," said a team employee who was close to O'Neal and summed up his view. "When Kobe makes a turnover it totally deflates the entire team. All 12 heads drop. Because he doesn't make a turnover while trying to help the team win. He makes a turnover out of selfishness. And it's never Kobe's fault. Kobe always has an excuse. It's somebody else's fault. That's why I think he belongs on a playground. He doesn't belong in the NBA."

Not addressing the issue directly, I asked Kobe about his turnovers. Was his youth a factor? "To me that's not an excuse," he replied quickly. "If you turn it over, you turn it over, that's all. I'm making bad decisions with the basketball. But that's gonna stop, and it will stop."

While it wouldn't stop (no one's perfect), his number of turnovers would decline over the spring. Essentially, though, the coaches understood that most of Kobe's turnovers came as he attempted to create offense for himself and for his teammates. On one hand he was being criticized for not sharing the ball. On the other, when he tried to pass and missed, that just brought more criticism.

"The way I look at it, sometimes I see a lot of things on the court," he explained. "Sometimes I'll see a little too much. I'll see a lane or a gap in the defense that's open. I feel like I can zip a pass through there. Sometime it will get through there. Sometimes it won't. Sometimes when it does get through there, my teammates are not ready for it. So I just have to understand when it's there and when it's not there."

When it did get through and everything worked beautifully? "Then nobody talks about it," he said and laughed.

"You gotta take risks," he said, still laughing. "But I want to minimize the trouble. You have to have more times where the ball gets through."

He knew that transition turnovers, where the other team got the ball in the open court and scored easily, were killers. "They can cost your basketball team a game," he said. "When we played Seattle in Seattle, I had a lot of turnovers because I left my feet. It turned out to be a six- to eight-point swing."

He did not sound like someone making excuses or blaming other people. But that impression deepened with O'Neal and his teammates as the season came apart in their faces. "He's a nice kid," said the team employee close to O'Neal at the height of the frustration. "He's a clean-cut kid, he's the golden boy, he's MJ reincarnated, he's management's chosen one. He's a little prick is what he is. Talented, but still a little prick. The kid has talent and he is competitive and he works hard. That's why management is so committed to him. The parts are there but not the whole."

This frustration would twice boil over into players-only meetings with the sole agenda of calling Kobe out on his selfishness on the court; only the players continued to address the issue in code. "Everybody knew what was being said," explained one witness.

What amazed Derek Fisher was Kobe's measured, low-key response, marked by few comments and no apparent anger. "He never really stepped up and said what he thought was the problem," Fisher confided later. "I always thought that was strange, that he never stepped up and said anything. I knew that he was competitive and that he wanted to win badly. I thought he would maybe even take control of the meeting because he has that ability."

But Kobe chose to leave so much unsaid, Fisher said, which left the feelings between him and his teammates perhaps worse.

Part of the explanation came from his parents. They cautioned him to proceed carefully, not to challenge O'Neal and get into arguments and make things worse. Kobe raised his eyebrows. They didn't have to tell him that, he said. He understood how to conduct himself. The secret was to build chemistry through tough times.

There are those who would look back on the circumstances and be struck by Kobe's maturity and mental strength in responding to the situation. Clearly, just about any other young player would have been crushed by the circumstances. Between his faith, his parents, and his unbendable will, he made his way through it without getting lost.

It was no wonder, Rick Fox would say as the season wound to a close, that Kobe chose to internalize the matter rather than resorting to fighting and fussing.

"I think it would be hard for him not to internalize it," Fox said, "if you feel that you're being singled out as the guy that everyone's waiting around for."

Although people wanted an open discussion of the issue, that wasn't entirely possible, Fox said. "You can't, because it's a losing argument. Both sides have a legitimate argument. Kobe has never come out and said that he knows everything or he's where he wants to be. I think his confidence in himself may at times be misperceived. It may be seen as arrogance, to the point that he knows everything and always has to be right. He strives for perfection."

The fact that the entire team was trying to blame its woes on one person indicated how far out of balance perspectives had fallen, Fox said. "I don't think in any year, especially this season, that a team should be about one person, in terms of success or failure. But it's focused around one individual. I think he's gotten a lot of attention positively and negatively. I don't know if that's great for a team, because I don't think it's all his fault when we lose, and I don't think it's all his credit when we win."

Besides, he added, Kobe was making solid progress at playing two guard, "especially when you consider all the things that have swirled around him as an individual and as a player, things that we as a team have had to deal with. Especially when you consider the fact that he's been pointed out as the guy we're all waiting around for him to come around so that we can contend for a championship.

"He doesn't externalize all this, but he should," Fox said.

Perhaps Kobe should have kicked and screamed. His teammates seemed to want some sort of reaction, but Kobe refused to give them that pleasure.

"I'm not gonna let them pressure me into rushing my career," he offered. "I'll take it year by year, step by step, then all of a sudden I'll be right under their nose, ya know what I mean?"

"In his mind," Fox said, "I think he's told himself to relax. He does understand that he's learning on the job. The only thing is, I think it frustrates the guys who are veterans because they think, 'Well, here's Shaq, and no one gave him time to adjust.' Shaq has only X amount of time left to win championships, and he doesn't want to be learning on the fly. But I think Kobe makes strides daily."

"I think Kobe recognizes his situation," Derek Fisher said after looking back on the matter. "I just really think he understands his age and where he is in his career. He's already made a movie in his mind of where his career is gonna go. It's already planned out, and he feels he's on pace with that."

Caught with a polarized team, Rambis seemed to grow increasingly offended that they couldn't or wouldn't or didn't find a way to respond to his pleas. On one side was O'Neal with his expectations and his impatience. On the other was Kobe, determined to survive and learn and succeed.

Never had he seen a better attitude for growth and adjustment in a player, Rambis said, the marvel clear in his voice. "You couldn't be better than he is. You ask him to come to practice two hours early. You ask him to watch videotape for two hours. You ask him to stay after practice. You ask him to work on his defense, his passing, his postups. He'll do anything you want him to do. And he despises to the core losing. He will pout after his team loses in an intrasquad scrimmage. What more could you ask out of a player?"

For his part West was not deaf to O'Neal's complaints. After all, no one wanted to win worse than he did. He verged on physical illness whenever the Lakers stumbled or blundered. Still, the team's vice president insisted on keeping the long view. "He is 20 years old," West confided as the debate within the team raged. "Some of the things he has done are incredible. He's certainly had some high points and some low points. The low points come when he tries to do too much, when he tries to beat everyone in the world."

Bryant's desire for greatness has the potential to create some team-versus-individual conflicts, West conceded. "For any young player there's always that conflict. But it's not a selfish motive at all for Kobe. Players are like anyone else. They want to be recognized."

Still, there was no question that the trade and the subsequent pressure it put on Bryant further alienated him from

O'Neal and some teammates. "He's so young and has had a lot of success," West said. "A lot of that success has come before his actual accomplishments."

West cited players such as Utah's John Stockton and Karl Malone, who had paid a high price trying to be champions. "Most of the players who have attained greatness, they've had a lot of personal sacrifice and a lot of pain," West explained.

He, of course, knew all about pain. And frustration.

"No matter how much you put into it individually, it's very, very difficult," West said. "Kids today have so much success at an early age. They arrive in the NBA and think it's gonna be easy. It's not easy."

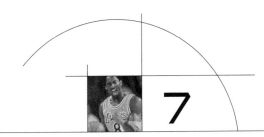

7

LEGENDS OF THE FALL

"It seems like there's a new test every week."
— KOBE BRYANT

I t was Saturday, March 13, hard on the heels of the big trade, that Dennis Rodman arrived very late to Lakers practice and informed Rambis that he was experiencing personal problems and would have to take a leave of absence.

The problems?

His Chicago friends said he had discovered that wife Carmen Electra was romantically involved with rock drummer Tommy Lee. Surprisingly, his friends didn't blame Electra. When she married Rodman, she had known that he would have substantial difficulty remaining faithful to her, and indeed he had almost flaunted his dalliances in her face. Perhaps her interest in Lee was a bit of a payback, but friends in Chicago said she obviously still cared for Rodman. He didn't take the circumstances too well, however, and went into something of a tailspin, just as he had done several years earlier in Detroit when he came home once to discover his first wife entertaining one of his Pistons teammates.

This night he burned through one cell phone battery after another in long, late-night conversations. He didn't want to deal with basketball and certainly not the fractured Lakers. So he told a stunned Rambis that he needed time.

"When we signed Dennis, we knew of his track record and

we knew that these types of situations may arise," assistant coach Larry Drew explained. "We, as an organization, were hoping it wouldn't happen. But we knew the possibility of it was very high."

The Lakers front office and coaches had wondered how they would deal with it if and when such a situation arose.

Now they were finding out.

In Chicago it was Michael Jordan who usually handled Rodman's characteristic bouts of doubt. Be with us or be gone, Jordan would quickly and impatiently tell the Worm.

Asked about that kind of leadership from the Lakers, Drew replied, "I don't know if we have it playerwise, if that's the type of responsibility that Shaq would want to take. Jerry West and Mitch Kupchak have always been the two guys to step forward in these types of situations."

What made the circumstances so hard was that many of the Lakers staff and players had quickly developed a genuine fondness for Rodman. Even Rambis, who was fighting a growing annoyance with him, found him charming. "He's done a good job dispelling all the rumors about him," the interim coach said. "He's talked with the players. He cares about this ball club. He's talked with me. He makes suggestions during the game. He's been incredible with that."

One senior staff member had been required to meet with Rodman over some administrative matters upon his joining the team and hadn't known what to expect. He was sweet and polite, introduced her to his bodyguards, then sat down and gave her his attention. It was the same manner he used with just about every staff person on every team he had played on.

"He's been great," Drew said. "He really has. He's a very likable guy. He really is, you know. And he always appears to be focused, no matter how much he stays away from the game. When he's in the locker room, when he's in a meeting, when he's on the floor, he seems to be focused."

And now he was focused on his personal problems and had decided on, it would later be revealed, a little self-medication, in the form of drinking and gambling in Las Vegas. Buss, who had called for the signing, was in the process of departing for Europe and told West to deal with Rodman however he saw fit.

The Lakers decided to respond by fining him $100 a day. For the team the timing was terrible. The Lakers were set to embark on a six-game road trip that would carry them from Sacramento to Minnesota to Cleveland to Philadelphia to Orlando to Dallas.

The Sacramento game would be the first time they had played the Kings this season and their first look at flamboyant rookie point guard Jason Williams. "He's spectacular," Kobe said. "People say he plays like Pistol Pete, and that's who he reminds me of, too. I had never heard of him. But what I like about him is that he's got the confidence to do those moves.

"He doesn't care what anybody says about him," he added appreciatively and laughed.

Asked what he would tell Williams about the hype that seemed to come with being young and talented, Kobe replied, "What would I tell him about the hype? Ignore it. You gotta keep on improving. And that's it. Don't worry about what people are saying about you today. You have to be concerned about the future."

As for his own dealings with the media, Kobe said, "That's fun. I really do enjoy it. It doesn't really add to the pressure. It's just a game. A chess game. I don't care what people are gonna say anyway. There's no question that it can bother you. None can bother me. If it's true, it's true. If it's not true, it's not true. You know what I mean?"

He would need that hard shell in the coming weeks as he alternately struggled and succeeded in his transition to playing the two guard position. That Sunday night in Sacramento he added another six turnovers to his totals, and the Lakers lost. From there it was a seething flight to Minnesota, where they beat the Timberwolves, 107–101, after Rice, himself faced with an adjustment, scored 8 quick points over the final minutes.

Kobe, too, turned in a nice box score with 21 points, 9 rebounds, and no turnovers, plus he settled the outcome with a driving layup, a 3-pointer, and 2 free throws. It all added up to an 11-point fourth quarter to go with Rice's big fourth quarter, and it left the impression that, given time, he and Rice would soon learn to complement one another.

Time, however, was not to be had in the zany season. They repaired next to Cleveland, where Kobe was shown a jolting lesson in the high screen and roll, which left him with a sprained ankle and the growing concern that teammates weren't entirely committed to calling out the screens and picks on his blind side. Then again, the Lakers had never quite gotten the hang of defending the screen and roll, and the Cavaliers happily reinforced that impression with a 100–93 win.

Next up was Kobe's hometown. The Lakers coaches had been concerned about the Philadelphia game, about Kobe's competitiveness against Allen Iverson. "Every time he comes home he wants to do well," Larry Drew explained. "He has the matchup to deal with, he has being home to deal with, he has everybody making the Bryant-Iverson comparison into The Matchup. He's fighting two or three demons. But we just try to tell him not to get caught up in that."

That was hardly a choice. Sixers coach Larry Brown had craftily moved the silver-quick Iverson to two guard and brought in a tall role player, Eric Snow, to play the point. Suddenly every team in the league seemed to struggle in contending with Iverson on the wing. Instead of being outmatched against opposing two guards on defense, the six-foot Iverson simply took the other team's point guard and turned the two guard defense over to the taller Snow.

For Kobe the Sixers had a new set of looks waiting, nasty screens and double screens. That and Iverson's quickness freed Iverson up to take a whopping 36 shots. The situation prompted O'Neal, who was battling Iverson for the league scoring lead and what both hoped would be MVP honors, to comment afterward, "Any shooter who shoots the ball 36 times every night should be the leading scorer in the league and should be an MVP candidate. I mean, I wish I shot the ball 36 times."

Kobe faced a disadvantage in that he had to guard Iverson, but Iverson didn't have to guard him. In the end Iverson would finish with 41 points and 10 assists, and Kobe kept pace, scoring 18 himself in the first half. But in the second half he strangely backed off that aggressiveness as the Sixers pulled away, 105–90.

"I wasn't getting as many looks as I was in the first half," Kobe would later confide. "I wasn't being as aggressive. I didn't want to force anything, you know what I mean? It's important for me to be patient and read and see where things are coming from. It was the first time, since I've been in the league, that the defense really keyed in on me."

The Sixers made a special effort to shut him down, leading him to realize later that aggressiveness is a funny thing. You think you're being aggressive, then you look back at the videotape of the game and realize that you let opportunity slip away. If he wanted, Kobe could have blamed the situation on his teammates not getting him the ball. But that wasn't the case, and he said so.

"That's something you must figure out, though, because it is the defense," he said. "You have to think. You wonder why the hell you aren't getting looks. It's the defense."

He also took the blame for the defensive breakdowns and had to tell the beat writers covering the team that it was his fault.

"It's a tough matchup having to defend somebody that small and that quick," Larry Drew conceded. "There are gonna be teams that have success against the Lakers and success against him. He'll take everything in stride. The first thing he told me after the Philadelphia game was that he really wanted to spend more time studying how to defend the pick and roll."

"They came at us with a lot of new stuff during the game," Kobe said. "I just do the best I can. If you fail, that's how you learn. Try new things, and if they don't work, throw them away, find something that works, and keep on using it."

He wasn't alone in this plight, of course. The screen and roll was a simple little play that teams had employed since George Mikan and Jim Pollard used it to help the Lakers rule the league in the 1940s and '50s. In the modern NBA the play was never the same with any team because every pair of players ran it differently. And when opponents didn't execute the screen and roll, they simply ran their two guard off a series of screens to get him open, a process that left the defender feeling like he'd been through blocking drills in football—without the pads.

"The screen and roll is something I've never had to guard before," Kobe said. "It's not Iverson or Pippen. It's the play. Playing small forwards is totally different. At two guard, when a guy comes off a screen, it's getting used to that."

One of his strengths with two guards was being more physical, but that, too, depended on the matchups. If he couldn't catch them, he couldn't be physical with them. "The hardest thing for me is not so much keeping up with them," Kobe said. "It's keeping up with the screens. That's my hardest part. It's not playing them. It's playing the screens."

"He knew when we made the trade that the two guard slot would be his position," Larry Drew said. "He knew that he would have to grow up pretty quick. With Eddie Jones having had that position for the last few years, Kobe knew he would have to step in and take over and that there would be huge, huge responsibility on the defensive end. He knew he would have to step up his game."

"Two is the toughest position in the league," Eddie Jones observed later when asked about Kobe's adjustment. "You got to defend the other team's best player every night. There's not many breaks. You've got to play defense on one end and create offense on the other. You gotta handle the basketball, and you're being defended. You gotta try to create for your teammates, to get things open for the rest of the guys. The point guard does a lot, but the two guard does the same things and also has to defend. Once Kobe gets adjusted to playing a lot, he'll get better."

Moving to two guard meant that Kobe had a front-row seat to the NBA's most entertaining show, an experience that kept him alternately wincing and giggling in delight. "It's a fun position to play, defensively, too, instead of being down there at the forward spot, banging and banging and chasing guys and everything," he observed. "It's a lot more intricate at two guard. So many two guards are so different offensively and defensively. It's completely different. It's crazy. It's incredible to me. Every night it's just completely different. A different challenge."

Even guarding Iverson was fun, he said, because of the challenge. Plus he liked Iverson. They chatted amicably, asked about each other's family.

Neither Kobe nor his teammates, however, were far removed from the questions about Rodman, who had missed four straight games. Without his presence the Lakers had posted eight wins against nine losses. "He'll be back," O'Neal promised, "and we'll get back on track. When he comes back, things will be OK."

"I think they need Rodman," Iverson told beat writer Tim Kawakami of the *Los Angeles Times*. "I see some chaos in their team. I won't elaborate."

Magical Interlude

Next up on Kobe's tour of two guards was Anfernee "Penny" Hardaway of the Orlando Magic. Kobe had idolized him as a teen and still maintained an appreciation for his game, Hardaway's flair and flamboyancy, but he made it clear that Hardaway presented nothing of the challenge that Iverson had.

In fact, he decided to take some rare time off in Orlando, to go, out of all things, to Walt Disney World. "Disney is like the greatest place in the world," he explained the next day, still wearing a black Disney hat. "It's like the happiest place on earth. If I could, I'd live there."

He used the time to buy a boatload of gifts for his baby niece, his sister's new child.

"I shook hands with Mickey Mouse, Minnie Mouse," he said. "I spent about three hours there. I bought a bunch of stuff for my niece. . . . You go there, and it takes all your worries away."

He felt particularly good that late March afternoon because practice had been good. The Lakers had actually had some time to work on things for a change. Upon Rambis ascending to command, Kobe had hoped that the coaching staff would make the effort to install split cuts in the offense. In fact he and Rambis had discussed the issue even before Rambis became head coach. But once he got the job, Rambis found his hands full with a dizzying season schedule.

"It's something I would like to do," the coach said when asked about split cuts, "but it takes practice to get that done. I can't just tell them, 'OK, you guys split,' because most players didn't grow up doing that. That's why Utah does it so effectively, because they do it over and over again. They practice it, and they do it in the games. They read the defense and all that stuff. It takes good, hard practice to figure all that out, how everybody's gonna get open, how you cut, how you move, who screens for who."

Instead, the coaches focused on adding some plays into the offense to get Rice the ball. A dazzling shooter, Rice explained that he liked coming off screens in set plays to get his shot, which didn't mesh so well with O'Neal's approach of getting the ball in the post, then flinging it out to spot-up shooters on the perimeter.

Whereas adding Rodman to the Lakers offense had been easy (he hardly ever took a shot), incorporating Rice presented quite a challenge, Larry Drew admitted. "That's not something that's gonna happen overnight either. Glen has always been a focal point of the offense in Charlotte, then he comes here where he's not the primary focus. That's a big adjustment. He has shown that he's willing to make that adjustment. It's just not something that's gonna come overnight. That's gonna take time."

It would also require a substantial sacrifice from O'Neal, Rambis admitted. "Shaq is saying and doing the right things. He is the focal point of our offense and our defense. He's the one that's wanted to get the acquisitions that we've had, so he's the one that has to sacrifice his ego; he's the one that has to sacrifice his limelight. Yet he's still the focal point of our ball club, so I think that says a lot for him as a leader. He makes no bones about the fact that he wants to win a championship, and he'll do whatever it takes for us to win one. He told me today, 'I don't have to be the focal point anymore. You can get me a couple of times, and you can go get Rice a couple of times. We can work our offense that way.' "

O'Neal's frustrations and the team's struggles would soon eat away at that resolve and leave him calling for the ditching of plays for Rice. But in the short term the coaching staff added the new looks, and it pleased Kobe.

"We had a real good practice going over some new sets," he confided in Orlando. "We put in some new stuff, back doors and guys reading each other off player picks and stuff. It was good."

Even so, the mood of the team was pensive. Above everything else the Lakers had shown they were a team with many frustrations bubbling just under the surface. While O'Neal was driven by his admitted impatience, the coaches somehow were able to fight off the pressures of their own impending futures to take special care of Kobe.

That was apparent in the wake of the Philadelphia game. "The most important thing at this stage is for him to learn as he goes along," Larry Drew said. "It's easy for a young guy to get discouraged when he has problems with different aspects of the game, but he has always maintained a positive attitude. He may be just a little disappointed. First of all, everybody's disappointed that we've lost three of our last four."

But everyone's spirits seemed lifted by word that Rodman planned to appear Sunday morning before their nationally televised game with Orlando. Even veteran Derek Harper, who had quickly become fed up with Rodman's antics and the team's handling of them, brightened at the news. "There's no need to panic right now," Harper said. "We knew this was gonna be a very tough road trip. Without Dennis we're a very different team. He has proven that. He's a big part of what we do."

Sure enough, the 37-year-old Rodman showed up at the team's meeting that morning. Kobe hadn't even noticed until he looked up and saw him sitting there. "We all said what we had to say to him, and he said he's going to be back the rest of the year," O'Neal explained later. "He said he had some personal problems. You never really know what that is, but you just have to respect the guy, and our organization was gracious enough to let him go to Vegas and gamble."

After the game Rodman would explain to reporters that it was his wife who prompted him to return. "Carmen told me . . . 'Dennis, go out there, suck it up, and do it, just do it. I know you love the game. Just go out there and do it,'" Rodman said. "This game ain't worth that much for me to lose who I am. So I could've stayed out and probably would've got kicked out of the state of California. But it don't matter. I've got to keep my head and my life together."

During Rodman's tenure in Chicago the Bulls had sought psychiatric help for him. And during the darkest hours of his absence, the Lakers had inquired about similar help. But Rodman said he didn't need it. "I saw a psychiatrist the last two or three years. I think that I know what I'm doing," he said. "I had to get away because I really didn't know if I wanted to play basketball. I'm different. I'm different—I do it my way."

"He had his game face on. I was just happy to see him back," Kobe said of Rodman before the game. "It's really gonna be wild. There's gonna be a lot of energy out there. When he shows up, he shows up ready to play. As long as all the other stuff doesn't affect the team mentally, as far as how they react to him, then we'll be all right. It bothers some more than others. Me personally, it doesn't bother at all. It's easy to focus."

When the Lakers rolled out into Orlando's arena that afternoon, Rodman was with them and sporting heavy bags under his eyes. As the crowd let loose a deep round of boos, he tugged nervously at his ear, he hopped into the layup routine, then somehow managed to slip into the background (he played 23 minutes, scored four points with six rebounds).

In the first half it was the Magic that took the spotlight by niftily executing their screen and roll. Part of their fun was pulling reserve center Michael Doleac away from the basket, where O'Neal was reluctant to chase him. The result was a career day for the Magic rookie, 25 points, and a 24-point second-quarter lead for the Magic. The Lakers gave up 63 points in those first two quarters, although they were able to cut the Magic lead to 20 by the half.

Even so, they walked off the floor looking like people flattened by a steamroller. The pick and roll so dazed Kobe in the first half that he was left disoriented even on offense and had managed just five points. In the locker room at halftime, there was heated discussion about defensive adjustments.

They quickly decided to come out aggressively in the second half and trap Orlando's pick and roll, which meant that O'Neal would have to become more active, shifting back and forth to the perimeter. It wasn't something he always liked to do.

"He did a great job trapping, and he had to rotate out of that," Rambis explained afterward. "For a guy who's that big, to ask him to do that, and then he did it so successfully, that's just a huge compliment to him."

Within the first few minutes of the third period, the Lakers had slammed shut Orlando's pick and roll, setting up a dramatic shift in momentum. "I just could not believe the turnaround . . . all the adjustments we made, the intensity, the guys helping each other," Rambis said. "It was beautiful to watch how they worked so well together."

With the Magic offense contained, Kobe fell into a shooting groove, making 13 of 16 shots in the final two periods.

"Teams have been giving me the open shot lately," Bryant said. "I hope they keep thinking like that, because I'm going to shoot. It's something I worked on all summer, hitting the open shot."

Watching from the bench, Derek Fisher saw the first jumpers fall and knew Kobe had settled into one of his scoring modes. "I knew if I got in the game I would be looking for Kobe coming off the screens and get the ball in his hands," Fisher explained.

Once on the floor, Fisher fed Kobe time and again. At one point in the third, after Kobe had feasted on several open shots in a row, Fisher sent the ball to him on the wing, but Kobe paused, thought better about it, and fired the ball back to Fisher. It was a subtle thing, but it showed a huge leap in maturity. Fisher waited for Kobe to set his feet again, and when the defender looked away, Fisher pushed the pass right back to him. Kobe again nailed the shot.

"Kobe's one of the best basketball players in this league, when he takes his time and picks and chooses when it's time to really go ahead and take the shot," Fisher explained later. "He showed the kind of potential he has to dominate basketball games night in and night out."

Rambis was equally elated by the sequence. "If they all just think of the team first . . . ," he said.

"I knew exactly how they were gonna play me," Kobe said of his second-half awakening. "I just wanted to relax. The first half I was rushing things a little bit because I felt really good. In the second half I just wanted to be more efficient, to cut back on my movement."

When it was over, he had scored 33 second-half points, a career-high total of 38 for the game, and the Lakers had wiped out the huge Magic lead to claim a 115–104 win. O'Neal had 31 points and 13 rebounds, and Derek Harper hit five

3-pointers down the stretch. "They are a traveling All-Star team," Magic coach Chuck Daly said. "Shaquille O'Neal is an All-Star of All-Stars. Kobe Bryant, we probably saw his coming-out party on national TV [NBC] today. We all know how good he is."

Despite all his activity, Kobe had sailed through the second half without a turnover. "They're just waiting for me to be myself, waiting more me to come to them," he said of defenders waiting on impromptu forays to the basket. "I'm not gonna do that anymore."

Just as he spoke, a Fox Sports Net reporter stepped up and asked him to do a live interview nationwide. Kobe turned to face the bright lights and smiled. Yes, he had had a big day, but the defense was what won the game, he said. And, no, he added, he wasn't getting the idea that he was the star of the team. "You're always gonna have to honor Shaq, I don't care who's hot," he said. "If I'm hot, Glen's hot, you're always gonna have to honor Shaq down there. He's our force in the middle."

As he spoke, a conservatively dressed young man quietly slipped into the Lakers locker room and sat on the bench beside him. Kobe turned away from the interview and jumped in surprise. "Peyton, what's happening, man? It's a pleasure to meet you," he said, obviously genuinely enthused about meeting Peyton Manning, Indianapolis Colts quarterback and fellow Adidas endorser.

"You, too," Manning said, smiling and looking a lot like a frat brother.

"Great season for you, man," Kobe told him.

"Thanks a lot," Manning said quietly. Obviously he didn't want to stir the interest of the numerous reporters milling about the room doing interviews.

"What you doing now, you working out?" Kobe asked.

"Yeah, working out," Manning replied. "Just down for the weekend. Adidas had a thing down here. Came to see the game. You guys put on a good show."

"Thanks, dawg. Thanks, dawg," Kobe said happily, then jumped with a question. "Hey, they let you meet Anna yet?"

Kobe harbored a deep infatuation with tennis star Anna Kournikova, who was also part of the Adidas team.

"Do what?" Manning asked, looking confused.

"They let you meet Anna yet?" Kobe repeated.

"Oh yeah," Manning said, his smile widening.

"What you think?" Kobe asked

"That's one of the benefits I like with Adidas," Manning said.

Kobe laughed with a deep hahaha, slapped his knee, then clapped.

"I like her. I like her," Manning said, laughing with him.

"That's great stuff, man." Kobe agreed, still laughing. "Adidas is a big family. All the men of Adidas are pulling for Anna."

For a few minutes the two young sports millionaires shared a wide-ranging conversation, with Kobe pumping Manning for information about training methods, pass routes, even the inside scoop on Colts roster moves, displaying a surprising knowledge of the NFL. Soon he had lapsed into a full fantasy, him playing quarterback and Manning running the wing for the Lakers.

Abruptly the session ended. The Lakers had a game in Dallas the next night and a plane to catch. Time to be wary again. "Just move on to the next one," Kobe said of his mind-set after the big game. "We got Dallas. We can't fall asleep that game."

Sitting nearby, 37-year-old Derek Harper looked very relieved. He shuddered to think what would have followed if the Lakers had folded at halftime. "Taking a trip to Dallas with no one talking to anybody and it tearing us apart as a team," he said, "because you lose a game like this the way we were on our way to losing it, and it can destroy you."

Playing Dallas meant Kobe would have to contend with Michael Finley, the next obstacle in his two-guard odyssey. "He plays with a lot of energy, takes a lot of shots," he said of Finley, "so you're going to have to be on your toes at all times."

Breakdown

The Lakers won that next night against Dallas, and Kobe held his own, scoring 21 points to Finley's 24. Then he and his teammates packed up and headed home, where two nights later they lost to Phoenix. Then for good measure they lost yet another two nights later, to Sacramento. At the time the players weren't sure what was happening to them, but they would soon come to understand that the period marked the rapid disintegration of Rodman's relationship with Rambis.

"I think it's shocked everybody," Larry Drew admitted after things had run their course. "Nobody anticipated all these things happening that have happened."

Rodman had the look of a man who had been on a Vegas binge when he returned to the team in Orlando ("I'm here for the rest of the season," he told reporters then. "I've used up my hall pass."), but he then had 17 rebounds in Dallas and led the team on the boards for another eight games. The numbers, though, didn't matter. He fumed whenever Rambis removed him from the lineup and kept him on the bench during games. At Rodman's request the team had provided an exercise bike to ride to stay warm during the periods, similar to the one he had taken to riding during the end of his tenure in Chicago. In Los Angeles the bike went unused.

His problems deepened with the Sacramento loss on March 26. Rodman led the Lakers with nine rebounds, but in a tiff he refused Rambis's request to return to the game after an extended period on the bench, saying he had grown stiff. With Rodman out, Kings power forward Chris Webber tipped in the winning shot with less than a second to go. It was a bitter loss that wasted Kobe's 26-point effort.

"I think you need to ask the people around here what is going on," Rodman told reporters afterward. "This is just completely ridiculous. I'm not used to this. I'm put in the starting rotation, and I only played 24 minutes."

Then he explained the team dynamic. "If we win, we win," he said. "If we don't, there will be more bitching and complaining about people." When he played, the Lakers usually won, and if they did, things ran smoothly. But when the losses mounted, so did the complaints about Kobe.

That next morning Rodman was better than an hour late to practice, and when he did arrive, he had his agent in tow for a meeting with Rambis. "I think we have come to an understanding that he is an important part of this ball club, and we need him to make a more concerted effort to be a part of this team," the coach told reporters afterward. "Be at practice, be on time, all of those things.

"I feel that it was a very positive discussion," the coach said. "I believe there's going to be a lot of positive things that are going to come out of that discussion. I understood why his frustration led him to be late. And we worked through his frustration, to what I feel is our satisfaction."

"They depend on me to keep this ship afloat," Rodman told *Newsweek*. "It's amazing to me that a person who doesn't score, doesn't make Michael Jordan–type moves, is expected to come in and win a championship for a team in total disarray. Am I a genius? Am I a miracle worker? Am I God? No— but I have a gift."

The next week brought three wins and reasonable calm, but it wouldn't last. First came wins over New York and Vancouver in which Rodman had 12 and 17 rebounds. In a tight win over Phoenix, Kobe distinguished himself defensively against Jason Kidd. "I truly believe he can be a stopper for us," Rambis said.

Even more important, Rice hit the winning shot and ran up 23 points for the night, a reward in that the team had struggled to include him in the offense.

That success, though, was followed by a humiliating home loss to Golden State during which the Lakers stars from the Showtime teams were honored at halftime. Then Kobe had 26 and Rodman contributed 17 rebounds in a Forum win over Denver, but the next day came news from Rodman's publicist that he and Carmen Electra had agreed to close up shop on their six-month marriage while remaining friends.

That night in Utah, Karl Malone had his way with Rodman, hitting all 12 of his field goal attempts in a Jazz blowout. Kobe had the same kind of trouble with Utah's Shandon Anderson, who broke him down for baskets.

Rambis responded to the team's anger by benching Bryant for long stretches of both halves. "I'm fine with it. I told Kurt, 'Man, I'm with you,'" Kobe told reporters. "Now, obviously, I don't like getting taken out of the game at any point. You want to play. But I'm always with Kurt. I respect Kurt because he has the [guts] to make those types of decisions. A lot of coaches, they would just panic and say, 'OK, regardless of what's going on, regardless of the mistakes that you're making, I'm just going to stick with you, because if we lose, I can say we lost with our best guys.' Kurt, he really doesn't care about any of that."

The outcome prompted the players-only meeting before the next game in Sacramento, the purpose of which was to call

Kobe out for his play. O'Neal then danced around the issue, but Bryant clearly got the message. He led the team in assists that night with seven, the only problem being that he also had eight turnovers. Still, the Lakers won and improved their record to 24–13. "What we're trying to do is playing to improve," Kobe said. "We're not even close to playing our best basketball. Not even close. And we're still in the hunt, still in the race, we're still playing good basketball."

But in the next game, a Friday, April 9, win over Utah at the Forum, Rodman again refused a Rambis request to return to the floor late in the game. The next day he was again late for practice, by an hour.

In the next game, against Seattle, O'Neal scored 38, his season high, Kobe had 25, and Rodman led the team with 13 rebounds, but they still lost.

The Lakers had gone 18–8 since adding Rodman (17–5 in games that he played), but the team seemed a shambles, unbridled and out of touch with itself, which prompted *Los Angeles Times* columnist Bill Plaschke to question O'Neal about his leadership. The center responded by saying that his attempts to discipline the team were undermined by Rambis. "I have said some things, done some things," he said. "But around here, it doesn't really work. Sure, I can get on a guy. But if that happens, Kurt can't go back up to him and talk all nice."

It was an obvious reference to Rambis's protecting Kobe from the center's wrath. "Do I think players should be yelling at each other? No," Rambis responded. "Kareem never said a word to us, but he didn't have to. We knew what we were supposed to do by just watching him."

O'Neal said he had also attempted to pull Rodman in line but had been told that Rambis would handle it. In the end, that's what the interim coach did.

The end was first marked by a blowout loss to Portland, in which the Blazers took advantage of both O'Neal and Rodman failing to get back in transition. "Their big guys weren't running the floor, and we took advantage of that," said Portland's Rasheed Wallace.

Rodman declined to play in the second half, saying he had a sore elbow and was recovering from the flu. "He said his elbow was bothering him, and I'll take it for that," Rambis said.

In their seven weeks with Rodman, the Lakers hadn't realized just how much they had in common with Carmen Electra, how they both had found and lost love in Rodman's nightmare of a funhouse.

Like Electra, the Lakers had attempted to ignore every sort of infidelity, but it finally got to be too much. He showed up late for Lakers practice on that Thursday, April 13, and couldn't find socks and shoes, the last in a long line of tests for the franchise.

"Just go home," Rambis told him.

Hours later West waived him, a pathetic ending to a distinguished career.

"At this time we feel it's in the best interests of the Lakers to end the relationship," West said in a prepared statement. "This obviously didn't work out like we had hoped, but we would like to thank Dennis for the contributions he did make to the team and wish him the best of luck in the future."

Asked for a response to his release, Rodman told Fox Sports, "They have to have a fall guy and I'm basically the fall guy. I wanted to play, and . . . the Lakers are cowards not to take the fall for some of the things that have happened this year. I hope I'm still loved by people here in the state of California."

He added that he would like to play for another team this season. "It depends on if somebody wants to take a chance on having a guy like me on a team that can win a championship—I will go and play with them," he said.

At the time Kobe told reporters that he understood management's decision. "I really didn't see the reason why they released him," he confided later. "It really shocked me." O'Neal, too, was privately upset and blamed L.A. print reporters for making a public issue of Rodman's transgressions with the team.

As Rodman had claimed, it would later become clear that he was hardly the heart of the Lakers' troubles. In fact there were those in the organization who still felt he was the team's best chance for winning. Without him the Lakers dropped into a tailspin. "We felt disoriented, really," Kobe explained.

It proved to be another mysterious drop, filled with even more unexpressed resentment and yet another team meeting.

Rodman's release was marked by their getting hammered at Utah in their very next game. They beat Vancouver in the Forum, then headed up the coast to Golden State and promptly fell behind the Warriors by 28 points in the second quarter.

Then O'Neal got ejected for shoving Warriors guard Bimbo Coles.

All of this happened as Michael Jordan watched from courtside, the guest of Golden State assistant Rod Higgins, an old friend and former Bulls teammate.

Pressing to impress, Bryant produced one misfire after another and finished the first half with a mere two points. Then at halftime he calmed and decided to change his approach. "I just wanted to relax," Bryant said. "We were rushing. We just had to calm down."

Relaxing meant that by the fourth quarter he could slip into his scoring mode. He rolled up 14 points, spurring a Lakers comeback that ate the Warrior lead right down to the wire. It was Kobe's 3-pointer that cut the deficit to 88–87 with 4.2 seconds remaining.

Then came the magical sequence. Unfortunately, Jordan wasn't there to see it, having left just before the end of regulation. The Warriors led by three after Coles hit two late free throws. Then Golden State fouled Rice so that he couldn't tie it with a 3-pointer. Rice made the first and intentionally missed the second, which allowed Robert Horry to get a hand on the loose rebound. Horry batted the ball to the right of the goal just as Bryant sailed in from behind the top of the key and tipped in the tying basket. "I saw the ball going to the baseline after Robert [Horry] got his long arm on it," Kobe told reporters. "I was just lucky it went in."

From that spectacular finish the Lakers would control the overtime period for a 106–102 win. Kobe had scored 25 in the second half to make it happen.

"It's unbelievable," Rambis said. "They showed great heart, great character, tremendous confidence. Kobe lives for games like this. It's what he dreams of. It's what he thinks of. If I ask Kobe if he could get a game like that every game, he would say yes. His coach wouldn't like it, but he would love it."

When asked later about Jordan's presence, Kobe smiled broadly. "Can you believe it? Isn't that wild?" he said. "And then he wasn't there to see it at the end."

The buzz from the big win lasted only a few hours, until Portland zapped them the next night by again resorting to a running game. Still, Kobe had obviously attempted to respond to his teammates' veiled complaints in their team meeting in Sacramento. In the previous eight games he had led the team in assists in six of them. He had gotten so much better at reading defenses and was such a threat that Rambis had increasingly taken to running Kobe at the point guard spot and shifting Fisher over to two guard down.

"I encourage him on a daily basis to get better, to make more right decisions at the right time," Rambis said. "He has the capability to do things on his own, do things that other people can't do. I think he's more conscious and aware when he has the ball in his hands of reading the defense. That's something we've been working with him on, to read and see and visualize and to anticipate. Because he could be very good at that. If he develops those instincts and those instantaneous reads as to where the ball should go, it's gonna make our team better, it's gonna make him better, and it's gonna make things easier for us. And him."

Even so, it was hard not to notice that his turnovers remained high, the coach added. "Sometimes he's trying to do the right thing, and sometimes he's trying to do too much. I don't expect him to be perfect. Nobody makes all the right decisions all the time. He still is developing. He still is learning. Some nights he has to deal with different things, so I don't expect it to be on a continual upward swing. That would be nice, but I know he's gonna take some steps forward and take some steps back. As long as he keeps his head in the right direction, that's all that I'm concerned with."

With a 27–17 record and a tenuous peace in the ranks, they headed to Texas to take on the soaring Spurs and the struggling Rockets. Asked what he would do if given the opportunity to do anything to improve the club, assistant coach Larry Drew said, "We've got to commit to one another. At times it looks like we've made that commitment to one another. Then at times it looks like everybody's got a different agenda."

It was the perfect wish. As they approached the final six games on the schedule, the Lakers' internal division remained deep. From Charlotte, Eddie Jones had kept in contact with friends on the team, except for Kobe, and he had heard the list of complaints. "I talked to Kobe after the trade, but I haven't talked to him in a while," Jones confided. "Everybody is saying this and that about his situation on the team. I won't say anything. I just want him to deal with it, make it right. Those things that people say will definitely make him grow up."

O'Neal remained obviously displeased. "There's a big responsibility," he said of Kobe. "He just has to adjust. We all just have to play team ball."

"With the turn of events that happened the way they happened, it can pull a team apart," Larry Drew observed. "We've had some ups, and we've had some downs."

The assistant acknowledged that the circumstances, the division, still left the coaches searching for an answer. "All the things that come into play as far as dealing with two different parties, those are things that can pull those parties further apart," Drew said. "You've got to find some kind of way not to allow that to happen."

For his part Kobe remained optimistic. "It's gonna be for the better eventually," he said of the Lakers struggles. "But right now we're going through it, as any team would. We're still fighting."

It had been a season of hard lessons, but he treasured them, he said. "All of them. You really do. Every little bit of them. You can't overlook any of them. It seems like there's a new test every week."

He laughed and said he could handle the criticism "because I don't really pay any attention to it. I know it's going on, but it doesn't really bother me. I don't let it grab me."

Although the team continued to focus on Kobe as a problem, Drew acknowledged that the team's defensive lapses had killed its momentum time and again, particularly the failure to get back to stop an opponent's transition. O'Neal's size was obviously a factor for him in the situation, but few of the other Lakers seemed focused on defending in transition. As a result, the scouting report against them said, "Run. Then run some more."

"We're still having that problem right now," Drew said of getting back. "And you can't have that. You look at the tape and you can see we haven't gotten back consistently. That's been a weakness of ours that other teams have exploited. They've come into games looking into getting us into an up-and-down game."

From the standpoint of the coaching staff, it was a touchy point to address with O'Neal. "If it's gonna take us getting on guys, telling them that they gotta get back, gotta do a better job, then that's something that we as a coaching staff have to do," Drew said. "We won't be going anywhere until we do that."

They found a Spurs team eager to exploit the situation and an Alamodome crowd of almost 32,000 roaring in delight as San Antonio ran away with a 27-point win. Hobbled by a sore left leg, Kobe played 38 minutes and scored 11 points on 5-of-14 shooting from the floor.

"We're trying to find ourselves as a basketball team," Derek Harper said afterward. "The cohesiveness is not where it has to be for us to be successful. Say what you want, we don't have to sleep with each other and go to bed with each other, but you need to be tied together as a group. Where it is, I'm not sure, but all of that aside, we gotta find a way to get things turned around."

Two nights later they visited the Rockets, another team caught in a funk, what coach Rudy Tomjanovich called the "negative energy" that can collect around certain teams as the playoffs approach.

During the shootaround before the Monday night game, I introduced Kobe to George Mumford, the sports psychologist that Phil Jackson had used for years to keep the Bulls functioning with a clear competitive mind. Kobe seemed stunned. "He brought you into practice?" he asked in disbelief.

Over the years Jackson had used a variety of strategies to battle the elements that subverted success. More than any coach, he seemed aware of the stresses that built up around competitive people. Jackson aimed to do anything possible to eliminate those stresses.

Mumford's approach was a mix of psychology, tai chi, meditation, and common sense. Beyond that Mumford was acutely perceptive about the details of group interaction. He often spent much time discussing with players how they saw themselves, how they saw each other, and how they viewed their relationships.

Mumford watched the Lakers in San Antonio and Houston and saw a disjointed group that had to clear away a substantial amount of mental debris before they could hope to compete.

That night Rick Fox said he was hoping an act of nature would do the trick. As he warmed up for the Rockets, Fox shook his head and said, "Somebody said there was a tornado in the area as we were riding over here. I said I hope it runs through this building and brings us back to the reality that basketball is just a game. Or maybe we could take a flight over to Kosovo.

"We're letting the little trivial things get in the way of the fact that, hey, we make a great living playing the game of basketball."

Like the Rockets, the Lakers had been zapped by negative energy, Fox said. "We haven't had anything positive really happen to us since the 10-game win streak. We've had all the situations with Dennis, all the situations with losing, with the trade. We're all walled up within our own mishaps and misfortunes and distractions. We've refused to lift our heads above all that."

To their credit, the Lakers would find the verve to make a brief recovery, although they got walloped that night in Houston, this time by 22, as the Rockets ran to their hearts' delight. Kobe opened the game by missing one shot after another, digging himself a deeper and deeper hole. He would finish with just nine points. Worst of all, he got into a snit with Rambis during a time-out with six minutes left in the fourth quarter. Kobe had his own thoughts about guarding Pippen, and Rambis raised his voice, telling him to do what he was supposed to do, double-team Charles Barkley in the post and leave Pippen on the perimeter. "Don't do it! Don't do it! Don't do it!" Rambis yelled loud enough for the *Los Angeles Times*'s Tim Kawakami to hear. Finally the coach shouted, "Fine, you're right! Do whatever you want to do!"

Once Rambis raised his voice, Kobe got up and moved to another spot on the bench.

In the locker room afterward, Derek Harper looked as if he had just bitten into a sour apple. "No defense. No passion to play the game," he said with disgust. "It's very, very difficult to explain. We've dug a hole for ourselves as a basketball team. You have to play defense on a consistent basis. Our focus tends to be offense, and as a result we lose every night because we don't care about defense."

As reporters were clearing out after their interviews, Harper stood by his locker and said loud enough for his teammates to hear, "Overrated m——f——ers."

Tex

By flatlining in Texas, the Lakers once again demonstrated their fragile nature. With the two losses, more of their chemistry problems spilled over into the L.A. newspapers. While the issue was still discussed in largely euphemistic terms, O'Neal grew bolder in his criticism of Kobe.

Bryant, for his part, continued to play the controversy down, as his parents had counseled him to do. He said that he didn't really know O'Neal off the court all that well but that their on-court relationship was solid.

O'Neal told reporters, "You know the real problem. You're just scared to write about it."

He told several media outlets that he simply didn't have time to wait for Kobe to mature.

Kobe, in turn, was taken aback by this continued lobbying, saying he believed such issues should be kept within the team. After the Sacramento meeting and the complaints that he needed to stay within the team concept, he had answered with a whirlwind of assists. It seemed that the only way to keep O'Neal off his back was to win every game. Besides, he knew the issue was more complicated than his and O'Neal's differing perspectives.

If nothing else, their squabbling festered in West's unhappiness. A number of critics called for the team vice president to emerge from his weeks of hiding to provide the team some leadership. Finally, at the insistence of Lakers media relations director John Black, West agreed to meet with reporters. It was an awkward session, to say the least, said veteran Lakers reporter Mitch Chortkoff. "It's easy," West offered when asked about the strange twists and turns of the season. "Just blame me. Isn't that what your job is, to assign blame for what the players do? So blame me."

Among West's critics was his former teammate, Wilt Chamberlain, who proved his strong Philly roots by phoning the *Los Angeles Times* to complain that O'Neal was unfairly blaming the situation on Kobe. "He needs to get down the court and play defense, instead of cherry picking by the basket for all those dunks," Chamberlain said. "Too often the other team is on offense, and Shaq is not even at half court. Everybody talks about his points when we should be looking closer at his rebounds and blocked shots and defense."

In the wake of the Texas disaster, Derek Harper called yet another players-only meeting. "It wasn't heated," Kobe explained afterward. "We were trying to figure out what happened, why we started spiraling downward, how we got to this point, how we're going to get out of this. It wasn't pointing fingers."

This time the agenda focused on O'Neal's unhappiness with Rambis's efforts to add the screen plays and other looks that featured Rice. The result, the center said, had been that the team was expending too much effort on offense.

So O'Neal informed Rambis that things had to change.

"I knew what the problem was," O'Neal confided later. "We went in and said, 'Kurt, this is how it should be. And this is how it's gonna be. We don't want to come down and call plays. I don't want to be on a team where we come down and call plays. If I'm on a team where we come down and call plays every time, then it's time for me to quit. Then I'm not gonna be an effective big man anymore.' If that's the case, then they're just using me as a token to set picks. I don't want to play like that. I want to run and get crazy and look at the fans and make faces. If I've got to come down and set picks and do all that, it's time for me to quit. Then I ain't got it anymore."

Their meeting evolved from the players-only discussion to a film session with Rambis where they reviewed their Texas failures. After that came more discussions.

The problem stemmed from their frustrations against Utah, which had left the coaching staff to conclude that the Lakers needed to do more cutting on offense and to feature some plays as Rice had requested. "Everybody said, 'We gotta cut, we gotta do this,'" O'Neal recalled. "But, you know, you really don't have to cut. You gotta let the defense dictate what your offense is gonna do. We got special guys on this team, guys that can draw double teams. When you got two guys on you, somebody's open. We have to keep it simple."

It would prove to be just the notion that helped them close out the regular season successfully. In a great sense, O'Neal was correct. Even the Lakers coaches conceded that they had too many plays. "I can't run 30 plays for Glen Rice," Rambis told reporters. "And he has to understand that. He can get his shots."

Simplifying was a process that needed to be done, but the Lakers still lacked a basic offensive system. As a result they would be left with no real means of making playoff adjustments, which would doom their hopes for yet another season.

Essentially O'Neal's system of posting up and passing the ball out of the double teams worked to a limited degree. Even he admitted that, conceding that it depended largely on the success of his team's jump shots. "When they're falling, everything's lovely," O'Neal said. "But they ain't gonna fall all the time."

Living on jumpers could be especially hard to do during tough stretches of the playoffs, when the pressure hit the high side.

In the short term, though, the stripped-down approach produced a rousing close to the regular season, a run of four straight wins, beginning with their blowing away Portland in the Forum, a game in which O'Neal matched his season high of 38 points and Kobe led the team with seven assists.

That was followed by a road win at Seattle with O'Neal scoring another 33 points and a Forum victory over Dallas where Kobe had 17 points and 10 assists, many of them to O'Neal, who again led the Lakers with 26 points.

The outburst had been enough for Los Angeles to take the fourth playoff seed from Houston, meaning that the Lakers would have the home-court advantage in their first-round matchup with the Rockets. On the last day of the regular season the Lakers again defeated the Blazers at home, another rousing victory, with O'Neal pushing his season high to 40 points. With the blowout Kobe played only about 20 minutes, and on the bench Rambis apologized, saying that he wanted to leave in the players who were playing well.

That was OK, Kobe replied, adding that he understood. But he told Rambis that he wanted a favor in return. He wanted the assurance that he could guard Houston's Scottie Pippen in the playoffs.

It was about this time that Kobe finally got around to phoning Tex Winter, the 77-year-old Chicago Bulls assistant. Even though Bryant didn't know Winter, they enjoyed a long, far-reaching discussion on basketball philosophy, including some professional evaluation that perhaps no one other than Winter could provide.

Winter was in his 53rd season of coaching and had a perspective to match. He had played against Jackie Robinson in junior college and later wound up at Southern Cal, where he was a teammate of Bill Sharman and Alex Hannum playing basketball for the legendary Sam Barry. Only an injury prevented Winter from competing in the Olympics as a pole vaulter. He served in the Navy during World War II and in the aftermath became one of America's premier college coaches, getting his first head coaching job at age 28. He devised the Bulls' famed triangle offense over his many years of coaching and deserved a substantial portion of the credit for the team's success in blending the supremely talented Jordan with the host of role players on the roster.

Winter was pleased that the young, highly talented Bryant would have such an intense interest in his offense. He and Kobe discussed Winter's dearly held principle that five-man basketball is far superior to the two-man isolation game prevalent in the NBA today, simply because five men in motion are far harder for teams to defend than two men standing still.

Winter confirmed for Bryant that his instincts were right.

"I don't think he's selfish at all," Winter, who had studied Bryant's play on videotape, said after the conversation. Rather, the lack of sophistication in the Lakers offense made Bryant's options rather complicated when O'Neal kicked the ball out to the perimeter with the shot clock winding down.

"The impression I get with him is his indecision, because they don't seem to have a system, other than to space the floor and move the ball inside to Shaq," Winter said. "I asked him if they had an identifiable system of play, and he said he didn't think so."

It was apparent that Kobe badly missed an offensive structure, Winter said. "I can see it when I watch him play. He doesn't know where to go and where his teammates are going to go. The roles aren't defined enough.

"There doesn't seem to be a true system. It's just get the ball in to Shaq and space the floor. But that's the pro game today. What you see with the Lakers is a symptom of what you see throughout the league. I don't mean to be critical. It's a pretty difficult situation for Kurt Rambis."

Rambis, Winter said, had inherited an impossible situation in the middle of a season. "A lot of those guys are lost. I know Del had a lot of plays. Pro sets and that stuff. He didn't run them much because of Shaq."

Bryant's idea of using split cuts would have been excellent for creating motion that would make it harder to defend O'Neal, Winter said. "But one of the things that cutting does, it means your center has to play differently. Instead of a scorer, the center has to be a feeder first, holding the ball and passing as teammates split and cut around him.

"I'm not sure that's what Shaq wants," Winter said. "As long as he can overpower people, run over 'em, and slam it in the basket, that's what he wants to do."

Just about everyone involved agreed that O'Neal needed to add a face-up jumper to his game, something to give opponents a different look to defend, something that would help open up the floor for his teammates. West acknowledged that as O'Neal aged and his physical skills declined, such a shot would be increasingly important.

Larry Drew pointed out that it was difficult for O'Neal's coaches to ask him to add those elements to his game because the Lakers already asked him to do so much for the team.

"I don't know why it would be tough," Winter said. As an assistant near the end of his coaching career, he occupied a unique position in the modern NBA. Whereas younger coaches had to coddle the game's young stars, Winter was that rare truth teller who never seemed to hesitate to offer his opinions to players about what they needed to do to improve. His nature had led him to clash with Jordan on occasion. And Winter, whom Phil Jackson revered as a mentor, had never hesitated to blister Jackson himself if the situation required it, especially during those characteristically long stretches during a game when Jackson liked to sit back and watch his Bulls players learn as they struggled during games.

At times Winter would lean into Jackson's ear and tell him, "You better get off your butt and do some coaching!"

Winter loved the game too much to let modern players think that their big salaries and big reputations meant that they didn't have to be serious students focused on improving.

"To be very honest with you, he's the real problem on that team," Winter said of O'Neal. "There's a lot of basketball he doesn't know. He's the best physical specimen in the game. But he's really not a complete player, doesn't have a complete feel for the game."

The often-discussed example of that was O'Neal's free throws. Winter acknowledged the center's reputation for dutifully working on foul shooting. "But he's practicing bad habits," Winter said. "That doesn't do any good, because he's not shooting them right."

Told that O'Neal had said he saw no need for setting screens and running plays, Winter said, "He seems to feel like he's doing his share when he's getting those stats. But in the final analysis the reason they can't win is they can't play defense. For the specimen he is, he's not the defensive player he should be. Nor the rebounder."

Winter's main concern after the phone conversation, however, was for Bryant himself. "I think he puts a little too much pressure on himself," the coach said. "He wants to excel so badly. He needs to relax a little more. He needs to be a little bit more of a 20-year-old and enjoy the game. Enjoy life a little bit. He's the kind of guy who could have a nervous breakdown over this stuff."

Winter said his concern really didn't have anything to do with Kobe's mental health but with the burden he faced. The greater the talent, the greater the burden, the harder it was for a player to find the format for that talent, Winter said. "He's great, and he's going to be even greater. But the expectations are so high, and he's brought a lot of that on himself. His basketball skills did that. They're so good that they build up the expectations. Probably the worst thing that ever happened to him was that All-Star game."

Winter acknowledged that his comments could be perceived as self-serving, because he had spent his life developing the triangle, or triple post offense, what he called "a sound offensive system for basketball."

"He needs to get that pressure off himself," Winter said of Kobe. "A system would do that. It's obvious that out on the floor sometimes he doesn't know which way to go. He's got such great individual talent. It's a question of knowing how to handle that talent. Michael had to learn how to handle it. To a degree, our system did that for him. He got to the point that he could rely on his teammates."

Winter, who coached Jordan for a dozen NBA seasons, admitted that both the superstar and Scottie Pippen had doubts about the triangle at first, as did many Bulls players, but Jackson had "sold Michael and Scottie on the idea they had to play in the system whether they liked it or not."

There was, of course, a strange and curious context to these conversations. Also phoning Winter on a regular basis was former Bulls coach Phil Jackson, who was taking a year's sabbatical from the game. Winter knew that Jackson wanted to return to coaching and that he wanted to coach the Lakers. Winter also knew that when he returned, Jackson wanted to use the triangle offense.

It was easy to see that Jackson would be a good coach for the Lakers. Beyond using the offense, Jackson knew how to deconstruct the walls that had built up between Bryant and his teammates. After all, Jackson had deconstructed similar walls between Michael Jordan and his Bulls teammates.

Beyond that, both Jackson and Winter were intrigued by the challenge of persuading a talented center like O'Neal to play within the triangle system.

Winter's college teammate at Southern Cal, Bill Sharman, faced a similar task in 1971 when he had to persuade Wilt Chamberlain to become a feeder and rebounder in the Lakers trianglelike system. Wilt frowned at the notion. Asking him not to score, he said, "was like asking Babe Ruth not to hit home runs."

But Chamberlain complied, and the Lakers won the 1972 championship. "Bill Sharman used a lot of the concepts of the triangle," Winter pointed out, "the main one being that the center is the apex of the attack. Chamberlain became a great team player, a rebounder and a feeder as opposed to being a big-time scorer. They became a great team because Sharman convinced him to play the team game and quit worrying about scoring. That was like Phil convincing Michael to play in our system."

The huge hitch in Winter's and Jackson's dream of coaching the Lakers was that over the final weeks of the 1999 season Jerry West had become furious with Jackson. On the final weekend of the Lakers' season, as they were about to be swept by the San Antonio Spurs, West was sitting in the nearly empty Great Western Forum when a reporter mentioned Jackson.

West responded by addressing Jackson with an epithet.

West wasn't alone in his disdain for the former Bulls coach. In New York, where Jackson had been cast as a potential replacement for Knicks coach Jeff Van Gundy, center Patrick Ewing had declared that he wouldn't play for the former Bulls coach. Ewing said he'd rather be traded.

It seemed odd that Jackson, who had coached Jordan's Bulls to six championships, could stir up such vitriol. After a bitter falling-out with Jerry Krause, Chicago's chief of basketball operations, Jackson had left the team and taken the 1999 season off to rest and keep a low profile, leaving his Bearsville, New York, abode only to make an occasional speech or to raise money for presidential hopeful Bill Bradley.

How do you take a low profile and still make so many people angry?

"I think he's burned his bridges," Winter said of Jackson.

It was something Jackson had done with a series of small fires. For example, in one of his rare interviews as the 1999 season opened, Jackson commented that the 1999 championship would be undervalued because it was a shortened season.

What he said was perhaps the truth, but folks around the NBA didn't like hearing it.

Then, in early May when he was honored by the Bulls at halftime of their final regular-season game, Jackson held a press conference beforehand and made reference to Rodman's release by the Lakers.

Jackson said Rodman hadn't gotten the same support in Los Angeles as he had gotten in Chicago, resulting in his release.

Although Jackson was seemingly referring to Rodman's off-court support, from agents and other professionals, West took Jackson's comments as criticism of the team's management itself. "Apparently we don't do things right," West retorted.

He remained livid for weeks. The Lakers did everything they could for Rodman, including paying the salaries of his two security guards, West said.

There were reports that Jackson could have upward of a half dozen different coaching jobs for 1999–2000. "The job he'd like to have would be the Lakers," Winter said, "but he might have burned the bridges. It's unfortunate. With the success he's had there's bound to be some natural jealousy. It behooves him to be humble and complimentary of other people.

"I think there's a lot of resentment in the league because of the success he had here in Chicago," Winter added. "People seem to feel that Phil was lucky to coach Michael Jordan. I don't think they give Phil the credit he should receive, but at the same time Phil should have been a little more humble. There was the impression that Phil rubbed it in."

The only hope for Jackson in Los Angeles rested with Lakers owner Jerry Buss, who had acknowledged his interest in

Jackson. The team was moving into the new Staples Center and had expensive skyboxes and season tickets to sell. Jackson would obviously be a marquee name in that regard. Buss, though, seemed understandably reluctant to force the issue. His efforts to get involved in the Lakers management had backfired disastrously. And there was a personal reason for Buss to hold off on a push for Jackson. The owner's daughter was close to Kurt Rambis's wife.

Rambis had been faced with an impossible task during the season, one that had given him no real chance to succeed. "Is it reasonable to judge what I can do as a coach given this season?" Rambis replied to a reporter's question as the playoffs neared. "I think as long as you understand that there are expectations that a team can have and as long as those expectations are real, that's the judge of whether or not a coach can bring out the best in the ballplayers. . . . I know the players listen to me. I know the players want to do the right thing."

That perspective seemed accurate enough. Plus the Lakers had long sought to be an organization that prized loyalty. With the team's apparent revival over the last four regular-season games, management took a wait-and-see approach for the playoffs.

What West and Kupchak saw against Houston in the first round was certainly encouraging.

Kobe got his wish with the Pippen defensive assignment and spent the first two games smothering the 33-year-old Rocket forward into misery. "It's fun," Kobe said. "I looked at him, and I told him that I was going to come at him with a lot of energy. I think he knew that, too."

It was Bryant's late free throws that provided the winning margin in the 101–100 series opener, but it was O'Neal's defense that determined the outcome. The Lakers center leaped to block Rocket rookie Cuttino Mobley's layup in the final seconds as the Forum crowd exploded in delight. It was his fourth block to go with 27 points and 11 rebounds. "The rumor is I'm not a good pick-and-roll defender," O'Neal told reporters afterward. "It's not that I'm not a good pick-and-roll defender. It's me being a big man and being a shot blocker, I'm just used to helping out the guards. . . .

"I mean, I can play defense."

The Lakers had trailed 100–98, and the Rockets had the ball in the last minute when Pippen attempted to drive on Kobe. He moved his feet to cut him off, then bumped the ball loose, and Fisher scrambled to cover it. O'Neal was fouled at the other end and made one of two free throws.

Later Bryant was attempting to drive with 5.3 seconds left when he collided with Houston's Sam Mack. The officials whistled a foul, which left the Rockets fussing, but Kobe dropped in both to put the Lakers up. With Kobe on the bench for long stretches in foul trouble, it was Rice who kept the Lakers in it with 29 points.

Game 2 brought more convincing defense from Kobe, who limited Pippen to just 3 points (he missed all seven of his field goal attempts), and a 110–98 win, putting the Lakers up 2–0 in the series.

"I don't think you've seen our whole team like this during the regular season," Derek Fisher told reporters.

"He's making me have to work to bring the ball and get into our set," Pippen said of Kobe. "I like to get the ball where I can catch the ball and be a threat, being able to drive, shoot, or pass. Right now, he's got me in the position where I bring the ball down. He knows there's only a couple things I can do. I can't drive the ball, because he's pressuring me so far out that he's running me into his help defense."

Observers knew that Bryant could hold a great player down for only so long, and that theory came to light in Game 3 in

Houston's Compaq Center. Kobe got in early foul trouble; Pippen finally found his form on the way to 37 points and a 102–88 Laker loss.

The Lakers, however, answered in Game 4 with a flurry of activity from everyone involved to close out the series. O'Neal even hit Kobe with an alley-oop pass for a dunk. It was Kobe's early offense—15 consecutive points from late in the first quarter to early in the second quarter as he fell into one of his trademark scoring sprees—that pushed L.A. out front early. Yes, he went through a stretch late in the first half with seven straight misses, but he fought back after halftime with key defense on Pippen and Michael Dickerson. He finished the game hitting 9 of 16 from the floor. "All those stories about me and Shaq, you can throw all of those in the garbage," Kobe said. "I mean, just look at us. We play great together."

Indeed, the big center was very pleased.

"Kobe is a competitor, and he showed that today," he told reporters happily.

Unfortunately the smiles would disappear quickly after that first-round defeat of the Rockets. Next up were the San Antonio Spurs and multidimensional big man Tim Duncan, who had a splendid post game and a face-up jumper that kissed nicely off the glass. He blew those kisses repeatedly at the Lakers through the series.

In Game 1 in San Antonio the Spurs employed a variety of troops to frustrate and entangle O'Neal. Robinson, Duncan, backup center Will Perdue, even six-foot-six reserve Malik Rose, all took turns bumping, grinding, and pushing the big Laker into making just 6 of his 19 field goal attempts. Later Jerry West would wonder why Rambis hadn't risen from the bench to protest the physical play. "The officials just let them beat the hell out of Shaq in that first game," he said, adding that it would have been good for Rambis to get thrown out over it, "just to get a technical, just to send the message that he wasn't going to put up with it, wasn't going to sit there and take it."

It was hindsight, and West knew a rookie coach could only learn from the experience. But he thought Rambis should have been fighting for his center. With O'Neal corralled, the Spurs used Duncan's 25 points and 7 rebounds to forge an 87–81 win. Afterward O'Neal had to be restrained from charging official Steve Javie (the NBA would later fine the center $7,500 for the incident). Still furious, O'Neal entered the Lakers locker room at the Alamodome and vented his anger by smashing a television and video player. That, in turn, made headlines the next day in the San Antonio paper.

"The only way to guard Shaq is to break the rules that the NBA is supposed to enforce," O'Neal complained. "But they never enforce them, which is fine. I've been getting played like that for seven years. But nobody's going to break me."

The Spurs were smug afterward, with former Bull Steve Kerr confiding that they knew the Lakers had no place to turn with their offense. Long schooled by Tex Winter, Kerr pointed out the obvious: The Lakers had no real system, thus no means of adjusting. They were wed to a stagnant, low-post format, and the Spurs simply stacked their huge front line against it, then used role players to fill in the gap.

The Lakers answer was to use talent and energy to overcome the circumstances, and that was almost enough in Game 2. O'Neal again was shackled by fouls, this time two quick calls at the offensive end when he led his drop step with an elbow. With only eight minutes gone in the first period, he was forced to sit and watch as the Spurs, driven by a stupendous wall of noise from the Alamodome crowd, pushed out to a 26–14 lead.

With Rice, Fox, and Kobe pressing the issue defensively, the Lakers narrowed the margin and even managed a brief lead in the second period. At the half, L.A. trailed by three, but the

Lakers had gained a measure of defensive confidence with Fox moving to power forward to confront Duncan. Although undersized, Fox used his low base and rooted the 6-foot-11 Duncan out of position in the post. O'Neal came back strong in the third period, and over the next 15 minutes the Lakers produced perhaps their most focused play of the season, getting stops on defense and forcing the issue at the other end. Kobe hit a jumper at the opening of the fourth to tie it at 61. The Lakers then tightened their defense while Fox, Rice, and Reid all scored to produce a 69–63 lead with nine minutes to go. Suddenly the Alamodome crowd of 33,000 grew anxiously quiet.

The ensuing sequence, however, would haunt the Lakers and stick in Jerry West's craw for a long time. Given the opportunity to break the game open, the Lakers forced a Duncan turnover, but in transition the ball went to Fox, who took an awkward shot and missed. West would lament that both Rice and Kobe, the team's premier finishers, were open but never got the ball. Instead Rose scored in transition off Fox's miss, and the lead fell to four. Then came a Rice miss and a Mario Elie basket for the Spurs that cut it to two. When Fox missed yet again and Derek Harper stepped out of bounds on another possession, the Spurs tied it and then took the lead, 71–69, on a David Robinson slam.

Watching it on television back in Los Angeles, West was sick. None of the shots in the run had been good ones. They had let their opportunity slip away, and with it the season. "It was a weird game," he would say later. "I've seen thousands of games, and this was the weirdest." In all, Harper would step out of bounds on three different possessions. How could a player with 16 years' experience make mistakes like that? West would ask himself.

The short answer, of course, was that no one on the roster

seemed to have found a comfort zone during this season of many changes.

On the next possession, Kobe snaked and juked his way to the basket to answer Robinson and tie it again. And later Duncan would score again, but mostly the defenses for both sides ruled, meaning that L.A. trailed 73–71 with 1:25 to go when Rambis called time-out and reminded them to go to O'Neal. The throng sent the noise pounding coming out of the time-out, but the Lakers center quieted things with a slam to tie it. Seconds later Robinson retorted with a slam of his own, and the Spurs led, 75–73. At 46.5 seconds, Kobe drove but was blocked. The Lakers retained the ball, but the shot clock had run low. Rambis called a 20-second time-out to try to draw something up. All night the Spurs' perimeter defense, led by Mario Elie and Jaren Jackson, had played like linebackers, bodying Kobe out each time he tried to drive. They again answered Kobe's attempt to drive with a body and corralled him on the deep right baseline as the shot clock clicked down, but with less than a second left and the deafening noise of the crowd, Kobe rose up, a remarkable elevation over the canopy of swarming arms, to lace in a three. The shot instantly stupefied the crowd, pushing the fans back into their seats, and gave the Lakers the lead, 76–75, with 34.2 seconds to go.

On that night Kobe had 28 points, his career playoff high. And things looked very good moments later when the Spurs muffed their offensive possession and were forced to foul Kobe with 18 seconds to go. He had made 22 of his 24 free-throw attempts in the playoffs, which suggested that L.A. seemed poised to take control of the series. The situation looked so good, in fact, that Ruben Patterson even juked a few steps with the Spurs' dancers during the ensuing time-out. But Kobe did a strange thing. He missed the first, watching grimly as it fell off. Then he missed the second, bringing the slightest smile.

The Lakers had the lead and would have to defend it with 18 seconds to go. They had a foul to give, and there would later be a debate as to whether Rambis reminded them of it. Eventually the rookie coach would acknowledge that he hadn't clearly articulated the circumstances. "He didn't spell it out," West would say later. "He didn't spell it out that they needed to foul."

"Kurt did a good job," team VP Magic Johnson would add later. "But you just can't make those mistakes that we made at a critical time during the playoffs. And he knows that."

Duncan was hardly challenged on the right baseline as he dropped in a sweet hook for the lead. The Lakers got the ball back down one with eight seconds to go, but Kobe and Fisher failed to connect on the inbounds. The ball hit Fisher's hands, bounced into his face, and fell to the Spurs on the floor.

Later Rambis would point out that another play had been called, that Kobe was supposed to send the ball elsewhere. The Spurs hit two final free throws to win, 79–76.

The Lakers had been so close to gelling with a huge playoff win, but they were a fragile team in those fragile moments. Where winning can solidify relationships, losing tears them apart, especially for teams that are searching.

They were all quietly disconsolate afterward, especially Kobe, but he gathered himself and spoke graciously with reporters.

"That's strange stuff," Kobe said of his missed free throws. "The last time that happened to me was in the eighth grade."

Asked if it would take him long to recover, he replied, "It won't take me that long. I'm obviously disappointed. You don't forget what happened here."

Reporters then asked him to reflect on the year, and he told them that because he had played so sparingly his first two seasons the 1999 campaign was almost the equivalent of a full rookie season.

"This year was way different from my first two years from the standpoint that I played a lot more and had the ball in my hands a lot more," he said. "I learned a lot more. You learn a lot faster with so many different situations."

One television reporter wondered if missing the free throw wouldn't prove to be traumatic. Kobe gave him a surprised look. "I'm just getting started," he said. "I'm gonna be in this league a long time and play a lot more basketball."

Like most players who aspired to greatness, Kobe would have to collect his share of painful lessons in the final seconds of big games. Bird, Magic, Jordan, West himself had all encountered that agony.

Perhaps none was worse than the blunder Isiah Thomas made for the Detroit Pistons in the 1987 playoffs. They had just battled the Boston Celtics to take a one-point lead in the closing seconds of an Eastern Conference Finals game at Boston Garden. On the verge of victory, Thomas faced the task of inbounding the ball under the Celtics' goal with three seconds to go.

Instead of handing Thomas the ball, referee Jess Kersey asked him, "Don't you want a time-out?"

"Gimme the ball," Thomas insisted.

Kersey gave him the ball, and Thomas watched in horror as Bird stole the inbounds pass and hit cutting teammate Dennis Johnson for the go-ahead basket.

With a second left on the clock, it was the Pistons' ball again. Kersey turned to Thomas and asked, "Now do you want a time-out?"

Now it was Kobe's turn to agonize. His free throws could have gotten his team over the hump. Asked about the trace of a smile that had crossed his face afterward, he said, "I was just shocked that I missed it."

His composure afterward impressed the Spurs' Steve Kerr, who had hit the winning basket for the Bulls' 1997 NBA title but had experienced his own share of disappointments over the years.

"He's willing to accept the responsibility after the game," Kerr said of Kobe. "I saw his interview, and he said, 'We can't look back. We gotta get ready for the next game.' That's impressive for anybody, much less a 20-year-old. He's willing to take the big shot, and that's the key. Michael, in his commercial a couple of years ago, told us how many times he had failed taking the big shot. Nobody's gonna make all of 'em, but if you're confident and you take 'em at every opportunity, you're gonna make your fair share. Kobe has done that, and he'll get better at those shots as his career goes along."

A reporter asked Kerr why Kobe might have smiled. Kerr smiled knowingly and replied that it was a typical response to a missed shot. "I've been smiling a lot this year," Kerr joked in reference to his own struggles in 1999. "I know exactly what he was saying with that smile. He was saying, 'I can't believe I missed those shots.' I've been there so many times. You have to laugh it off. You can't put your head down and get all bummed out. You just have to kinda laugh it off."

What was especially admirable was Kobe's fearlessness, Kerr explained. "Some guys have it, and some guys don't. The guys who have it are generally the most talented players. They're also the most fearless. Maybe that's a generalization. Michael obviously had it. I think Karl Malone has it. It took me a few years to feel comfortable in that situation because I would get the ball with the game on the line about once a year. When it did happen to me, I was a little anxious. You finally realize that the chances of the shot going in are much greater if you just kind of throw caution to the wind and say, 'Screw it. If I'm open, I'm gonna fire.' When you do that, if you're a 50 percent shooter in the regular season, you're likely to shoot 50 percent of 'em. You're gonna miss some, you're gonna make some."

The important thing about being fearless was figuring out when to do it, Kerr said. "Michael went through that in Chicago his first five or six years. When to shoot, when to pass, when to make the move. And Kobe's 20, you know, so give him a little time, and he'll figure it all out."

Mainly, the Lakers seemed shackled by their lack of offensive sophistication, Kerr said. Told that Kobe wanted the team to install split cuts into the offense, Kerr raised his eyebrows. "He's a smart guy," he said. "I'm glad to hear this. I mean I knew he was smart, but I'm glad to hear he's so intrigued by the teams that really execute. Split cuts are so difficult to cover."

Told that the turmoil of the season meant that the Lakers coaching staff had no time to add such features, Kerr acknowledged, "It takes perseverance, and it takes a coach to stay with it and do it every day. The Jazz have done it every day for 12 years. The big lesson there is obviously continuity of a team, keeping a Stockton and Malone together for that long. And the framework of the offense for that long. You keep the same guys doing the same things, any offense is gonna get better if you keep guys together long enough.

"The offenses that are run around the league don't lend themselves to much organization," Kerr said. "It's dump it in and spread out and wait for the double team. It doesn't allow for much direction and focus."

Still, it wouldn't be all that hard for the Lakers to add split cuts, he said. "The split cut is really simple if you watch it. You got a guy at the wing who passes the ball to the post. And Shaq would be perfect to run those split cuts with. What happens now is, they throw it in to Shaq and everybody basically stands. The defenses are all looking at Shaq, and they kind of decide when to double-team. On the Spurs we decide to go once he starts dribbling. But if you set up a split cut—let's say

Kobe is on the wing, and he dumps it in to Shaq—rather than standing, Kobe is immediately rushing to the lane to set that cut for the other guard at the top of the key. The other guard sets his man up and comes off. Those two defenders are scrambling to cover those screens. Now all of a sudden Shaq's going to work down low, and the defenders don't have time to react. If they do, then you got a guy wide open for a jump shot. I think it would be perfect for Shaq."

That, of course, was a thought for another season. The 1999 campaign came down to one final weekend for the Lakers. Down 2–0 in the series, they returned to the Forum that Friday afternoon to prepare for back-to-back games on Saturday and Sunday.

Kobe had put on a brave face, telling reporters, "All season has been an uphill battle for us. We've been building our character all season to get to this point. We're not gonna stop now."

An hour before his team was set to practice that Friday, West sat courtside in the virtually empty Forum. The building, the scene of so many of his great games as a player, was to be sold after the season as the Lakers made plans to move into the new Staples Center.

"It's gonna be a big weekend," West said as he watched a TV crew doing a stand-up report on the court.

It would all depend on how the young Lakers mentally approached the game. If they saw how much they had to gain, they might have a chance. On the other hand, if they allowed their fears to overtake them and focused instead on how much they had to lose, there would be little chance.

For his part, West knew how much they had to gain. Stockton and Malone and the Jazz were showing their age in their first-round series against the Sacramento Kings. The Portland Trail Blazers had shown they couldn't contend with O'Neal. If only the Lakers could tough it out against the Spurs, they could reach the NBA Finals. And if they reached the Finals, they could win it.

On the other hand, it was hard, even for West, not to look back over the long, troubled year and ask himself, What if they had kept their team together? What if they hadn't made all those changes? The Rodman situation had been painful for the franchise. "He didn't want to play," West said of the curious forward. "Our owner talked him into it."

It was obvious to West that Rodman had lost his quickness. Then came the personal problems, and Rodman started coming to practice late and still intoxicated from his late-night lifestyle. West simply couldn't stomach that, not with this fragile young team.

Then there was the Eddie Jones trade, the move that still irked the fans. Jones was "a nice young man," as West saw him, but he was going to demand a starter's salary, and he wasn't going to be worth it, at least not in L.A., West figured, because Kobe would clearly win the two-guard job.

All the moves had had a disastrous effect on the team, he acknowledged, evidenced by the Lakers terrible play during the Texas road trip. "They just quit playing," he said. "In the middle of a tough season, you're gonna have stretches where things fall apart. That's where they fell apart."

Still, the season had offered the opportunity for Kobe to grow as a player, and he had done that, especially late in the schedule, when Rambis had taken to playing him at the one with the ball in his hands. It's not that he was a one guard, rather that he harkened back to West's day when guards were simply guards, designated not as ones or twos but as well-rounded players, capable of doing all the necessary chores.

That's the way West still liked to think of them.

"He's just a guard," he said.

As such, Kobe was already the best guard in the league, West said, adding that he considered it an outrage that Kobe hadn't been selected by Basketball USA to play on its Olympic qualifying team.

"I've seen 'em all, and I haven't seen anybody better," West said.

"I would have loved to have done that," Kobe said of the Olympic qualifying team.

Yes, Kobe was only 20 and he was still experiencing some trouble in reading defenses, but his skills were amazingly complete.

His work ethic meant that he had pushed the schedule on his development years ahead.

"The only thing is sometimes he tries to do too much," West said.

O'Neal, too, was a player with a lot of confidence, he said, adding that that confidence sometimes got in the center's way, that it sometimes created a blind spot.

Perhaps it was the end of the Lakers tenure in the Forum, perhaps it was the fact that they faced an uphill battle against the Spurs, but as West talked he seemed to acknowledge that the franchise he loved was poised on the verge of another transition.

"This is a big weekend," he repeated.

It was an odd mood that settled on the Lakers in those final hours of the 1999 season. "I haven't been in a situation before as strange as this," observed Rick Fox before Game 3. He had spent eight years in the NBA, much of it with the Boston Celtics, where he had seen the final days of Larry Bird's career and the subsequent retirement of Kevin McHale and the death of Reggie Lewis. Fox had been on fine teams at the University of North Carolina and watched the Tar Heels struggle with expectations. He thought he had seen it all, until the Lakers chaotic season unraveled before his eyes.

"It's made for an interesting year," he said. "When you have turmoil over the course of a season, you sometimes forget the task at hand. Our chemistry is actually better than has been documented. It's a lot better than it was in the middle of the season. I think we actually realize that we do need each other and that we care for each other."

That perhaps was true, but for a team to thrive in the play-offs it had to have real togetherness, something the Lakers hadn't come close to experiencing. Their defensive efforts against Duncan that had worked so well in Game 2 didn't work as well the next time. Duncan shrugged off the Lakers effort and scored 37 with 14 rebounds in Game 3 in the Forum. That meant the Lakers had to battle to stay close most of the afternoon, which they managed to do mainly because O'Neal was strong in the post and Derek Fisher played masterfully at point guard. Sadly, Fisher marred his afternoon with a rushed three-pointer late in the game that allowed San Antonio just the breathing room it needed to escape.

Even the officials felt bad for the third-year guard who had played with so much heart.

Kobe, meanwhile, had spent much of the day shackled by the Spurs. He had repeatedly gone to the basket, where the contact was clearly physical. Kobe kept fussing and cussing the officials about not getting the foul call, but Jess Kersey and the crew figured that Kobe was initiating the contact with the defense.

Then Kersey cautioned Kobe to watch his language, and if he didn't, the veteran official threatened to tell his father. After all, Kersey told Kobe, "Jelly Bean was never impolite or disrespectful."

Kersey had playfully issued this warning in the hallway outside the locker room at halftime, and Kobe smiled in response, saying, "Oh, no, don't tell my dad."

Kobe's wasn't the only foul language ringing in the Forum

that day. Sitting in his courtside seat, Jack Nicholson left the officials wincing with his yelling and cursing, all apparently aimed at Kurt Rambis.

"It's all about execution," Kobe said when asked about the frustration oozing from the Lakers bench. "It's about knowing what you're going to run to counteract what the defense is doing. With us, we're in a difficult situation because we don't know what we're going to run every time down the floor."

Afterward, Kerr expressed shock at how much the Lakers had deteriorated physically, particularly O'Neal. "They used to seem so talented," he said. "Now they don't seem so talented."

This frayed atmosphere made for a dismal means of closing the Lakers tenure in the Forum, the scene of so many of their triumphs. Rambis, for his part, seemed caught in a downward spiral and had decided the entire season should be blamed on the media. "Because we are in such a tremendous media spotlight, you guys are not allowing this team to grow and develop," he told the beat writers covering the team. To a man, Tim Kawakami of the *Los Angeles Times*, Howard Beck of the *L.A. Daily News*, and Brad Turner of the *Riverside Press-Enterprise* had all found themselves reporting one fantastic event after another. But Rambis now accused them of prodding negative answers out of his players.

It was no wonder that the circumstances had finally gotten the better of Rambis, Kobe said. "I'm surprised his whole head didn't turn gray. I think he did an excellent job, actually, for all the changes that were made. You have to put yourself in his shoes, with all the press, all the hype, all the changes, all the blah-blah-blah stuff that was going on."

The "blah-blah-blah stuff," as Kobe called it, was a veiled reference to the tension between Kobe and his teammates. Before Game 4, Rick Fox offered the opinion that Kobe had warmed a bit in his relationships with teammates. "Kobe's starting to talk more," Fox said. "He's opening up more."

At the same time, he needed to open up even more, Fox said. "In team sports, I think you have to have something of a relationship with at least a few guys on the team. I can't be sitting across the locker room from you wondering what you're thinking, because on the court I'm gonna be wondering the same thing. That doesn't make for cohesive play.

"You have to be able to read each other without speaking to each other. I definitely feel that as he goes on in his career he's gonna have to open up and feel the need to communicate."

There was steady progress in Kobe's willingness to involve his teammates, Fox said. "I think he's learned throughout the course of this season. He's much better now than he was at the beginning of the year. And he'll be much better next year. There's a progress there."

Game 4, though, produced little evidence that the Lakers were making progress as a team. Duncan scored 33, and O'Neal outdid him with 36. But as they had all series, Jaren Jackson, Mario Elie, and the other Spurs role players cut the Lakers up from the perimeter.

Kobe scored 16 discombobulated points and was met with nasty boos from the Forum crowd as the Lakers were routed, 118–107.

"We shut down the Forum, baby!" Elie crowed. "I want a piece of the floor."

The fact that this sad display marked the Lakers last in the grand old building particularly grated on West. "I think we should schedule an exhibition game here next year against the Globetrotters or Washington Generals," he told reporters disgustedly, "so we can leave the building with a win."

"It's very embarrassing," O'Neal said, his voice in its usual postloss whisper. "Every time I've been sent home it's a sweep. It's very embarrassing. I hate saying, 'Well, we played hard.' No, now it's over."

Kobe's performance evoked the harshest of appraisals from

the one veteran Lakers staff member who was his relentless critic. "It was bullshit," he said, "that scene of him in the last game, standing there, moving his head through a series of fakes, beating the ball in the floor, with everybody standing around trying to figure out what he was going to do, because you never know what he's going to do.

"Finally he dribbles into three defenders, leaves his feet, and makes a pass that nobody can catch. Then he gives his teammate a look like 'Why didn't you catch it?' It's never Kobe's fault.

"You have to blame him unless you want to blame the people who are directing him. Del always said that the folks upstairs gave him his marching orders to play Kobe. The people upstairs said that wasn't the case. They apparently believe in him. But you have to wonder. Is it just a marketing thing? Do they need his star power to sell seats in the Staples Center? You have to wonder."

Asked about the roles on the team, O'Neal replied, "That's up to the coaching staff to let people know their roles. Everybody on this team knows their role. It's up to management to enforce it."

Afterward reporters came at Kobe with pointed questions. "What would the team need to develop more cohesiveness?" one asked.

"Just by playing together, I guess," he replied. "I can't really pinpoint one thing, because I've never been in this situation before."

Would cohesiveness develop if Kobe learned how to get other players involved? "I've done a pretty good job at penetrating and kicking out," Kobe replied. "But it's not something that I'm going to harp on. And it's not something I'm going to put my head down over, because people will think that I don't do it."

Then Kobe issued a promise. "You're always gonna see the scoring," he vowed. "You're always gonna see the flashiness." They were part of who he was, and he was not going to deny them, not going to be changed. It was as if Jordan were whispering in his ear, "Stay aggressive."

At the same time Kobe acknowledged that his approach was destined to draw criticism and that he was quite willing to live with it.

"The only way you shut that up," he said, "is by winning championships. That's gonna be there my whole career."

Another reporter pointed out that Kobe was only 20, while O'Neal was 27 and didn't have as much time to win titles. "Are you as impatient as Shaq?" the reporter asked.

"If I wasn't impatient," he said, "I'd be in college right now."

After the disappointing game, a frustrated Magic Johnson had also weighed in on the team's failures. "This is just disgusting," he said, adding that it was hard to close the Forum on such a low note. "I'm embarrassed. They should be embarrassed. To get swept again on national television. When are we gonna learn?"

Johnson cited the team's lack of offensive organization. The Lakers needed some type of system, including the split cuts that Kobe had asked for. "Oh, man," Johnson said, "I'd love to see it."

More than that, though, Johnson called for a rise in the Lakers' maturity level. "I'm tired of everybody pointing the finger at everybody else," he said. "We look for excuses."

The series outcome absolutely stunned Derek Fisher, who had been certain that his team had awakened and was on its way to the league championship series. Three weeks later in a wide-ranging interview, Fisher would offer his view of what the Lakers needed to shake loose of their chemistry. He addressed the walls that had risen up between Kobe and his teammates. Those walls could come down, Fisher said. "I think it's gonna take time, and it's gonna take a huge effort on his part to break that barrier. He's so important to the scheme of things that he needs to be more vocal. He needs to set an example to be more unselfish, knowing that his status and his future are set."

That example would make a large impression on his teammates who have a lesser status on the team, said Fisher, himself a free agent and unsure at the time he spoke what the Lakers planned to do about his own contract. "I think that was where Michael Jordan took off, when he finally got to that point where he understood that his doing a little less would be more."

Fisher pointed out that communication among players was difficult with so many conflicts pulling at them. It was difficult, he said, to go to a team's star players and suggest that they change their approach.

Having acknowledged that, he went on to express that both Bryant and O'Neal needed to grow and change. "He gives up a lot, and we ask a lot of him," Fisher said of O'Neal. "But he has areas of his game where perhaps he needs to give. I'm not saying that he's not good enough in what he does. It's not about what he does now not being good enough. It's about improving our team. If he can add a face-up jumper or improve his free-throw shooting, that can open things up for us as a team."

For Kobe those sacrifices might well mean not resting so tightly in his dream's embrace, Fisher said. "You could tell when Kobe came into the league that he felt he had a lot to prove at this level. I think Kobe recognizes his situation. I just really think he understands his age and where he is in his career. He's already made a movie in his mind of where his career is gonna go. It's already planned out, and he feels he's on pace with that.

"Sometimes," Derek Fisher said, "you have to put the individual things on hold to help the group. That's where it is with both of these guys, Kobe and Shaq."

Change Again

Right after their second-round playoff ouster at the hands of the Spurs, someone in the Lakers organization leaked the idea that the team might bring Rambis back. That stunned staff members across the organization. "I think everybody knows Kurt's in way over his head," said one staffer. "That's why it blows me away that they're thinking about bringing him back."

But as the Lakers came to terms with their disastrous exit from the playoffs, West examined the situation and decided to put away his anger with Phil Jackson. Having guided and guarded it so many years, he cared too much about the franchise to let anything prevent him from seeing it through to success.

In an interview, he acknowledged that the team was looking beyond Rambis. "We're still exploring some possibilities," West admitted. He explained that the Lakers had to determine whether to select a young coach and let the team "grow with him or whether [we need] a coach who's had some success."

Whatever the choice, West said, "We need to be more stable here. We don't need to be changing coaches every year."

He was referring to the fact that whoever the Lakers selected must come in and improve the chemistry between O'Neal and Bryant.

There has been increased talk out of O'Neal's camp that he might opt out of his massive Lakers contract with the hopes of returning to the Orlando Magic. "If he does that, he'll have to do it for about $1 million a season," West said. That, of course, would have been a vast pay cut from the Lakers contract that paid O'Neal better than $20 million per season.

Orlando executive Pat Williams agreed with the circumstances. O'Neal still had a home in Orlando, and his mother still lived there. "But we have no money," Williams said.

The Magic organization was also trying to find a coach in the wake of Chuck Daly's retirement. The top two candidates were Phoenix Suns assistant Scott Skiles and broadcaster Doc Rivers.

The Magic probably wouldn't make an effort for Jackson, who was said to be asking for a contract that paid around $6 million per season, Williams said. "We can't afford that."

Having Daly's substantial salary the last few seasons taught the Magic the economic realities, Williams said. "Chuck did a great job, but it just kills your bottom line."

At the same time, Williams acknowledged that hiring a cheap young coach brought enormous risk for a team, evidenced by Rambis's struggles with the Lakers. "Last year, Rambis was the hot name," Williams observed. "This summer it's Doc Rivers and Scott Skiles."

That realization seemed to have settled on Lakers management, which helped explain the effort to engage in a preliminary dance with Jackson. The Lakers, after all, were entering a new $350 million arena at the Staples Center and needed to make a strong move to settle down their young stars and to sell skyboxes and other corporate ticket packages.

Both Bryant and O'Neal made it clear to West that they would view Jackson's hiring favorably. "Our job is just to continue his track record," O'Neal would later say of Jackson. "And we will."

That seemed reason enough for West to quell his anger over Jackson's comments. Jackson had the status and the skill to make both Bryant and O'Neal realize that they needed to grow beyond their current games.

In mid-June the Lakers announced Jackson as their new coach in a press conference at the Beverly Hilton Hotel. "I feel like a very lucky man today," Jackson told reporters. "Of all the jobs that were sitting out there this year, this was the one that piqued my interest." He had signed a five-year, $30 million deal.

"We think he's the preeminent coach in America," West told the gathering.

Asked to evaluate his players, Jackson responded with his typical trademark frankness. "Shaq has not really developed into a leader at this point," he said. "I feel for him a little bit. I think he could be better than he is. He could be the most valuable player in this league."

Then he added, "I've been very intrigued with Kobe Bryant, who I think has Michael Jordan–esque type of ability yet is a player who is still uneducated in basketball and in life."

Rambis would later put the finishing touches on his dejection by going into the Forum after hours to clean out his office. Larry Drew and Bill Bertka were to be kept on the scouting staff, but with the change they lost their roles as assistant coaches.

Most in the organization, though, were elated with the change.

At the press conference Magic Johnson was ecstatic. "Now we'll see," he told reporters.

Kobe, too, had expressed his delight over the news by going out and purchasing Jackson's autobiography, *Sacred Hoops*. Then, when the new Lakers coach came to L.A., Kobe slipped up to his hotel room to tell him how excited he was about the opportunity to work with him.

It had been a dramatic turnaround since that dismal last Sunday of the 1999 season, after which Kobe had taken a lonely walk down the hallway to the exit tunnel, pausing along the way to answer a chorus of fans calling for an autograph, then slipping away and striding out into the harsh light of a southern California afternoon.

As Kobe asked the attendants to bring his car up, a reporter stepped up and asked what his plans were for the summer.

"Basketball," he replied. "There is nothing else."

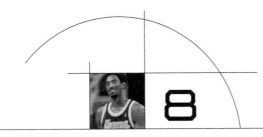

8

LOVE TRIANGLE

> *"I think they're gonna be happy with Phil. He's gonna give them a certain structure and a certain guidance."*
>
> —MICHAEL JORDAN

Three months after his conversation with Kobe Bryant, Tex Winter left the Bulls to become Jackson's assistant with the Lakers. It was a difficult decision. For years he had been a friend and mentor to Bulls VP Jerry Krause. When Krause and Phil Jackson began to grow apart after the 1996 season, Winter had faced the difficult task of holding them together to keep the Bulls moving forward.

Now Winter had decided to leave the Bulls for Jackson's new team. The Lakers presented an excellent opportunity to stress to the NBA his deeply held beliefs about five-man basketball.

Besides, Winter knew that Jackson needed him.

"Tex makes things a lot easier for Phil," one of their close friends pointed out.

Jackson would put much of his focus to getting the Lakers to play withering pressure defense, while Winter would grumble and teach the triangle.

They both knew it would be a tremendous challenge selling the young Lakers stars on the offense and teaching it to them. It had been a tremendous challenge with the Bulls.

And as the 1999–2000 NBA season approached, Winter would be greeted by his 78th birthday. Never mind that he looked just 60, the grind of an NBA season wore hard on him. He was determined to coach just one more season. He knew there would be a tough period of adjustment to his offense. But like O'Neal, Winter wanted to win badly.

The mix of toughness and integrity and grandfatherly charm was his trademark. "Tex is a few years younger than my parents and a product of that Depression era," explained former Bulls trainer Chip Schaefer, who joined the Lakers staff with Jackson. "To say that he is frugal would be an understatement. Johnny Bach used to call him penurious. I think that's a very apt description of him. But I think Tex in a lot of ways is the way we all should be. He doesn't like to see things get wasted. He takes that attitude at the dinner table, too. If there's a little bit of meat on your bone, he may just pick up your steak bone and finish it off for you."

"Tex saves shoe boxes, he's so tight," Bulls equipment manager John Ligmanowski once pointed out, laughing. "We had a meal one time when we were bringing in Larry Krystowiak. I think it was the first time we had ever met Larry. Jerry Krause was there. Tex was there. Larry wasn't finished with his food, and Tex goes, 'You gonna finish that?' Larry goes, 'Yeah, I'm gonna finish that!' That was funny. Tex thought he was gonna get a few scraps. Jimmy Rodgers one time got Tex this fork that he could put in his pocket, and it extends out like an antenna."

"Basketball is his absolute passion in life," Schaefer observed. "That's what keeps him going. There's times when he'll look tired, and I'll wonder if he has the energy for it. Then all of a sudden practice will start, and he's out here barking at these guys like he's coaching the K-State freshman team and it's 1948.

"Tex has three or four real passions in life. One of them's basketball. Certainly one of them's food. He really enjoys his finances. He pores over the business section of the paper as intensely as he does the sports section. He's a real joy. I hope he keeps on going."

"He's an innovator," explained Bill Cartwright, who had worked with Winter first as a player, then as a fellow Bulls assistant. "He's a really unique person in this sport. He absolutely loves basketball. And it's really fun to be around him, because whatever situation you see on the floor he can talk to you about it, because he's seen them all.

"You recall that everyone used to wear those Chuck Taylors, those canvas Converse shoes," Cartwright said, "and you talk to Tex, and he'll tell you, 'Oh yeah, I knew Chuck Taylor.' "

Over his 53 seasons on the bench, Winter had been the head coach at five colleges—Marquette, Kansas State, Washington, Northwestern, and Long Beach State—and had served as head coach of the San Diego/Houston Rockets.

The Bulls pulled Winter to Chicago with a handsome salary in 1985, but Jerry Krause couldn't find a head coach willing to listen to Winter's advice. First, Stan Albeck declined to buy into Winter's view of the game. Then came Doug Collins, who saw the triangle as unworkable in the modern NBA.

Discord on the coaching staff mounted to the point that Collins blocked Winter from being involved in practice during the 1988–89 season. "Tex was basically out of the picture at that time," Jackson recalled. "He did some scouting for Jerry Krause and took some road trips. He didn't go on all of our game trips. When he was with us, he sat in a corner and kept notes on practice and didn't participate in the coaching. He was out of it."

This discord, however, did little to stifle the growing Jordan phenomenon. But like O'Neal, Jordan harbored substantial frustration over the team's seeming inability to compete for a championship. Writers and reporters often compared Jordan to

Larry Bird and Magic Johnson by pointing out that Bird and Johnson were the type of players to make their teammates better while Jordan often seemed to be playing for himself. This criticism infuriated Jordan. Then, in 1989, the Bulls fired Doug Collins and promoted his assistant, Phil Jackson.

Without question, Winter said, it was the rise of Jackson to the position of head coach that made the use of his triangle offense possible. It was not, however, an easy transition.

Winter had spent years developing the triangle. It was an old college system that involved all five players sharing the ball and moving. But it was totally foreign to the pro players of the 1990s, and many of them found it difficult to learn. Where for years the pro game had worked on isolation plays and one-on-one setups, the triple-post used very little in the way of set plays. Instead the players learned to react to situations and to allow their ball movement to create weaknesses in defenses.

Among the offense's strongest questioners was Jordan.

"I've always been very much impressed with Michael as well as everyone else has been," Winter once explained. "I've never been a hero worshiper. I saw his strong points, but I also saw some weaknesses. I felt like there were a lot of things that we could do as a coaching staff to blend Michael in with the team a little bit better. I thought he was a great player, but I did not feel that we wanted to go with him exclusively. We wanted to try to get him to involve his teammates more. Until he was convinced that that was what he wanted to do, I don't think we had the chance to have the program that we had later down the line."

"Tex's offense emulated the offense I had played in with New York when I was a Knick," Jackson said. "The ball dropped into the post a lot. You ran cuts. You did things off the ball. People were cutting and passing and moving the basketball. And it took the focus away from Michael, who had the ball in his hands a lot, who had been a great scorer. That had made the defenses all turn and face him. Suddenly he was on the back side of the defenses, and Michael saw the value in having an offense like that. He'd been in an offense like that at North Carolina. It didn't happen all at once. He started to see that over a period of time, as the concepts built up."

"It was different for different types of players," recalled former Bulls guard John Paxson. "For me it was great. A system offense is made for someone who doesn't have the athletic skills that a lot of guys in the league have. It played to my strengths. But it tightened the reins on guys like Michael and Scottie from the standpoint that we stopped coming down and isolating them on the side. There were subtleties involved, teamwork involved. But that was the job of Phil to sell us on the fact we could win playing that way."

"Everything was geared toward the middle, toward the post play," Jordan said, explaining his opposition. "We were totally changing our outlook . . . and I disagreed with that to a certain extent. I felt that was putting too much pressure on the people inside."

"What Michael had trouble with," Jackson said, "was when the ball went to one of the big guys like Bill Cartwright or Horace Grant or some of the other players who weren't tuned in to handling and passing the ball. They now had the ball. Could they be counted on to make the right passes, the right choices? I brought Michael in my office and told him basically, 'The ball is like a spotlight. And when it's in your hands, the spotlight is on you. And you've gotta share that spotlight with some of your teammates by having them do things with the basketball, too.' He said, 'I know that. It's just that when it comes down to getting the job done, a lot of times they don't want to take the initiative. Sometimes it's up to me to take it, and sometimes that's a tough balance.'

"All along the way it was a compromise of efforts," Jackson said. "Everybody made such a big issue of the triple-post offense. We just said, 'It's a format out of which to play. You can play any way you want out of the triangle.' Because if it's a sound offense, you should be able to do that. One of the concepts is to hit the open man."

Jordan's presence also stretched the flexibility of Winter's concepts and challenged the older coach's thinking. "There were times when Michael knew he was going to get 40 points," Jackson said. "He was just hot those nights. He was going to go on his own, and he would just take over a ball game. We had to understand that that was just part of his magnitude, that was something he could do that nobody else in this game could do. And it was going to be OK. Those weren't always the easiest nights for us to win as a team. But they were certainly spectacular nights for him as a showman and a scorer."

"It took some time," Paxson recalled. "Michael was out there playing with these guys, and unless he had a great deal of respect for them as players, I think he figured, 'Why should I pass them the ball when I have the ability to score myself or do the job myself? I'd rather rely on myself to succeed or fail than some of these other guys.' The thing I like about Michael is that he finally came to understand that if we were going to win championships, he had to make some sacrifices individually. He had to go about the task of involving his teammates more."

"A lot of times," Jackson said, "my convincing story to Michael was 'We want you to get your 30-some points, and we want you to do whatever is necessary. It's great for us if you get 12 or 14 points by halftime and you have 18 points at the end of the third quarter. Then get your 14 or 18 points in the fourth quarter. That's great. If it works out that way, that's exactly what it'll be.' Who could argue with that? We'd tell him, 'Just play your cards. Make them play everybody during the course of the game and then finish it out for us.' I think that's why sometimes Michael has downplayed the triangle. He says it's a good offense for three quarters, but it's not great for the fourth quarter. That's because he took over in the fourth quarter. He can perform."

"Phil was definitely set on what we were going to do, and he wouldn't waiver," Winter recalled. "Even though the triple-post offense evolved through my many, many years of coaching, Phil was sold on it even more than I was at times. There's times when I would say, 'We should get away from this. Let Michael have more one-on-one opportunities.' And Phil was persistent in not doing so. It's to his credit that we stayed to his basic philosophy of basketball."

The team's effort with the offense intensified over the early months of the 1990–91 season, and by February the players and Jordan clicked in their understanding, which resulted in impressive displays of execution. They finished that February with an 11–1 record that included a host of road wins during a West Coast trip. "We had been on the road for something like two weeks," Jordan recalled, "and it just came together. I could feel it then."

"I remember we were on a West Coast swing before we really started kicking it in and getting some really nice action off of it," recalled Bill Cartwright. "It was fun. People started seeing that. We were getting dunks and wide-open jump shots. But before that, it took a lot of time and patience for us to grow."

From that early growing period, the Bulls won the first of their titles, soon to be followed by two more consecutive championships.

Asked to explain how the triangle factored into these championships, John Paxson replied, "The NBA game is not a system game. The NBA is a play game. You have sets, and you have called plays. You see coaches running up and down the sidelines all the time making a play call, which to me, especially in playoff series, plays into your hand. If you scout well, you know how to defend against those set plays. Phil sold us, then made us believe, the more subtle you are on your offense, the more successful you're going to be. You can do some damage if you're reading the other team's defense and reacting rather than worrying about calling some play that the coach wants from the sideline. That's really what happened. That's what this offense is all about. I'm a believer in it. I think it's a wonderful way to play a game."

"It may sound sort of self-serving," Winter said, "but I think the offense has very definitely been one of the Chicago Bulls' strengths. Because the program has perpetuated itself. Even when Jordan left us, I think people were amazed—and we were too—that we could win 55 games."

Jordan had never discussed the offense with Winter and had never acknowledged its importance. When the superstar returned to the Bulls in 1995 after his 18-month retirement, both he and the team struggled in the playoffs that spring, leading to speculation among the media that perhaps it was time for Chicago to find a new offensive system. Even Winter himself had doubts. In the wake of the loss to Orlando in the 1995 playoffs, Winter pushed Jackson to discuss the issue with Jordan in the season-ending conference Jackson held privately with each player.

"With his impulsiveness, Tex said, 'Phil, I'd like you to ask him, does he think we need to change the offense,'" Jackson recalled. " 'Is it something we should plan on using next year? I want you to ask him just for me.' So I did, and Michael said, 'The triple-post offense is the backbone of this team. It's our system, something that everybody can hang their hat on so that they can know where to go and how to operate.' "

Indeed, the offense played a key role in Chicago's success for the next three seasons, but that didn't mean the debate ended. If anything, the issue seemed to become more pronounced with the passing of each NBA season.

In 1958, Winter's Kansas State team defeated Wilt Chamberlain and the Kansas Jayhawks in the Big Eight Conference, preventing the dominant giant from returning to the NCAA tournament his junior season. Chamberlain was so disappointed by the loss that he withdrew from school and spent a year touring with the Harlem Globetrotters.

Decades later, Winter would joke facetiously that he "drove" Chamberlain from the college game. Still, his team's victory over Kansas in the basketball-crazy Midwest was one of the great upsets of that era. In some ways the success of his team play against the individual brilliance of Chamberlain was a theme that still resonated every game night as the Bulls sought a balance. There was Jordan's individual mastery, and there was Winter, extolling his triangle offense and the purity of team play. Their careers had evolved to a nightly give-and-take on the issue.

"It's a balancing act is what it is," Winter said in 1998. "Every game is a thin line; it's a thin line as to how much freedom you want to give a player who has as much talent as Michael has. And how much do you want him to sacrifice his own individual talents to score to involve his teammates more?"

Asked if Jordan and his coaches ever actually debated the issue, Winter replied, "I think he understands, but Michael wants to score when he touches the ball. And he feels like he's got the ability to. So, consequently, why should he give up the ball? He probably doesn't have the trust in a lot of his team-mates he should. He'd rather put it on his own shoulders to bear that load."

Jordan's teammates often felt that lack of trust, Winter said. In fact, Jackson's film sessions and postseason preachings about togetherness were often meant primarily for Jordan, Winter said. "He understands. Michael understands. He's a very smart basketball player. It's just that he's such a competitor that he likes challenges. And when he catches that ball, if he feels like he can, he's gonna try to score. And oftentimes he does. Even when he goes one on one, most of it comes out of the concept of the offense. He's not going off on his own and completely abandoning our principles. We won't let him do that."

If Jordan's competitiveness raged to the point that he bordered on killing chemistry, Jackson would usually caution him that he was trying to do too much. "That's usually about all it takes," Winter said. "Phil will remind him to involve his teammates. Phil will let him know that he missed a teammate that was open."

The triangle offense was the apparatus that provided for the ball movement necessary to defuse Jordan's competitiveness when it reached toxic levels. As Jordan book collaborator Mark Vancil pointed out, most fans never would have heard of the triangle offense if not for Jordan's individual mastery. That certainly was true. On the other hand, there was a strong argument that Jordan would never have realized his potential as the leader of a championship team if he hadn't molded his game to fit within Winter's team approach.

Jackson later synthesized the argument. Often the team struggled in executing the offense, he pointed out, but "we were still philosophically in tune with one another because of it. And it shows.

"A lot of times," Jackson said, "it's all right to say from a coaching standpoint, 'You know we executed offensively in these games, and it's really a matter of great function of the team.' But the reality is that the triangle offense works great because Michael Jordan has an ability to move between five different positions and sail by double teams and knows how to function in this thing so that he can always bail out the offense in the last five seconds. That's made it really a great offense for a superstar."

The Bulls would often use the offense for the first 20 seconds of a possession, then turn the ball over to Jordan to execute one-on-one moves as the shot clock wound down. The friction between the individual and the system brought still more innovation.

Despite their great success together, Winter readily acknowledged the fear that his triangle offense might not last much past Jordan's career itself, at least not in the NBA. In the women's college game, however, the offense was thriving. Coach Pat Summitt had successfully incorporated it into her approach at the University of Tennessee, the dominant program in the women's game. The University of Connecticut, another top women's program, also made use of the triangle. Winter said that was an indication of the dedication of female athletes and their coaches and their drive to teach and learn the fundamentals of the game. The NBA, however, seemed to be another story, with both Phoenix and Dallas having tried the offense and failed miserably.

The issue raised questions about the legacy of Jordan's great Bulls teams. Certainly Jordan had brought vast changes in the economics of the game, but in many ways the prosperity he brought to the game also threatened it. As far as his individual style is concerned, there were legitimate questions about the ability of Kobe Bryant and other younger players to duplicate it successfully. More important was the style of the team itself. Had the Bulls brought any lasting changes as a group? Would the team's style of play eventually force other teams to change?

Ron Harper was one of many Bulls who had struggled mightily to adapt to the offense after coming to Chicago. He was asked in 1998 if he would use the triangle if he became a coach. "I don't know it too well," he replied. "Is that an offense that I would try to run? Some of it, yeah. It depends on the kind of ballplayers that my team has. There have been other teams that have tried it. On this team you got Michael, Scottie, myself, guys who can go play on any team with any kind of offense and fit in. So that's a big key, I think. I don't know if it would be good with a young basketball team. There's a lot to this offense. If you got young ballplayers who can only play one way, or one phase of basketball, it would be tough.

"If I was a coach, there would be some part of this I would try, I think," Harper added. "But it's a challenge. On this team you've got to know the spots for all five guys. I can go to the five-man spot and be a center. I can be a four, a two, a point guard. You have to have guys who are interchangeable, more complete players. If your player is a good isolation guy, if that's what his skills are meant for, that's what you're gonna need to do. But in this game, where the defenses are very solid, you need to get things that change up here and there. The way we play is a new kind of style. It's old school, too. But it's so old it's new. The Bulls have been seen all over. People are seeing how we do things. But in Dallas, it didn't work. What they tried to do in Phoenix, it didn't work. It worked sometimes, but they didn't have enough success. Some teams have some players who've gotta have the ball all the time. On our team, guys don't have to have the basketball all the time. Here you very seldom see a guy hold the ball all the time. You have to pass and move yourself. You got to learn that you won't have the basketball on this team here."

Scott Burrell, who had also struggled with the triangle, said learning the system required immense patience because it leaves new players feeling out of sync. "It just makes you off balance and not ready to go out and play," he said. "It drops your confidence 'cause you can't really go out there and play like you could. I think players lose with it because they don't have faith in it. You gotta have faith in it. It's hard to sell. You gotta have faith that it's gonna work.

"You just gotta have the right people," Burrell said, "and everybody's got to have the right frame of mind. And everybody just has to have a lot of different skills at a lot of different positions. It makes the game a lot easier for less skilled persons. It's great for that kind of player."

But the offense also forces players to become more complete because they have to show great flexibility, Burrell said. "Everybody has to know the right pivots, the right passes, the right moves. With this team everybody functions and does well off that, playing as a team."

Former Bull Jud Buechler, rumored to be headed to Los Angeles from Detroit to help Jackson install the offense, was an unabashed admirer of the system. "Are you kidding me?" Buechler said when asked about it. "The triangle has given me a chance to play in this league. All the offenses in the NBA now, everything is so one-on-one, get the ball in isolation. As a player, it's not a very fun style to play, because if you're not that guy with the ball then you're just standing around out there. I was the guy standing in the parking lot on the other side of the floor going, 'Illegal defense!' the whole time to the referee. I came to Chicago, and all that changed. The way the triangle is set up, you pass, you move, you make decisions. It's more of a team game; it gets everybody involved. It's an exciting way to play. It's the way every player would like to have it. Who wants to turn on a game and watch the ball go into the post and watch a guy back a guy down, a guy spaced out on the other side standing around? Those games aren't very fun to watch. It's not a very fun style."

Buechler said he understood that Phoenix and Dallas failed in using the triangle, "but they didn't give it any time. It's not something you can throw out there for half a season. It takes years. It took this team two or three years to get it down and figure it out."

"It is the type of offense where you need time," agreed Bill Cartwright. "You need time with it. You need people to run the offense at maximum speed. They must be able to recognize the cuts, who's open and who's not. They must be able to read defenses, and all of that takes time."

And that, in itself, helped explain why so many NBA teams opted to run isolation offenses. They're put together with quick assembly, while the triangle required many hours of intricate work. It's the age of McDonald's, of fast food, of quick turnaround. The isolation offense was quick process in an age of quick processes. The triangle, on the other hand, was much more involved. The circumstances presented a question: How would the young Lakers, already so frustrated, handle a period of learning and possibly losing?

"What's happening is that the NBA is a superstar league," Winter said. "It features the players, which it should. But in so doing, the superstars are the ones who make the money and get the recognition. Consequently they're the ones who set the example for everyone who comes along in the league. What happens is, you don't get team play.

"You see," he said, "I think this offense is very simple, but it's so basic that these players with these great individual talents and skills that they've developed on the playground don't want it that simple. They want to make it their contest one-on-one against somebody, and that's the thing the NBA is going to have to guard against. Showmanship is important. There's no question that people came to see Michael Jordan play and to see him score. It's a superstar league, but I think it has to get back to where the team becomes more important than the individual.

"The thing that's happening," Winter said, "is that basketball's a game of habit, just like life is a game of habit. Most of your younger players, the younger talent, they've played an awful lot of pickup basketball, playground basketball. And playground basketball really defies the basic principles of sound offense. They learn to play in a crowd, in congestion, all the time, and they're very good at it. But they play on top of each other all the time, and they're not concerned about the principles of a sound offense and a five-man situation. So they're nurtured that way, and it's very difficult for them to come into a situation where they've got to play differently. They've got to learn new skills, new techniques. They're not permitted to play in congestion like they're used to doing. There's times, of course, where it's a good thing to know how to play in a crowd. In any offense you get an awful lot of scrum situations.

"But they develop skills playing in a crowd," Winter said. "And that's the way they like to play, playing one-on-one basketball, trying to beat somebody. Get the ball and try to beat their opposition one-on-one. Instead of letting the offense, the flow of the offense and the ball movement, create shots for them, they like to create it one-on-one. They like to create it themselves."

Would the Lakers be able to alter their approach to allow Winter's offense to work for them?

That question enveloped Lakers fans over the summer of
1999 as Jackson, Winter, and assistants Jim Cleamons and
Frank Hamblin came to Los Angeles and watched the Lakers'
summer league team struggle to run the triangle.

Steve Kerr, a close friend of Jackson's, acknowledged that he
and Jackson had discussed using a triangle with the Lakers
long before Jackson was named their coach. "I've talked to
Phil about it before," Kerr said. "I said, 'If you had Shaq,
would you run the triangle?' He said, 'Absolutely.' He said he
felt like the offense was adaptable. He would give Shaq more
post-up opportunities in the triangle. He thinks it would be
perfect. And I think so, too. Because Shaq is a much better
passer than he was a couple of years ago. And he's so big,
When you get him the ball on the block, rather than having
four guys standing there claiming that the defense is illegal,
and rather than having the defense standing there looking at
him, you'd have his four teammates cutting all around him.
And all of a sudden he can pick you apart."

The same concepts that helped Jordan would apply to
O'Neal because Jordan was a great post weapon, like O'Neal,
Kerr said. "It's the same principle, that you want to keep the
defense occupied. You want to also keep your teammates occupied. The worst thing in basketball is to stand there and not
do anything. Then, by the time you do get the ball, you're not
into the game. But if you're constantly moving and cutting and
being involved in the offense, you're much more mentally
focused and you're much more likely to make a shot when you
get it."

But would the young Lakers have the patience and take the
time to learn the offense? "That's the big question," Kerr said.
"Phil told me he thinks it takes two years, two years to learn
the triangle. You tell me what NBA coach has two years to fid-
dle with an offense? Most of them get fired before then, and I

think that's a big reason why you're seeing the same offense all over the league."

Jim Cleamons, Quinn Buckner, and Cotton Fitzsimmons had all lost their jobs trying to teach pro players the triangle. Perhaps Jackson would have the status and stature to make it work in Los Angeles, Kerr said.

Whatever path the team took, one thing was clear: the young Lakers knew they better be ready to work—in practice. "The difference with the Bulls from every other place that I've been—every coach I've been with in the NBA has been very well organized—the difference in Chicago was the focus on fundamentals every single day," Kerr said. "We started every day with basic drills, footwork, passing, ball handling. Every single day."

He admitted that it was hard for coaches to get modern pro players to do that, which was why the leadership of Michael Jordan and Scottie Pippen was so valuable. "The first time I saw Michael and Scottie standing 15 feet apart throwing two-handed chest passes back and forth for 10 minutes, I realized the Bulls were really going to focus on fundamentals," Kerr said. "It's the foundation of the game, and if you don't work on 'em, you're not gonna have that foundation."

So much of Jackson's success in Los Angeles would depend on O'Neal. How would he feel about stepping away from the basket routinely and developing a face-up jumper?

"That is something I would love to see him develop," Larry Drew said of an O'Neal jumper, "but the key word is *develop*. It's something you really have to spend time with. It's something you have to work on. When Earvin [Magic Johnson] came into the league, he wanted to develop a right/left-hand hook shot. So he spent the entire summer developing that. He spent time with it and came back, and it was a very big piece of his offense. Can Shaq develop a step-out, face-up shot? I don't know, but if there's any type of change he wants to make to his game, it has to happen over the summer, where he can spend numerous hours working on it. Then hopefully he can come back the following season and use it."

Adding such a shot would be a major development, Drew said, adding that O'Neal could face the same performance anxiety in his face-up jumper that he has in his free throws.

"It has to be something that he will be confident doing," Drew said. "It can't be a sometime thing. He has to have confidence. Plus it's hard to go out and ask a guy to develop something when he's already scoring 30 points a game for you. What more can you ask? He's shown that he can score 30, maybe 40 points with what he's already got."

Facing such questions, Winter, Jackson, and their disciples came to Los Angeles with the fervor and delight of missionaries, men who wanted to save pro basketball from stagnation. "I have this discussion with everybody, because I love talking about it," Kerr said. "I think the game is going down the tubes. The beauty of the game has been lost. The triangle is one of the offenses that maintains that beauty, the ball movement, the rhythm. It's become such a stagnant game now, and it's all based on one-on-one.

"I remember Phil saying we didn't run the triangle for Michael and Scottie. We ran it for the rest of us, and that always struck me. Kobe's so good, he's gonna average 25 points per game or whatever wherever he goes. As his career goes on, he'll always be able to score. But I'm pretty sure that he knows his career will ultimately be defined by how many championships he wins."

The situation, the questions, awaited the best efforts from both Kobe and O'Neal.

With Winter's phone number, I had given Kobe another number—Jordan's. Having Jackson as a coach meant that he just might have Jordan as a mentor. Psychologist George Mumford held the belief that such a mentorship would be vastly important to both Jordan and Bryant, that in retirement Jordan had the need to contribute, that Kobe would need adult role models beyond that provided by his excellent parents.

At the end of June, I tracked Jordan down for a few questions, and one of the first points he wanted to make was that he had no plans to return to the NBA as a Los Angeles Laker.

He did, however, have some kind words of advice for the young Lakers who soon would be working with Jackson. The Lakers should keep an open mind about Jackson's quirky approach to coaching, including his use of Zen Buddhist philosophy, Jordan said. "It can relieve a lot of tension in your life, and I'm pretty sure they got a lot. Actually I think they're gonna be happy with Phil. He's gonna give them a certain structure and a certain guidance that they probably need. They got the talent. It's always been there. It's just how you utilize the talent in a focused situation. And I think Phil is good at that."

When I spoke with Jordan, Bryant had left a message with him that day. Jordan said he hadn't had a chance to return Bryant's call, but when I told him that Kobe wanted to know about incorporating math into the game, Jordan smiled his most competitive smile.

"I can teach him that," he said.

INDEX

Abdul-Jabbar, Kareem, 81, 91, 99
Abdur-Rahim, Shareef, 76
Adidas, 101, 249
Adidas ABCD All-America camp, 54–55, 57
Adidas Big-Time Tournament, 57
Akiba Hebrew Academy, 49–50
Albeck, Stan, 297
Allen, Ray, 76
All-Star weekend, 1998, 14, 127–28, 158–64
American Basketball Association, 29, 59
Armato, Leonard, 97

Baker, Charles, 42
Baker League, 42, 43
Baltimore Claws, 60
Bannister, Anthony, 147–48
Barkley, Charles, 31, 218
Barnes, Marvin, 28
Battle, John, 37
Baylor, Elgin, 86, 90

Bernstein, Andrew, 139–42, 146, 187–88, 194
Bertka, Bill, 211
Bibby, Henry, 29
Bibby, Mike, 57
Bickerstaff, Bernie, 62
Big Eight Conference, 303
Bird, Larry, 279, 298
Black, John, 81, 262
Blount, Corie, 113
Boston Celtics, 82, 84
Bradley, Bill, 42, 43
Brandy, xi, 76
Brown, Howard, 55
Brown, Larry, 238
Bryant, Joe "Jelly Bean," xi, 8, 20, 25–35
  coaching Akiba Hebrew Academy, 49–50
  coaching Lower Merion High School, 49
  at Golden State Warriors, 27–28
  at Houston Rockets, 33–35
  on Kobe's NBA decision, 74

at Philadelphia 76ers, 28–32
playing in Europe, 39
playing in Italy, 35–36
at San Diego Clippers, 32–33
Bryant, Kobe
Adidas contract, 101
at All-Star weekend, 127–28
born, 31
childhood in California, 32
college opportunities, 18
confidence, 7–13
contract, 1999, 193–94
first All-Star game, 158–64
first NBA field goal, xii
first NBA score, xii
high school academics, 18
Lakers playing time, 123–24
leisure time, 21
rookie year, 111–36
second NBA season, 137–80
shadow basketball, 38
Shaquille O'Neal against,
185–90
"Showboat" nickname, xiii,
121
at Sonny Hill Community
Involvement League,
41–46
star quality, 139–40
summer leagues, 1997, 140
trying out for Lakers, 94–95
women and, 23–25
work ethic, 3
Bryant, Pam, 20, 27, 51, 76
family life, 146–47
on Kobe's NBA decision, 74
Bryant, Sharia, 101–2
Buckner, Quinn, 311
Buechler, Jud, 307–8

Burrell, Scott, 307
Burton, Willie, 56
Buss, Jerry, 4, 87, 91, 104, 170
Jerry West and, 170–71

Camby, Marcus, 76
Campbell, Elden, 113, 116, 221
Carr, Chris, 128
Carrawell, Chris, 73
Carter, Fred, 29
Cartwright, Bill, 297, 301, 308
Catchings, Harvey, 29
Caught in the Net (Locke), 60
Ceballos, Cedric, 113
Chamberlain, Wilt, 42, 59, 72,
90–91, 99, 262, 269, 303
Charlotte Hornets, Bryant
trade to Lakers from, xii,
77
Chicago American Gears, 99
Chicago Bulls, 259–60
triangle offense, 10–11,
295–312
Chortkoff, Mitch, 100, 121–22,
125, 212, 262
Cleamons, Jim, 310, 311
Clemson University, 59–60
Collier, Jason, 69
Collins, Doug, 29, 60, 298
Cooke, Jack Kent, 88, 90, 91
Cooper, Michael, 94
Cowens, Dave, 77
Cox, John "Chubby," 27, 45–46
Cox, Pam. *See* Bryant, Pam
Crossover dribble, 1–2
Cunningham, Billy, 31–32

Dabney, Emery, 68
Daly, Chuck, 19

Daugherty, Brad, 32
Dawkins, Darryl "Chocolate
    Thunder," 29, 30–31, 60
DeCourcy, Mike, 75
Denver Nuggets, Nick Van
    Exel trade to, 178–79
Denver Rockets, 59
Detroit Gems, 88–89
Divac, Vlade, 77, 97
Doleac, Michael, 246
Downer, Gregg, 46–47, 49, 52,
    67
Downey, Mike, 98
Drew, Larry, xiv, 3, 10, 21,
    102–3, 119, 120, 121, 140,
    212, 311–12
Duke University, 72
Dunleavy, Mike, 29
DuPree, David, 199

East Bank High School, West
    Virginia, 86
Electra, Carmen, 235, 252
Erving, Julius, 29, 31, 42
Eskin, Howard, 75
Europe, Joe Bryant playing in,
    39
Ewing, Patrick, 270

Fila Summer Pro League, 102
Finley, Michael, 128
Fisher, Derek, 105–8, 110, 132,
    181–84, 190–91, 214
Fitzsimmons, Cotton, 311
Fox, Rick, 8, 16, 20, 144, 231,
    260
Franklin, James, 66–67
Free, Lloyd "Prince of Mid
    Air," 29, 31

Furlow, Terry, 29

Garciduenas, Rudy, 111
Garnett, Kevin, 57, 62, 69
Golden State Warriors,
    27–28
Graboski, Joe, 58

Haley, Jack, 202, 207
Ham, Darvin, 129
Hamblin, Frank, 310
Hamilton, Richard, 70
Hardaway, Anfernee "Penny,"
    95, 242
Harlem Globetrotters, 59
Harper, Derek, 17, 192, 199,
    249–50, 259, 263
Harper, Ron, 152, 306–7
Harris, Del, xii, 3, 15–16, 104,
    114, 122, 125, 132, 134
    Bryant conflict, 142–43
    firing, 179–80, 184,
        208–11
    at Rockets, 33–34
    Van Exel and, 120
Hartman, Sid, 91
Haywood, Spencer, 59
Hearn, Chick, 86
Heathcote, Jud, 26
Heisler, Mark, 91
Higgins, Rod, 255
Hill, Brian, 95
Hill, Grant, 151, 161
Hill, Sonny, 35, 41, 43, 141
Hinson, Roy, 32
HIV announcement, Magic
    Johnson, 39, 92
Horry, Robert, 113, 135,
    166

Houston Rockets
  Del Harris and, 33–34
  Joe Bryant and, 33–35
Hundley, Hot Rod, 177–78
Hunt, Donald, 42

Italy, Joe Bryant playing in,
  35–36
Iverson, Allen, 13–14, 76, 238

Jackson, Phil, 9, 191–92, 211,
  215, 259–60, 267, 269–72
  Lakers hiring, 292–93
  triangle offense and,
    298–305
John Bartram High,
  Philadelphia, 26
Johnson, Larry, 198
Johnson, Magic, 24, 25–26,
  34–35, 37, 73, 91, 97, 99,
  111
  HIV announcement, 39, 92
Jones, Bobby, 31
Jones, Caldwell, 29
Jones, Eddie, 46, 109, 113, 116,
  118, 119, 169, 221–26,
  257–58
Jordan, Michael, 7, 9–13, 62,
  73
  on Bryant, 152–56, 313
  heirs, 151
  on Lakers, 219–20
  last All-Star game, 158–64
  retirement, 197
  return to NBA in 1995, 63
  on Shaq free throws, 125–26
  triangle offense and,
    300–304
  on young players, 145

Kansas Jayhawks, 303
Kansas State University, 303
Kawakami, Tim, 261
Kemp, Shawn, 61–62, 149, 164,
  173
Kempton, Tim, 112
Kerr, Steve, 279–81, 310, 311
Kidd, Jason, 121
Knight, Travis, 106, 112
Konchalski, Tom, 65
Krause, Jerry, 270
Krzyzewski, Mike, 19
Kupchak, Mitch, 53, 106, 170

L.A. Sports Arena, 90
The Lake Show, 116–24
Larry Bird rights, 203–4
LaSalle University, 26, 50, 72,
  141
Layden, Frank, 130
Lee, Tommy, 235
Ligmanowski, John, 296
Locke, Tates, 60
Los Angeles Lakers, 4
  1997–98 playoffs, 4
  1997–98 record, 4
  history, 88–93
  Lake Show, 116–24
Lower Merion High School
  basketball, 47–49, 52, 54,
    56, 65, 67
Lucas, John, 63
Lynch, George, 97, 120

Mahorn, Rick, 56, 73
Malone, Moses, 33, 59
Manley, Dwight, 204–5
Manning, Peyton, 248–49
Marbury, Stephon, 76

Matkov, Matt, 71
McCloud, George, 113
McDonald's high school All-
America team, 73
McGinnis, George, 29
McGrady, Tracy, 131
McHale, Kevin, 185
Michigan State University, 26
Mikan, George, 90, 99, 185
Miner, Harold, 151
Minnesota Lakers, 89–90
Mix, Steve, 28
Mohs, Lou, 90
Monroe, Earl, 42
Morris, Speedy, 141
Mumford, George, 259–60

Narberth League, 50–51
National Basketball
Association (NBA)
1998–99 lockout, 181, 184
collective bargaining
agreement, 1999, 192–93
environment, 19
rule for leaving college early,
59
National Basketball League, 99
National League, 88
NCAA, 61
New York Knicks, 82, 270
New York Times Magazine,
146
Newell, Pete, 85, 86, 87
Nicholson, Jack, 91
Nixon, Norm, 24

O'Neal, Jermaine, 57, 129
O'Neal, Shaquille, xiii, 9, 116,
122

Bryant and, 183–84, 185–90,
214, 262–63
injuries, 126–27
at Lakers, 95–100, 102
Rodman and, 216–18
Van Exel and, 120
Orlando Magic, 95–96

Packer, Billy, 130, 145
Palestra, Philadelphia, 67, 70
Parade high school All-
America team, 73
Patterson, Ruben, 190
Paxson, John, 299, 301–2
Peeler, Anthony, 97
Perkins, Sam, 174–75
Philadelphia Daily News, 65
Philadelphia 76ers, 14, 30–31
Joe Bryant at, 28–32
Philadelphia Inquirer, 47,
54–56, 64–65
Philadelphia Warriors, 59
Phillips, Richie, 28
Pippen, Scottie, 5–6, 151, 158,
214–15, 272–73
Plaschke, Bill, 147
Pollard, Jim, 90, 185
Portland Trail Blazers, 134

Rambis, Kurt, 110, 184,
212–14, 215, 222, 225, 228,
256
Rodman and, 250–55
Reid, J. R., 184
Rice, Glen, 184, 221, 226–27
Richmond, Mitch, 169
Rider, Isaiah, 134
Robinson, Cliff, 134
Robinson, David, 207–8

Rodgers, Guy, 42
Rodman, Dennis, 6, 184, 197,
  201–7, 214–20, 223–24,
  244–45
  leave of absence from
    Lakers, 235–36
  Rambis and, 250–55
  Russell, Bill, 84, 99

Sampson, Ralph, 33
San Diego Clippers, 32–33
Schaefer, Chip, 296
Schaus, Fred, 84, 104
Scott, Bryon, 109, 119, 132
Scott, Dennis, 158
Seattle Super Sonics, 59, 62
Seymour, Paul, 57–58
Sharman, Bill, 84, 269–70
Shields, Tee, 44
Short, Bob, 90, 91
"Showboat" nickname, Bryant,
  xiii, 121
Shue, Gene, 30, 31, 33
Sikma, Jack, 100
Silas, Paul, 33
Smith, Dean, 18, 64
Snow, Eric, 238
Sonny Hill Community
  Involvement League,
  41–46
The Sporting News, 77
Stackhouse, Jerry, 63–64,
  151
Sterling, Donald, 32–33
Stern, David, 62, 198
Stockton, John, 136
Strickland, Rod, 167
Summitt, Pat, 305
Sura, Bob, 128

Tellem, Arn, xii, 77
Thomas, Isaiah, 279
Thomas, Tim, 51, 57
Threatt, Sedale, 97
Tomjanovich, Rudy, 57, 259
"The Tonight Show," 102
Treatman, Jeremy, 47–55, 64,
  67–71, 73, 75, 133, 146
Triangle offense, 10–11,
  298–300
Tyson, Mike, 147

University of Arkansas, 72
University of Connecticut, 305
University of Kentucky, 61
University of North Carolina,
  72
University of Tennessee, 305
USA Today's High School
  Player of the Year, 73
Utah Jazz, 4, 6, 134
Utah Stars, 59

Van Exel, Nick, 4, 113, 116,
  119, 121, 122, 125, 138,
  178, 200
  Del Harris and, 120
  Shaquille O'Neal and, 120
  trade to Denver, 178–79
Van Gundy, Jeff, 270
Vancil, Mark, 304
Vitti, Gary, 25, 111

Walt Disney World, 242
Walton, Bill, 30–31
Webber, Chris, 167
West, Jerry, xii, 4, 24, 38,
  79–94, 96–98, 101, 104,
  111, 114, 131, 140

Buss and, 170–71
new contract, 196
Phil Jackson and, 270
West Virginia University,
83
Western Conference All-Star
team, 14
Westhead, Paul, 26
Whitsitt, Bob, 62
Williams, Jason, 237

Williams, Pat, 27–28, 30, 32,
99
Winston, Maury, 89, 91
Winter, Tex, 12–13, 18, 192,
265–71, 295–303, 308–9
Wise, Skip, 59–60
Women and Bryant, 23–25
Woods, Loren, 57
Woods, Tiger, 144
Worthy, James, 111